D0404860

Also by Richard Hugo

A Run of Jacks

Death of the Kapowsin Tavern

Good Luck in Cracked Italian

The Lady in Kicking Horse Reservoir

What Thou Lovest Well Remains American

31 Letters and 13 Dreams

The Triggering Town: Lectures and Essays on
Poetry and Writing

Selected Poems

White Center

The Right Madness on Skye

Death and the Good Life (novel)

Making Certain It Goes On: The Collected Poems of
Richard Hugo

THE

REAL WEST

MARGINAL WAY

A Poet's Autobiography

THE

REAL WEST

MARGINAL WAY

A Poet's Autobiography

RICHARD HUGO

Edited by Ripley S. Hugo,
Lois M. Welch, and James Welch
With an Introduction by
William Matthews

W · W · NORTON & COMPANY · *New York* · *London*

Copyright © 1986 by Ripley S. Hugo
All rights reserved.
Printed in the United States of America

First published as a Norton paperback 1992

The text of this book is composed in Baskerville.
Composition and
manufacturing by the Maple-Vail Book Manufacturing Group.

Library of Congress-Cataloging-in-Publication Data

Hugo, Richard F.
The real West marginal way.

1. Hugo, Richard F.—Biography. 2. Poets,
American—20th century—Biography. 3. Poets—
Authorship. I. Hugo, Ripley S. II. Welch, Lois M.
III. Welch, James, 1940– . IV. Title.
PS3515.U3Z476 1986; 811'.54 [B] 86–5299

ISBN 0-393-30860-X

W. W. Norton & Company, Inc.
500 Fifth Avenue, New York, N.Y. 10110
W. W. Norton & Company Ltd
10 Coptic Street, London WC1A 1PU

2 3 4 5 6 7 8 9 0

For Matt, who saw those sea lanes out.

1961–1984

Contents

❧

Preface

RICHARD HUGO intended at one time to write an auto-biography, then didn't. He discovered he disliked the genre. He also discovered he liked writing essays. This collection of essays is the autobiography he envisioned and had essentially completed by the time he was struck down by leukemia in September of 1982.

"Your way of writing locates, even creates, your inner life," he said in *The Triggering Town*. This collection of essays, as it weaves together autobiographical details and poems, sketches more than a double arc of personal history and publication. It dwells continually on the relationship between the two for a poet who was fundamentally uninterested in the merely factual aspect of history. Truth wasn't enough for him; he felt it had to sing.

While a chronological progression would have violated the intimate relationship between events in the various layers of his own history, we see here events related to time, but not necessarily in sequence. A history is duller than a plot because the precious drama of arrangement is missing: an event finally understood today re-arranges your purely chronological understanding of your own life.

These essays were written over a period of perhaps 15 years, and were certainly not composed in the order used here. "Catch 22," probably the earliest, dates from the early seventies. We have arranged them in an order as close to the biographical as possible. "Ci Vediamo" is reprinted from *The Triggering Town*, his volume of essays on poetry and writing, because it covers so well a period of his life that would otherwise be omitted from this autobiographical trajectory.

When there were problems, we tried to solve them by following Hugo's lead. Some of these essays existed in various forms; we have chosen the ones which seemed most final.

For example, the two essays "Small Waters and Tiny Words" and "Some Kind of Perfection" were originally one essay, entitled "Influences," which was never published. As Hugo attempted to define his influences, the density of the themes and the breadth with which he covered them apparently led him to rewrite, separating the various strands. This pair of essays was his final form. Certain unpublished, even handwritten, essays were complete and required only minor editing. The James Wright essay and the "St. James Lutheran 5" required some editing decisions, due to redundancies and other changes which Hugo himself would no doubt have made, had he finished this project. Those interested in the various forms of these essays can consult drafts and manuscripts now in the archives of the University of Washington Library; these make clear Hugo's extensive reshaping of the various essays.

Parts of different essays interweave—cover again territory which has been covered elsewhere. (For example, parts of the essay "Statements of Faith," published in *The Triggering Town,* were included in "The Problem of Success.") Straight autobiography probably would not do this. Hugo clearly had recurrent interests; he would have called them obsessions. He urged his students to listen to their own obsessions—as though obsessions were the bedrock of one's inner life. To have edited out those sections with recurring themes would have, we felt, violated his sense of the very shape of his life.

"Self-Interview" originally appeared in *New Salt Creek Reader* as an interview conducted by a second party. However, since Hugo actually wrote it as a self-interview, we have restored it to its original format. Hugo invented the questions he wanted to answer.

We have included two poems with the essays. "The Milltown Union Bar, (Laundromat and Café)" not only coordinates usefully with the essay "You Could Love Here," it provides its first line. "Last Words for James Wright" uses the Ed Bedford persona whose origin Hugo explains in the essay "James Wright." Together, the two pieces describe this enduring friendship between poets which dated back to graduate school days in Seattle.

A chronology has been included as well, in order that the reader locate in history the events which are discussed without dates. (For example, "The Problem of Success" opens with the line "One morning a few years back in Iowa City," and a reader might well wonder a few years back from when? The chronology provides answers to such questions.) We hope also that it gives little bonuses, such as making clear that Hugo legally changed his name to that of his step-father when he was 19.

Finally, we have assembled a number of photos from different periods of Hugo's life. The house in which he grew up. A winsome baby photo. Hugo with baseball pals and army pals and fish and (other) loved ones. While he might never have considered these for inclusion, we offer them unapologetically.

The volume concludes with a "Dialogue with Richard Hugo" which resulted from an interview with fellow teacher and writer, William Kittredge in the winter of 1982. It is not precisely autobiography. In it, Hugo steers the discussion towards certain subjects which were important to him that winter when he was worried about his failing health. He is clarifying for himself what he had thought about over the years, and summarizing what he intended to do in the future. We chose to include this piece because it gives a sense of ways in which he was still developing, and because it concludes with the title he had chosen for this collection. He was still going strong: "Making Certain It Goes On" and the "Stone" poems were sent to APR in August, the same month he sent "Salt Water Story" to the *The New Yorker;* it appeared in November of 1982.

As Hugo said in his "Elegy" for Harold Herndon, proprietor of the Milltown Union Bar: "I tried to remember his life. He gave it to me in pieces over the years. . . ."

The Editors

ACKNOWLEDGEMENT

John Benedict was editor and friend to Richard Hugo through the poet's ten most productive years of writing (1972–1982), welcoming each new manuscript as it came. In 1983, one year after Dick's death, Benedict published the collected poems as he had promised, choosing the title *Making Certain It Goes On* from one of Dick's last poems. The editors would like to thank John Benedict for his encouragement and assistance in seeing this present collection of essays into print. We have depended on his loyalty to Dick's work.

Introduction:
Old Haunts

A WRITER is neither born nor made, but written. Thus one of the pleasures of reading these autobiographical essays by Richard Hugo is to watch one of our central poets recapitulate, late in his life and at the peak of his powers, the long process of building a life's work (q.v., *Making Certain It Goes On: The Collected Poems of Richard Hugo*, Norton, 1984). But in writing the essays, the poet has the accumulated momentum and insight of the poetry. He knows how the story comes out, and thus at relevant points in the narrative he can quote aptly from his own work. *Yes,* he seems to be saying in pleased recognition, *that's the man I became.*

So this remarkable book is neither a conventional autobiography, nor that rarer thing, the autobiography of a body of work, but, rarest of all, it is an extended meditation on the relationship between the life and the work.

The life, after all, could be given in brief synopsis. Dave Smith has a wonderfully acute and empathetic paragraph in his essay "The Man from White Center."

Fatherless and abandoned by his teenage mother, Hugo was raised by elderly, severe grandparents in White Center, Washington, then a semirural, poor suburb of Seattle. Enforced churchgoing left him feeling he owed something, that he was spiritually dunned all his life. Shy, awkward, and isolated, he believed himself not only the cause of his ill fortunes but also unregenerately weak, worthless, and ever "a wrong thing in a right world." He grew up admiring local toughs for their violent courage. He extended this admiration later to sardonic movie stars, detective heroes, and British Royal Air Force flyers, who seemed to have a stylish, right manhood. He feared, hated and coveted girls and compensated by making himself a skilled baseball player, fisherman, and dreamer. His tutelary spirits appeared early and never abandoned him—waters, sky, hills, ocean, fish, birds and drunks. All meant unimpeachable and continuous acceptance, private dignity, and sweet, if unrecognized, belonging.

Tutelary spirits pervade these essays. "The Anxious Fields of Play" is perhaps the most unsentimental hymn to baseball in English, and Hugo's love of waters, fishing and friendship is everywhere in this book. I remember Hugo settling contentedly before a television set in anticipation of an afternoon of baseball. "As you know," he pronounced, "work is ridiculous."

Hugo had the loner's natural gift for friendship, and he watched baseball, drank, fished and made excursions with a remarkable number of people. His outings were famous, and the fifteen poems called "Montana with Friends" and eleven poems called "Touring with Friends" from *The Lady in Kicking Horse Reservoir,* each poem dedicated to somebody who shared the triggering event, are testimony to how gregarious Hugo taught himself to be.

"Ghost in a Field of Mint," dedicated to Sister Madeline DeFrees (DeFrees was then a nun), is a good example of the genre.

> The old man on the prison work release gang
> hoeing asphalt followed us to Wilkeson
> and those cyrillic graves, to Carbanado
> and that one long empty street, Voight's Creek
> and then Kapowsin and our picnic
> in a field of mint. Wherever we went, old haunts
> I wanted you to see, he hung there grim.
> I ruined him with theory: sodomy, infanticide.
> His bitter face kept saying we die broken.
> Our crab patè seemed bitter and the sun.
>
> In old poems I put evil things in Carbanado
> where I'd never been because a word that soft
> and lovely must be wrong, must hide what

really happened, the unreported murder
in the tavern, faithless wives. Clouds were birds
of prey. The cell door clangs before we know
we're doing wrong. The stern click of the calendar
damned us long ago to take pain on the tongue.

One day, alone in an asylum, I will find
a door left open and the open field beyond,
a wife beside that road the map forgot
waiting as prearranged.
She'll say, I'm crazy too. I understand.
From then on we will seek the harboring towns,
towns you never find, those flowers dying
certain the forlorn die wise. My sister,
we have been released for the entire day.

The old man is a characteristic figure in Hugo's poems—
someone fallen irremediably into solitude, exile and wretched-
ness, an emblem of pure self-pity. Each picnic or excursion is
a ceremony against his baleful possibility. If pain is our daily
bread, then here's how we live with it.

It's interesting to note the poem's prediction of Hugo's
later happy marriage. But it's not a wistful hope or an uncanny
foreshadowing. The ceremonies of friendship and outings were
a preparation for happiness, and it was not *for* but *by* such
good behavior that a reprieve longer than a day was achieved.

The essay on James Wright is a moving portrait of Wright's
and Hugo's rhyming temperaments, and another glimpse of
Hugo practicing affection. The last years of his life he came
frequently to Seattle—in those days I was living there. Sometimes we'd go to the Kingdome and watch through condi-
tioned air baseball being played indoors, an event even more
ridiculous than work. Sometimes we'd just drive around. There
were old haunts he wanted me to see—White Center, the Pike
Place Market, and a place where a houseboat he'd lived on
long ago had been moored. I was glad for the looks into his
life, and for his company, but I knew the jaunts were as much
for him as for me. He was always homing.

The last time he was in Seattle, I'd go to the hospital to sit with him and watch baseball on television. He watched through the playoffs and then into the Series, but between the sixth and seventh games his condition grew suddenly far worse and he died swiftly. Baseball, its fans love to say, is the only team sport not played with or against a clock. But no game is more about mortality. Fouling them off, a batter is said to be staying alive. He only gets, according to conventional wisdom, one good pitch to hit per appearance at the plate. A team has only twenty-seven outs to spend. And in the box score the next day one of the statistics the game will have produced is how long it took to play the game. Hugo's life wasn't anywhere near long enough for the many who loved him.

And he died with many loving him, with a wonderful body of work, with the marriage and family he struggled so hard to feel worthy of. He was in many ways a single-minded man. His work shows a similar consistency. He found a unique and flexible style early, and rather than modify it he clarified and simplified it, making familiar and capable what at first might have seemed idiosyncratic.

A late poem, "Glen Uig," begins with a couple on an outing to the Faery Glen. Here's the last stanza.

> Believe the couple who have finished their picnic
> and make wet love in the grass, the wise tiny creatures
> cheering them on. Believe in milestones, the day
> you left home forever and the cold open way
> a world wouldn't let you come in. Believe you
> and I are that couple. Believe you and I sing tiny
> and wise and could if we had to eat stone and go on.*

These essays don't give us a different autobiography from the poems because the primary interest of the essays, after all, is not autobiography per se but the relationship between a poet's life and work.

If the book took on the obligations of conventional auto-biography, it would require substantial reference to Hugo's

---

*The last sentence of this poem appears on Hugo's gravestone in the St. Mary's Cemetery, Missoula, Montana.

first marriage, for example. The title poem of *What Thou Lovest Well Remains American* gives us these chilling lines.

> Lawns well trimmed remind you of the train
> your wife took one day forever, some far empty town,
> the odd name you never recall. The time 6:23.
> The day: October 9. The year remains a blur.

Hugo's poems tell us how much his happy marriage to Ripley Schemm kindled and warmed his last years, and how thoroughly involved he became with her children from a previous marriage. But except for the sense of guilt for the failure of his first marriage that pervades all but his late poems, what do we know of his first wife? Little from the poems and less from the essays. At the memorial evening for Hugo, sponsored by the Academy of American Poets in the spring of 1984, Carolyn Kizer spoke of Hugo as lucky to have been married to two wonderful women.

My argument here isn't that Hugo should have included an essay on his first marriage, but that its absence tells us a great deal about how to understand the relationship between his life and work.

Surely Hugo felt loss and even abandonment, and surely he was fiercely and sometimes helplessly (the ferocity may well be in direct proportion to the helplessness) loyal to the circumstances of loss and abandonment. But this is a book about trying to get home. It is a given, here as everywhere in Hugo's work, that we're all lost and abandoned.

Isn't our fascination with loss dangerous to us precisely because what we most grieve for is not what we honestly lost, but what we never had, and which therefore no amount of imaginative fervor can ever restore to us? It's too much to lug home.

"In a way, all towns you look at could be your home town," Hugo said in his *Ohio Review* interview. We know the towns, or town, he meant. Some of its names are Kalalock, La Push, Gooseprairie, Mukilteo, Tahola, Bear Paw, Philipsburg, Nine Mile and Ten Sleep. There are Italian names (Tretitoli, Maratea, Acquafredda) and Scottish names (Uig, Ayr). There are more specific locations: West Marginal Way, 1614 Boren, the Milltown Union Bar and Spurgin Road Field. They are names of places, poems, and whole states of mind, all at once: "Helena, Where Homes Go Mad," "Where Jennie Used to Swim." "What the Brand New Freeway Won't Go Past," or "Where Mission Creek Runs Hard for Joy."

The meaning of the profusion is not just a rich life and a bottomless longing for connection, though Hugo had both. And the meaning isn't primarily that Hugo could find emblems of the collision between communal optimism and private degradation, between planning and loss, between courage and failure, wherever he turned his gaze.

The meaning of the profusion is that the process is endless. For to say "all towns you look at could be your home town" is not only to say you are homeless but that you are potentially at home anywhere. It is to say along with Whitman that you can, by continuous imaginative appropriation, belong to America, however beautifully and terrifyingly vast it is. And it is to say that the continuous reclamation of a hometown, the original mystifying poise between self and others, is the lifelong imaginative project to any adult.

There are specialized ways to carry out this work more formally and purposively than usual, and Hugo used two of them: psychotherapy and writing. Here and there in the poems we see residue from psychotherapy.

> You conquer loss
> by going to the place it happened
> and replaying it, saying the name
> of the face in the open casket right.

This passage reminds us of those moments in Hitchcock's films *(Psycho, Marnie)* where the complexity of personality and psychic life is suddenly compromised by a need for explanation. And it seems to be the nature of self-regard that it is a process without a clearly definable product or explanation.

The passage about the open casket fits psychoanalytic theory neatly enough, and that's finally the problem. It has the relationship to the process that theology has to God. What's interesting about Hugo's urge to write the lines is the explicit parallel between whatever he learned from psychotherapy and his relentless homing, which is not explained by his poems or these essays, but is beautifully embodied by them.

Seen in this light, all Hugo's work (including his book of pedagogical essays, *The Triggering Town,* and his mystery novel *Death and the Good Life*) is the work of ceaseless reclamation.

Each town was a new opportunity. I remember driving with Hugo from Boulder to Fort Collins to conduct a workshop in 1976. When we got in, we took motel rooms and then convened in Dick's room to watch baseball and eat ice cream. Dick went in for flavors whose names ended in *brickle, twirl* or *ripple.* He liked things stirred up and impure. At the workshop he would criticize a sentiment like "I want to hold you forever," not by describing it as a cliché but by asking "What will you do when you need to pee?" But this was ahead of us. We were driving along the Colorado foothills and Dick was reading out the names of the small towns we passed through. "Damn it!" he called out after a few miles. "Who cares what altitude they're at? Why don't these signs give the population?"

I think he wanted to know not how many but how few people lived in those towns. Always room for one more.

—William Matthews

A CHRONOLOGY OF
RICHARD HUGO'S LIFE

DECEMBER 21, 1923   Richard Franklin Hogan born to Esther Clara Monk Hogan & Franklin James Hogan in White Center, a community on the south side of Seattle, Washington.

AUGUST 1924   Brought to live with maternal grandparents, Fred & Ora Monk, and raised in their home.

1927   Esther Monk Hogan, now divorced, marries Herbert F. Hugo. His mother does not take Richard to live with them.

NOVEMBER 30, 1942   Richard Hogan changes name legally to Richard Franklin Hugo.

1943–48   Army Air Corps, Mediterranean Theatre: Bombardier, 35 missions. First Lieutenant. Air Medal with 3 Oakleaf clusters. 5 Bronze Battle Stars, Distinguished Flying Cross.

JUNE 1948   B.A., University of Washington. Takes the first 2 poetry courses Theodore Roethke taught.

JUNE 1950   Finishes graduate work, but forgets to pay graduation fee.

JUNE 1952   M.A., University of Washington.

1952   Marries Barbara Williams.

1951–63   Technical Writing, The Boeing Company, Seattle.

1961   *A Run of Jacks*, Univ. of Minnesota Press.

1963   Trip to Italy with wife, Barbara.

1964–65	Visiting Lecturer, University of Montana (wife Barbara returns to Seattle in the fall of 1964; they divorce shortly thereafter.)
1965	*Death of the Kapowsin Tavern,* Harcourt, Brace & World.
1966–67	Subject of Dave Smith's film *The Lady in Kicking Horse Rervoir.* Black & White, 16 mm. ½ hour.
1967–68	Rockefeller Fellowship for Creative Writing; travels to Italy alone.
1965–69	Assistant Professor at University of Montana.
1969	*Good Luck in Cracked Italian,* The World Publishing Co.
1969–70	Associate Professor, University of Montana.
1970–71	Visiting Poet, University of Iowa.
SUMMER 1971	Roethke Chair, University of Washington.
FALL 1971	Buys his first home, on Agnes Street in Missoula.
1971–1982	Professor & Director of Creative Writing, University of Montana.
1973	*The Lady in Kicking Horse Reservoir,* W. W. Norton. Nominated for the National Book Award.
OCTOBER 26, 1973	Meets Ripley Schemm Hansen.
JULY 12, 1974	Richard Hugo marries Ripley Schemm in Coeur d'Alene, Idaho. He moves to Wylie St. where they live with Ripley's children, Matthew & Melissa, various dogs, cats & horses beside Rattlesnake creek.
1974–75	Visiting Professor, University of Colorado.
1975	*What Thou Lovest Well Remains American,* W. W. Norton. Nominated for the National Book Award.

1976	Roethke Poetry Award.
1976–77	Subject of Annick Smith's film *Kicking the Loose Gravel Home.* Color, 16 mm. One hour.
1977	Appointed editor of the Yale Younger Poets series.
1977–78	Guggenheim Memorial Foundation Fellowship: Dick & Ripley & Melissa spend the year on the Isle of Skye, Scotland.
	Runner-up for the Pulitzer Prize.
1979	*The Triggering Town* (essays), W. W. Norton.
	Selected Poems, W. W. Norton.
1980	*The Right Madness on Skye,* W. W. Norton.
	White Center, W. W. Norton.
FALL 1980	Visiting Distinguished Professor Chair, University of Arkansas, Little Rock.
1981	*Death and the Good Life* (a novel), St. Martin's Press. Nominated for the Pulitzer Prize.
	Awarded Academy of American Poets Fellowship.
JUNE 1982	Honorary Degree, Doctor of Letters, Montana State University.
JUNE 1982	Distinguished Scholar Award, University of Montana.
OCTOBER 22, 1982	Richard Hugo dies of leukemia at Virginia Mason Hospital in Seattle.
1983	*Sea Lanes Out,* Dooryard Press.
	Making Certain It Goes On: The Collected Poems of Richard Hugo, W. W. Norton.
1985	Richard Hugo's papers acquired by the University of Washington Archives.

—Compiled by Lois M. Welch

Certain I
Remember
Everything Wrong

(—"White Center")

The Real West Marginal Way

IN MANY of my early poems, the speaker is, I am, somewhere along West Marginal Way, the slow lower reaches of the Duwamish River, the last two or three miles before the river ends in Elliot Bay, Puget Sound. Reading these early poems, one might think I spent much time in that area and had an intimate knowledge of the place, but that's not true.

I lived in White Center, several miles south of the Riverside area where these early poems locate themselves, and was only partially familiar with the landscape. This is the first of a series of Duwamish River poems I published:

West Marginal Way

One tug pounds to haul an afternoon
of logs up river. The shade
of Pigeon Hill across the bulges
in the concrete crawls on reeds
in a short field, cools a pier
and the violence of young men
after cod. The crackpot chapel,
with a sign erased by rain, returned
before to calm and a mossed roof.

A dim wind blows the roses
growing where they please. Lawns
are wild and lots are undefined
as if the payment made in cash
were counted then and there.

These names on boxes will return
with salmon money in the fall,
come drunk down the cinder arrow
of a trail, past the store of Popich,
sawdust piles and the saw mill
bombing air with optimistic sparks,
blinding gravel pits and the brickyard
baking, to wives who taught themselves
the casual thirst of many summers
wet in heat and taken by the sea.

Some places are forever afternoon.
Across the road and a short field
there is the river, split and yellow
and this far down affected by the tide.

Making Certain It Goes On, p. 5.

After all these years (I wrote many of the poems in that first
volume—*A Run of Jacks*—long years before the book was finally
published), it strikes me as a confident poem, especially for a
time when confidence in writing or much else was hard to
come by. Though the area is small, the view seems panoramic.
Poems closer to home usually limited themselves to a single
person.

Neighbor

The drunk who lives across the street from us
fell in our garden, on the beet patch
yesterday. So polite. Pardon me,
he said. He had to be helped up and held,
steered home and put to bed, declaring
we got to have another drink and smile.

I admit my envy. I've found him in salal
and flat on his face in lettuce, and bent
and snoring by that thick stump full of rain
we used to sail destroyers on.
And I've carried him home so often
stone to the rain and me, and cheerful.

I try to guess what's in that dim warm mind.
Does he think about horizoned firs
black against the light, thirty years
ago, and the good girl—what's her name—
believing, or think about the dog
he beat to death that day in Carbonado?

I hear he's dead, and wait now on my porch.
He must be in his shack. The wagon's
due to come and take him where they take
late alcoholics, probably called Farm's End.
I plan my frown, certain he'll be carried out
bleeding from the corners of his grin.

Making Certain It Goes On, p. 44

I've already written in detail elsewhere about my early life
and growing up with my grandparents who were ignorant,
sentimental and innocent, worn by a life of hard work and by
raising five children of their own. Here it should be sufficient
to summarize. I was subjected to gratuitous beatings and dis-
torted, intense but, by any conventional standards, undemon-
strated affection by my grandmother, who, I was convinced
years later, had not been right in the head. My grandfather
was a silent man, at times a defeated one who sometimes sat
in a wood straightback chair in the kitchen and stared at the
floor, his head bowed. He occasionally threatened to turn me
out of the house. I saw my mother sporadically. She had left
me with my grandparents when I was less than two. She had
divorced my father by then. I first met him when I was thirty.

By the time I was a young man I was a mess. I had the
normal urge to show girls affection and the normal need to
receive affection in return. But with my hatred and fears of
women, normal relations with them were impossible. My
behavior around girls was uncontrollably affected and con-
voluted, and for a long time I was convinced I would know
the disdain of women all my life. By clowning and obsequious
displays of generosity, I set out to make friends with men
everywhere, sensing that being liked by others insured survival. The dignity and self sufficiency I longed for, I found

on the baseball and softball fields, or when I was alone. It is no accident that the speaker in many of my poems is alone and that the people he has relations with are usually dead.

Years later my neurosis was so advanced it threatened to be crippling and I sought help. The doctor told me that writing was the luckiest sort of adjustment and that given my life it was a miracle I was not a criminal. Our alcoholic neighbor was no idle curiosity. I believed that I might very well end up that way, and the idea isn't unattractive.

I'd best try to clarify some topography. West Marginal Way parallels the Duwamish River for several miles, but the part I used in my poems is a stretch of about three miles from the foot of Boeing Hill (now renamed Highland Park Way) north to Spokane Street where it ends, a half mile or so from the river mouth. This stretch runs along the base of a high steep hill thickly wooded with alders, maples and evergreens. The north end of this hill, that part near Spokane Street, is called Pigeon Hill. Traveling on West Marginal Way, just before you reach Spokane Street, you come to Riverside, a cluster of drab frame houses. Many immigrants lived there in the 30s, Slavs and Greeks mostly. The homes huddle together and climb the east side of Pigeon Hill, up into alders and ivy. The names, Popich, Zuvela, Petrapolous, were exotic, and the community, more European in appearance than any other in Seattle, always seemed beautiful to me.

I was ready to believe all stories I heard about Riverside. The Greeks who distrusted banks and kept huge amounts of cash in their houses. The Slavs who bought cheap bourbon in the liquor store, then mixed it with pieces of raw fruit in mason jars which they put on their roofs all summer for the sun to work on. The results were said to be staggering. Succulent dishes the immigrant women prepared with eels, cod and sole the river provided. Old John, the Greek fisherman, whose feats of strength had become legend along the river. He had killed a bear in an exhibition wrestling match in Alaska. He could throw the bow rope over his shoulder and walk away from the river hauling his twenty foot fishing skiff onto the dry land. He had once knocked two thieves senseless, then carried them, one over each shoulder, a quarter of a mile to

the rundown Riverside grocery on Spokane Street where he
called the police.

Between The Bridges

These shacks are tricks. A simple smoke
from wood stoves, hanging half-afraid
to rise, makes poverty in winter real.
Behind unpainted doors, old Greeks
are counting money with their arms.
Different birds collect for crumbs
each winter. The loners don't
but ought to wear red shawls.

Here, a cracked brown hump
of knuckle caved a robber's skull.
That cut fruit is for Slavic booze.
Jars of fruit-spiked bourbon bake
on roofs throughout July; festive tubs
of vegetables get wiser in the sun.
All men are strong. Each woman knows
how river cod can be preserved.

Money is for life. Let the money
pile up thirty years and more.
Not in banks, but here, in shacks
where green is real: the stacks of tens
and twenties and the moss on broken piles
big ships tied to when the river
and the birds ran painted to the sea.

Making Certain It Goes On, p. 60.

On the other side of Pigeon Hill, the west side, sits Youngstown (now renamed Delridge) where many of the Riverside
residents worked in the Bethlehem Steel Mill, and where the
children went to grammar school. The school was called
Youngstown then. Now it's called James B. Cooper. In White
Center, those of us who lived inside the Seattle city limits,
attended Highland Park Grammar School.

The boys of Youngstown-Riverside and the boys of White Center shared at least one concern. Many of us felt socially inferior to children of West Seattle. If the girls of our district felt that, I never heard them express it but then I seldom spoke with girls. There, directly west of Youngstown, sat the castle, the hill, West Seattle where we would go to high school. What a middle class paradise. The streets were paved, the homes elegant, the girls well groomed and simply by virtue of living in West Seattle, far more beautiful and desirable than the girls in our home districts. Gentility and confidence reigned on that hill. West Seattle was not a district. It was an ideal. To be accepted there meant one had become a better person. West Seattle was too far to be seen from White Center, but for the children of Youngstown and Riverside, it towered over the sources of felt debasement, the filthy, loud belching steel mill, the oily slow river, the immigrants hanging on to their odd ways, Indians getting drunk in the unswept taverns, the commercial fisherman, tugboat workers and mill workers with their coarse manners.

When people from White Center applied for work in the 20s and 30s, they seldom mentioned White Center, either in the interview or on the application form. The smart ones said they lived in West Seattle. White Center had the reputation of being just outside the boundary of the civilized world. This stigma remains and as recently as ten years ago a movement started but failed to change the name to Delridge Heights or something equally offensive in its sorry try for respectability.

The reputation was not without reason. White Center was tough. Roxbury Street, the city limits, splits White Center, and following the repeat of prohibition, drinking laws were far more lenient outside the city. Just south of Roxbury street the taverns flourished. People came to White Center from miles around to have a good time and a good time often involved a good brawl. When I was fourteen, I would go to the roller rink, not to skate but to wait for a fight to start. I had my heroes, Bill Gavin, Tommy Silverthorn. Many of the White Center toughs, like Gavin, came from Youngstown or Riverside. Fights started in the rink with a challenge by someone who had suffered insult enough to serve as an excuse, and ended outside with somebody senseless and bloody on the gravel. I idolized those tough guys but I was too frightened to fight. I stood outside that brutal world, a fascinated witness, winning vicariously. Those battlers from Youngstown and Riverside seemed super masculine, and I wanted to be one of them.

I had two direct connections with West Marginal Way. One was with the Duwamish Slough where I often went fishing when I was nine, ten, eleven, twelve. Duwamish Slough, long ago filled in by progress, sat along West Marginal Way at the foot of Boeing Hill, now renamed Highland Park Way. What fishing that was. Porgies, shiners we called them, were so numerous there that after the out-tide drained the slough, we continued to catch them out of the small puddles left standing in the mud flats. I remember vividly the bloated dogs we used to find in those flats, gunnysacks of rocks around their swollen necks. During the Depression, people killed their pets to save the expense of feeding them. An old shingle mill stood beside the slough, but it was seldom operating when we fished there beside it. A cat lived at that mill, a mascot of the mill crew. He was so tough he used to dive into the slough and catch shiners for his meals. I make reference to him in the last stanza of a poem called Duwamish Head. West Marginal Way bridged the slough just south of where it crossed Boeing Hill. Someone, probably the mill crew, had built an outhouse that hung over the slough under the bridge. Sometimes we fished through the toilet down into the water. It made no difference. Shiners nibbled wherever we fished. Along the back part of the slough stood an abandoned brickmill. It was a large low red brick building, and when we were bored catching fish we, chums from White Center and I, explored the mill. We never got far. There were only a few small openings, doorways a grown man had to hunch down to pass through, and little light got inside.

But that is not the West Marginal Way of my poems. My speaker, I, whoever, was downstream at least a mile, alone on the bank with the reeds, birds, the ponderous tugs towing huge log sections upstream, the usual gray sky of Seattle turning the river gray. I saw people who never were, in a place I had never been.

No Bells to Believe

When bells ring, wild rain pelts the river.
Who rings bells in the abandoned chapel,
once a school, once a shed where hide
was stored? The painter painting reeds
a private color, poppy farmer,
and the seiner folding autumn's nets—
they hear the bells and don't look up.

Mad Sam, the nutty preacher rings the bells.
He remained despite that mess, twelve
years back—the squaw—the poisoned wine.
Not Sam. He drowned beneath a boom.

No bells. Even when Mad Sam went mad
with God each Sunday and the women wept
to hear their imperfections yelled across
the river while a drum knocked Jesus
senseless and the tugboats tooted home.
No bells then. None now. What rings here
is something in the air unnamed.

The wild rain rings. The painter's reeds
run down the canvas in a colorful
defeat, the seiner's nets gain weight
and poppies wash away. The women told
Mad Sam before he ran out on the logs,
you must accept the ringing like the day.

Making Certain It Goes On, p. 51.

Where did that come from? I may have been thinking of that "crack pot chapel" from the poem "West Marginal Way" when I dreamed Mad Sam. But I'd dreamed that chapel too. I don't know if nutty religious groups operated along West

Marginal Way. They certainly operated around White Center. I must have been transplanting.

I know where I got the way Mad Sam died. When I was in the first grade, an Indian boy, a classmate, drowned in the Duwamish. He had been playing on a log boom and fell into the river, got trapped under the logs and died trying to find an opening. His mother flipped and for years called him to dinner every evening in prolonged fits of scream. They lived close to Highland Park School, and her afternoon screeching gave neighbors the creeps.

I see myself in the poem, "the painter painting reeds a private color." I considered myself a private poet in those days, almost to a point of arrogance. If someone didn't understand my poems, I was pleased. Could I have been the poppy farmer? Did I have some egomaniacal Coleridgian notion that my poems might offer the euphoric glory of opium? I hope not for christsake, but it's possible. The seiner folding autumn's nets must have been me and my sexual timidity, the fishing season over and the nets empty, able to gain weight not from a vital catch of thrashing salmon but only from the rain they soaked up lying useless on the ground. Certainly I was Mad Sam, ringing bells no one responded to, remaining on the scene of a shameful past hoping in time to be accepted, prejudiced against women, feeling the only salvation possible was through self-acceptance and equally convinced that only women, with whom I could not communicate, could tell me the truth about self-acceptance. I and my poems were doomed. The paint would not hold on the canvas. Any chance for happiness would be cut off at the source as the poppies and their promise of euphoria washed away.

But why did I have to go to the river to find the poems? Why not around White Center, the district I knew so well? Somehow, along those lonely marshy banks I dreamed, I could exercise the suspended cynicism necessary to write a poem. Some might say that once I got away from home I had some distance on myself, but that is misleading I think. If anything I got closer to myself. One thing is clear: along the Duwamish I made no distinction between the odd things I created, Mad Sam, the poppy farmer, and those things endemic to the scene, tugs, commercial fish nets. I always wanted to be tough, like those young men who lived near the river and came to White Center to fight, and in my poems I could get tough, at least with myself. Once I imagined myself along the river, my language got hard and direct.

Duwamish No. 2

Mudhens, cormorants and teals take
legal sanctuary in the reeds,
birds and reeds one grey. The river
when the backed-up tide lets go
flows the only north the birds believe.
North is easy. North is never love.

On the west hill, rich with a million
alders and five hundred modern homes,
birds, deep in black, insist the wind
will find the sea. The river points
the wrong way on the in-tide
and the alders lean to the arid south.

Take away all water. Men are oiling
guns beside ripped cows. Wrens have claws
and clouds cascade with poison down
a cliff mapped badly by an Indian.
Tumbleweeds are plotted to stampede.
Where there is no river, pregnant
twice a day with a tide, and twice each day
released by a stroking moon,
animals are dangerous as men.

When the world hurts, I come back alone
along the river, certain the salt
of vague eyes makes me ready for the sea.
And the river says: you're not unique—
learn now there is one direction only—
north, and, though terror to believe,
quickly found by river and never love.

Making Certain It Goes On, p. 61.

I don't like the poem much, but the last stanza demon-
strates a tough way of addressing myself. Those "vague eyes"
I wanted to escape were the eyes of nineteenth century sentimentality I'd inherited from my grandparents. In the third
stanza, the loneliness I felt to be an unattractive force along
the river seems a kind of protection against a brutal world I
felt I could not live in and survive. I know what north means,
what it always meant. In Seattle the obvious flow is north. Wind
is usually from the south, so clouds go north, trees and grass
bend north. Big ships leaving port go north to exit from Puget
Sound through the Straits of Juan de Fuca. The Duwamish,
Seattle's one big river, flows north. As a child I believed life
was a northern journey and at some unknown point far to the
north, all things end.

My other direct (real, not imaginary) connection with West
Marginal Way and the river was through a boy named Don
Crouse. Don, and his older brother Ray, would come up from
the river to Highland Park to play ball on our Park League
team. They even came for practice despite the long trip, which
they often covered on foot. Don played shortstop and Ray
played first base. Both were good players and when they
appeared, I felt our team was complete. Later Don and I played
American Legion and High School ball together.

Don invited me salmon fishing. He owned a boat and had
won a motor in a salmon derby. Morning, around four, I caught
the first bus from White Center and rode to Riverside. I walked
the hard dark autumn morning down the hill and along West
Marginal Way to Don's house. I had never been salmon fishing before, but Don had plenty of extra tackle, and we putted
down the foggy steaming Duwamish to the bay. Dawn lit up
the fog until it was blinding pink. The river was alive with
salmon. They rolled and splashed everywhere. I could hear
them in the fog, and some I could see, huge shadows that
climbed the air and slipped back into the water so close to the
boat I could have touched them. It seemed impossible that we
could fail to catch a fish, but we caught nothing. We trolled
the bay for hours and gave up. The salmon surfaced close
around us and everywhere I looked after the fog burned away,
but none took our plugs. The motor gave up too, and the out-
tide was pouring down the river. I tried rowing but made no

headway. Don took over and with patient relentless strokes took us home. Years later when he had become a commercial fisherman, we chanced to meet and I saw his arms had grown to be enormous. I thought of the day he'd made that long tortuous row.

Another day I visited Don, he took me to a bird sanctuary. At high tide it was an island, but not after the out-tide drained the water from the channels next to the mainland. Don brought his shotgun, and we walked through the reeds and tall grasses where grebes, teals, ducks, pigeons, doves and other fowl were nesting or catching a nap. Don shot a few birds and carried them in plain sight home along West Marginal Way. He seemed unconcerned about getting caught, and that day I got the idea that no one cared what you did along the river. West Marginal Way was a world outside the mainstream of city life, isolated and ignored. Once you left the heavily industrialized area at the Spokane Street Bridge and started upstream from Riverside toward Boeing Hill, West Marginal Way was, in those days, a curious combination of the industrial and rural. A brickyard, a saw mill or a sand and gravel company operated here and there. More often they were idle, abandoned beside the slow river. The street itself was an old worn concrete road with cracks and hunchings. Homes were mostly scattered, like remote farms, with wild thick lawns and roofs heavily mossed. I can't recall a mowed lawn or a kept yard, or even a defined one. It was as if the people had no concept of property. The natural took over, blackberry bushes, snakeweed, scotch broom. Houses were allowed to weather year after year.

Hideout

In the reeds, the search for food by grebes
is brief. Each day, inside the shack
the wind paints white, a man keeps warm
by listening to ships go by, keeps sane
by counting European faces
passing north in clouds. Tugs deposit
miles of logs outside. A tax collector
couldn't find this place with holy maps.

When salmon crowd each other
in the river, and the river boils
with re-creation's anger, what tall man
re-creates too clearly domes of mills
downstream, and the gradual opening
as if the river loved the city
or was crying loudly "take me" to the sea?
What odd games children play.
One shouts himself into a president.
Another pins the villain salmon
to the air with spears. A rowboat
knocks all night against a pile.

Morning brings a new wind and a new
white coat of weather for the shack.
The salmon moved upstream last night
and no bird cuts the river, looking
for a smelt. Ships sail off to Naples
and the bent face bobbing in the wake
was counted in another cloud gone north.

Making Certain It Goes On, p. 64.

Except for two or three trips to Don Crouse's in my early teens, and those earlier fishing trips to the slough, West Marginal Way and the Duwamish River remained unfamiliar and lived only in my mind all those years, ready for use when finally I was writing poems good enough to get published. Much that I visualized came from stories I heard from boys who lived there. Our subjects choose us, I suppose, if we let them. Certainly, our landscapes do. They must. And writing a poem finally may be a form of self-acceptance in alien country.

Duwamish

Midwestern in the heat, this river's
curves are slow and sick. Water knocks
at mills and concrete plants, and crud
compounds the gray. On the out-tide,

water, half salt water from the sea,
rambles by a barrel of molded nails,
gray lumber piles, moss on ovens
in the brickyard no one owns.
Boys are snapping tom cod spines
and jeering at the Greek who bribes
the river with his sailing coins.

Because the name is Indian, Indians
ignore the river as it cruises
past the tavern. Gulls are driving crazy
where boys nail porgies to the pile.
No Indian would interrupt his beer
to tell the story of the snipe
who dove to steal the nailed girl
late one autumn, with the final salmon in.

This river colors day. On bright days
here, the sun is always setting or obscured
by one cloud. Or the shade extended to the
far bank just before you came.
And what should flare, the Chinese red
of a searun's fin, the futile roses,
unkept cherry trees in spring, is muted.
For the river, there is late November
only, and the color of a slow winter.

On the short days, looking for a word,
knowing the smoke from the small homes
turns me colder than wind from
the cold river, knowing this poverty
is not a lack of money but of friends,
I come here to be cold. Not silver cold
like ice, for ice has glitter. Gray
cold like the river. Cold like 4 P.M.
on Sunday. Cold like a decaying porgy.

But cold is a word. There is no word along
this river I can understand or say.

Not Greek threats to a fishless moon
nor Slavic chants. All words are Indian.
Love is Indian for water, and madness
means, to Redmen, I am going home.

Making Certain It Goes On, p. 44.

For me, that poem illuminates my need to return again
and again to West Marginal Way and the river for poems. I
seem to relive my early personal sense of defeat out to some
sort of poetic fulfillment. My assumed right to self-pity in my
youth later became my license to write a poem. I could create
something out of my past personal sense of futility in language hard enough to prohibit wallowing in melancholy. And
it must have occurred to me, at least unconsciously, that to
have remained with my grandparents in that austere home
long years after I had reached the age where I should have
left, was a kind of madness. For all purposes, we had stopped
speaking to each other years before grandmother died, and I
moved away. And years later imagining myself there along
the river, I could convert myself into a Greek tough enough
to survive my disdain, and into an Indian long enough to tell
myself the truth. For the duration of the poem, I became a
man sufficiently honest to warrant my own approval.

If I once subjected girls to cruelty in fantasies, of vengeance for the pain and rejection I had suffered at the hands
of women, I could also turn myself into a snipe and dive
heroically out of the sky to rescue them. I would be better
than I felt I was, better than a boy who fantasized himself into
violent roles and snapped tom cod spines and who, out of
insecurity, jeered at the foreign and the strange. The latter
was what middle class people did. Did I really want to be a
part of West Seattle? Or did my poems keep me honest to my
isolated self, away from the smooth pavements and even
smoother girls of the respectable well-kept hill to the west?

I'm aware of the dangers of locating poems in overly
familiar territory. Too much memory remains to interfere with
the imagination. I think the West Marginal Way I created was
a place where I could melodramatically extend and exploit
certain feelings I had about myself and ignore others that,

had I tried to root my poems in White Center, would have gotten in the way. Did a lone tug struggling to haul acres of logs against the out-tide flow of the river represent some melodramatic picture I had of myself? Was gray wind bending marsh grass a force I fantasized within me, persistent as it was futile? I believe I went to the river for poems because I could imaginatively realize self-acceptance there that I had not felt closer to home. I could accept there those parts of self that elsewhere would have unwelcome handicaps. Perhaps every poet has his West Marginal Way somewhere. For some it may not even be a place, in the geographical sense. Along that river my defeats and fears turned into a raw ore, my loneliness became a dramatic ploy, my desolation made me a citizen of that ignored and unique world, even one with the fish in the brackish water backed up on the in-tide from a bay that, on our best days, glittered blue and clean to the north.

The St. James
Lutheran 5

IN THE late 30s, the St. James Lutheran church of White
Center, Washington, had a basketball team. Just barely. Just
barely because we had only five players, and just barely because
we had no coach, no plays, no organization. We didn't have
uniforms either. We played in our trousers, stripped to the
waist. The few times we won, we won by luck, a little defense
and, for 13- and 14-year-olds, some rough play under the
boards. But mostly luck. Elmer Matson and I were the best
shots and we were terrible. We just came closer than Benny
Fiedler, Karl Schalka and Eddie Nelson.

We lacked experience of even the most basic kind. Highland Park grammer school, which we all attended, had no baskets. How impoverished St. James Lutheran came to have
baskets, I don't know. They hung at either end of the small
rec room that served as the church auditorium and social hall.
For several years, the high point of a church social affair came
when Mr. Clark, who was related to Benny Fiedler in some
way, sang "We Just Couldn't Say Goodbye." We clapped and
clapped when Mr. Clark had finished. I never remember Mr.
Clark singing any other song. If we applauded long enough,
Mr. Clark sang "We Just Couldn't Say Goodbye" again.

Our team was not in a league. The wind forbid. Once we
were defeated 42 to 3 at the Seattle downtown YMCA by a
bunch from West Seattle. They'd attended schools that had
baskets and basketballs, and they'd picked up some fundamentals along the way. Little things we didn't know, like
breaking for the basket, screening, passing and shooting.

I started Sunday School at St. James when I was three.
Grandmother saw to it I did not miss. I hated it and went
under the threat of a beating if I resisted, since Grandmoth-

er's beatings were no laughing matter. I never stopped hating
it all ten years I had to attend. I detested every step through
the woods on the trail that led from our backyard to 16th,
though I loved that trail itself, then south a half block on 16th
to Cambridge, and west on Cambridge to 18th where the old
frame brown church sat on the crest of the small hill. I ran
every loving step of freedom back the same route when we
were finally released.

One day in Sunday school we were discussing right and
wrong, good and evil, and I eagerly pointed out that Eddie
Cantor was a good man because he gave newcomers a chance
to sing on his radio show. Both Deanna Durbin and Bobby
Breen got their start there. "But," Mrs. Brandt, our teacher,
said, "Remember Eddie Cantor is a Jew, and a Jew's right
hand always knows what his left hand is doing." I was hurt
that my contribution had been rejected. Why wasn't Eddie
Cantor good if he did good things? And what did hands have
to do with it? What was a Jew, anyway?

As I got older I found some saving things about the church,
namely the baskets, the basketball and a kitchen window I
could jimmy. I would shoot baskets alone for hours inside the
locked church. The thud of the ball on the floor echoed
spookily in light that seemed gray once it entered the small
windows. Once when I had stopped to rest, the church bells
started to ring. I froze in fear as the room filled with clangs,
and I imagined the bells ringing themselves. When the bells
stopped I bolted home without locking the door or putting
the ball away.

The degradation I associated with the church, with the
pitifully small congregation of the early and mid 30s, the spir-
itless self-conscious singing of hymns, as if the singers were
afraid they might be heard, the two posturing insecure sons
of a woman who had a mustache and hairs growing from her
chin, the torn yellow wallpaper (or was it flaking yellow plaster?), was never more felt than when I was thirteen and had
to take confirmation. If I didn't take confirmation I was assured
I'd be thrown out of the house to make my own way in the
world. That was threat enough. I had little courage or character.

I was the only boy in the confirmation class. That reinforced my suspicion that religion was unmanly and only for girls. Grandmother was ultra-religious while Grandfather was indifferent. He went to church seldom, and when he did he looked uncomfortable and bored.

The five or six girls in the class and I sat in the church kitchen under the bare overhead lightbulb and took religious instruction. At least the girls took it. I didn't read any of the assignments. During class I stared at the floor, embarrassed and depressed, and refused to speak. I didn't listen to the others, and if called on mumbled anything that would get them off my back so I could return to whatever fantasy I was playing before the interruption.

One day at grammar school, some of my colleagues on the softball team told me they had spied on the class through the kitchen window. Shame flooded my stomach and my face burned. I wanted to lash out at them, their grinning faces. I wanted to run away forever. God damnit, other boys didn't have to take confirmation. In the confirmation class picture I looked as uncomfortable as I felt.

If the church and religion were feminine, basketball was not. The high points of the season were when we beat Fauntleroy twice, both times by one or two points. I'm not sure how we did that. They were boys from affluent homes two miles west of White Center, and they were disciplined players, well coached and drilled in fundamentals. Were they psyched out playing boys from the legendary tough White Center district? I doubt that. We weren't tough, except for Eddie Nelson, and he was not a hostile boy.

We played both times at Fauntleroy. We never played anyone at St. James, since the gym there was not really a gym. There were no seats, or even room for seats, and no showers. Fauntleroy's gym was modern, with tiered stands where Fauntleroy's well groomed mothers and staid looking fathers in suits and ties (really, or am I making that up?) came to cheer their sons on.

What a good team Fauntleroy was. Their passing dazzled and befuddled us as they broke plays that to our untutored reflexes seemed performed in dream. Eddie and I picked up the boy streaking to the basket with the ball just in time, when we did. I suppose we beat them both times because their shooting was off and Eddie and I, the two biggest boys, grabbed our share of rebounds. Our offense consisted of standing around with the ball looking for someone to pass to, hoping Elmer Matson could find room and time for a shot. Yet both times we left the Fauntleroy parents disappointed when we headed back home happy with our narrow victory.

It was around the time of the short lived St. James Lutheran basketball team that Frank Capra's *Lost Horizon* came to George Shrigley's White Center Theatre. How I admired Ronald Coleman. What class. And how I wanted to be like him, calm and detached while being kidnapped, the plane headed who knows where deeper and deeper into the mountain ranges of west China. But I was like the others, concerned, nervous, frightened, unable to summon any dignity in the face of the uncertain and unknown.

And think of Shangri La, where people are always nice to each other, where you have a right to be simply because you are alive, where people live to be hundreds of years old protected from this mean world by gorgeous mountain ranges. It was almost too much for this 13-year-old. Don't leave, Mr. Coleman. Don't ever leave. But he did, and suddenly a lovely young woman was an old hag dead in the snow, and he was wandering aimlessly through the bitter weather alone. And then, just when all hope seemed gone, he found it again, that secure valley of paradise, and the bells rang, and Mr. Coleman's eyes glowed with the hope of all people, and blubberer that I was I've never blubbered harder in a movie. I was shattered. It took the whole newsreel and the cartoon which I'd already seen, before I was composed enough to go out into the streets of White Center.

Karl Shalka lived closest to us. He was an even-tempered boy who seemed to get along with everyone. He lived in a big house on the crest of First Hill, two blocks east of us, on what, for us, was the eastern horizon. His house might have dominated the landscape but it was obscured by the thick near tropical growth of the Pacific Northwest. Karl looked a little bit like the actor Jimmy Lydon, who played Henry Aldrich in the movies.

I knew Benny Fiedler best. We were in the same class in grammar school. Benny was a talented child and his mother saw to it he took music and dancing lessons. By the time he was seven or eight he had tapdanced on the stage of the Orpheum Theatre in downtown Seattle. Benny was a bit sissified in grade school, and since dancing itself was not considered masculine, some of the boys in our class disdained him. He seemed to have few friends when he was little and he wasn't good at sports though he could run fast. He may have been on the track team at Highland Park, I'm not sure.

Elmer Matson was small, graceful, quick. He had delicate features as a boy and suffered much of the time from colds. He overdressed, sweaters, jackets, overcoats, and he often wore rubbers at his mother's insistence. He was the only boy I knew who wore rubbers. The one time I remember being in his house it was suffocatingly hot, and I suspected Elmer wouldn't have so many colds if he weren't overheated most of the time. He looked like he might be temperamental but he wasn't. I remember him as unusually civilized for a boy in his beginning teens.

Eddie Nelson lived alone with his father. I think his mother was dead. Eddie's father was a house painter, I believe. Eddie was blond, near albino and husky. He had little personality and few complicated emotions. You'd expect him not to be temperamental and you'd be right. I can't imagine Eddie being psyched out in a game, his play affected by moods or the reputation of the opposition. He was rugged and simple.

When I thought about White Center, I often thought of the Tonkins and Wilbur Fordyce and Mr. and Mrs. Baker. I think Wilbur was Mrs. Tonkin's son by another marriage, and the Bakers were related also but I don't know how. The Tonkins and Wilbur lived across the street from us in the house long occupied by the Brockermans before they finally moved away to Bremerton. They were coarse people. That's a funny adjective for me to use but I can't think of another one that is so fitting. I seldom think of people that way and I imagine anyone who knows me would be surprised to hear me use the word 'coarse' when speaking of people. Yet, as a young boy, that's how I saw them. Jack Smith, who lived in the other house across the street, broke me up one day after the war when he remarked that he had been so hard up at times during the war that he could have given Wilhelmina Tonkin a bad time.

She was a huge unattractive woman with a loud voice. Mr. Tonkin limped badly.

The Tonkins, the Bakers and Wilbur seemed such low class people that living in the same neighborhood with them was a source of degradation. Junk littered their yard. An old car partly torn down. Cooking pans. Mr. Baker beat Louise and Buddy, his children, frequently, harshly and often for less than cause. Once after Buddy had done something quite minor, Mr. Baker yelled, "bend your ass over that car," and when Buddy complied across the fender, beat him with a thick rope knotted at the end. The rope looked like something from a Russian prison.

Mrs. Baker was a young woman who looked old. Her hair was gray and stringy, and her clothes were faded and limp from too many washings. She was a sad looking, silent woman, someone who had been defeated always, and she aged daily it seemed, almost as you looked at her, as if she were in another cycle of time.

Wilbur was around my age but I had little to do with him. He was gone much of the time, maybe back to some other place he'd lived where old friends remained. Wilbur seemed crude and ill mannered, tough too, and a trifle bitter. I found myself as intolerant of him as I was of the others.

One night in the White Center Theatre, I saw Mrs. Tonkin grinning inanely at a terribly produced, unfunny Marie Wilson comedy. I saw that as typical of White Center and my own heritage. No Taste. No Class. The evening Louise came out onto the gravel road that was our street, weeping violently, I mocked her and yelled "Louise got a spanking." For years I was haunted by my sudden cruelty. And when I remembered that, I realized I was from White Center too, as vile, as crude as I considered the others, and I made private vows to better myself. For many years whenever I did something I was ashamed of, I felt, in addition to the shame itself, a sense of failure. Would I ever be any better?

When I started high school in West Seattle, I found a place that seemed in more ways than just miles far from Wilbur Fordyce, the Tonkins, the Bakers. The streets, unlike ours, were all paved, and the homes were middle class, freshly painted and well kept, with trimmed lawns, some with clipped hedges. Both Elmer Matson and Karl Schalka were from middle class homes but that didn't impress itself on me. I wanted to pull away from all things White Center which I lumped into one undesirable past. I tried to cultivate new friends among the boys from West Seattle, and so in the next few years I lost contact with the members of the St. James Lutheran basketball team. It was a big high school, around 2000 students, and so it was possible to look for other circles in which to move. If I was to find any dignity, any confidence, any self-improvement, it would be with people from West Seattle. It didn't occur to me that the gang I found myself a part of in my senior year had no one as genteel as Matson, Schalka or Fiedler. I was so prejudiced toward places, I generalized beautiful girls in White Center into homely ones, plain girls in West Seattle into glamorous sirens.

For me, Betty Bolin epitomized the social superiority of West Seattle. Petite, pretty, well groomed, poised, she lived in a large home on top of the Admiral Way hill. Below her home, Elliott Bay, and across the bay all Seattle opening like a gift against the far backdrop of the Cascade mountains. I would never have had the nerve to ask her for a date but over a long period I developed an obsessive urge to speak to her. The day I finally found the courage to try I was so frightened words began to gush out faster than I could think. Her stare was as level as her posture, and I couldn't meet it for even a second it seemed. I stammered out of control until I was so embarrassed it was impossible to go on. I walked off fast, sweating and blushing, not realizing then that my fears were not just juvenile but signs of a sexual timidity that would cripple me for many years to come, and I found some remote spot where I could regain some composure. I hated Betty Bolin, not being sophisticated enough to know that it was really me I hated for having humiliated myself.

Benny Fiedler had gotten interested in tumbling early and by the time he was a junior in high school he was a muscular young man. His shoulders were wide and his chest and arms were huge. But as his body developed his eyesight, never very good, got worse. He made the football squad and sat on the bench until late in the season when the coach sent him in at defensive guard. I felt warm when Benny ran onto the field.

The sissy boy from Highland Park in a high school football game. When the ball was centered, Benny knocked the opposing lineman down and raced into the backfield so fast it seemed impossible that he hadn't been offside. There he was, a lone West Seattle player in the middle of a play that was just forming, with a chance to throw the play for a big loss. But he didn't. His eyesight was so bad he couldn't find the ball carrier.

Eddie Nelson filled out and became a very fine first string player for West Seattle, a defensive bear who either made all city or came close to it. He was savage on the field, quiet off of it. Given the accidental development of social affairs at that age, I found myself one night at a party with Eddie in West Seattle. Eddie's well-built date teased him into dominating her and he easily wrestled her to the couch as she giggled and protested unconvincingly. I was impressed with Eddie's masculinity, ashamed of my lack of it.

All five of us from the now defunct basketball team graduated from high school in the early 40s, and we all went into the service in World War II. Eddie and Karl joined the marines. Elmer Matson joined the navy. Benny Fiedler was drafted into the Army, and I joined the Army Air Corps. Three of us came back.

Benny Fiedler was killed in Belgium. The citation said that with the rank shot out from the front of the company, Benny led a charge of 1000 yards across Belgium soil under heavy German tank fire before he was cut down. I got that from Benny's father who took some pride in it. Since I came back with a DFC for a mission where the bombs fell in some remote Alpine region that might have been Switzerland, I was cynical about citations, but I didn't let Mr. Fiedler know it. In Benny's case, I hoped the citation was true, that those sneering bullies from Highland Park Grammar School would be wrong forever. But I was young then and at times righteousness was vital.

Benny had no business in the Army at all. The Army drafted him despite his bad eyesight and assured him he would see only limited service. Mr. Fiedler told me this with bitterness. Those were the days when a clerk inadvertently using the wrong rubber stamp on your records might seal your destiny.

Eddie Nelson bought it at Tarawa in the invasion assault. One day I ran into Ed Jersey, a White Center boy, in an old tavern down by the Duwamish slough. Ed had been in the Marines and was in sorry shape. He suffered from malaria and the depression some men experience after being frightened too many times in combat. He said he thought he had seen Eddie Nelson's body at Tarawa but he couldn't be sure. The body he'd seen had been in two pieces and he hadn't stopped to study it.

I saw Eddie's father after the war, in the streets of White Center. He was shuffling aimlessly along as if he had no destination. I didn't speak to him. He seemed so forlorn I imagined the immediate air about him looked gray.

A year or so after the war, I saw Elmer Matson. He had recently married and was living in an apartment only a couple of blocks from our place in White Center. He seemed happy and on his way to a full life, and I envied him. I thought he couldn't miss, a well-mannered, good-looking young man like that.

And it was in the first year after the war that I was drinking beer with a couple of old friends from White Center in the Swallow Tavern when Mr. Baker was suddenly at our table, the way people are suddenly at your table in taverns. Mrs. Baker had just died and he wanted to talk about it with someone. He hated himself for the hard life he'd given his wife, and he blamed himself for her death. Now and then his eyes misted up. We sat and drank beer late into the night and talked intimately like old friends.

I was no longer interested in the church but I heard about it now and then from Grandmother. It rode the post-war religious revival to modernization. Now it was a large brick building, not the old frame one, and the congregation had multiplied. The old timers still came, many nearing death, those strange sad people who had kept the church going during the Depression years. But now successful business people from White Center attended. Some assumed positions of power in the church. At one point the Fiedlers thought of finding another church. Some of the new, "highly respectable" members ridiculed Mr. Fiedler for the way his face looked when he passed the collection plate. He had passed the collection plate for years but now his expression wasn't dignified enough. Too matter of fact.

Betty Bolin looked no different when I saw her in 1960 at a University of Washington football game. She introduced me to her husband. Both looked like well-heeled alumni. They were living in one of the fashionable suburbs that had developed east of Lake Washington after the war. We fell into a brief conversation. When she told me how hard it was becoming to cross over the lake to Seattle, I said, "Don't worry, you'll have a second bridge in a matter of forty years." She laughed brightly. It was a local joke. Authorities had been discussing and seemingly doing little else about a second bridge for years.

How easy it was to talk with her. Maybe it always had been. She was just a nice woman, down to earth and unaffected. As she disappeared into the crowd making its way back for the second half, I wondered if she had remembered that day, at least twenty years before when I'd humiliated myself in front of her. If she did, she had the graciousness not to show it.

In those years I was living a sort of dual life. I dressed up and went to work in the office at the Boeing Company, the middle class man hoping for anonymity, hoping my surface was conventional enough to pass myself off as one of the rest. But we lived, my wife and I, in run down, old out-of-the-way houses we found to rent, where we could let things go, the yard outside, the rooms within. We made plenty of money and we lived as if we were poor. Both of us were irresponsible with money and we managed to spend all we got. So, in a way, we kept ourselves poor enough to belong where we lived. When we decided to go to Europe it took but a little over a year to save 8000 dollars so we could make the trip.

I saw Karl Schalka in 1963. Someone organized a neighborhood reunion party at a downtown hotel. Men only but not a "stag party." No girls or dirty movies. We drank in a banquet room into the night and talked about our lives. My wife and I were planning to leave for Italy soon and I was glad we hadn't gone before this affair. It was good, though in some cases sad, to see what had become of some of the White

Center-Highland Park bunch. Karl and I happened to sit next to each other.

Deep into the evening Karl said to the group, "I'm not surprised Dick became a poet. Dick always had things to say and we always used to listen to Dick. He seemed to understand things." I was drunk enough to show that I was pleased but not so drunk that I wasn't surprised and a little embarrassed. When you hear something that contradictory to what you remember, you know everything you write is a damned lie. I looked back on my life and could remember few moments when I found any wisdom to call on. More than anything, I remembered a series of phony roles, an attempt to imitate men I admired who seemed to be making it through life with confidence and dignity, silly posturings calculated to make me look masculine and courageous, posturings calculated to change me into someone other than my inadequate self, a life based often on fantasy because reality was elusive and would not do.

New businesses and many new people have moved into White Center, the neighborhood streets were paved long ago, and one White Center restaurant is reputed to be pretty good. Modest, nice homes sit close to each other where I remember woods, ponds and swamps. West Seattle, mostly built up by the 40s, has seen fewer changes. The widened thoroughfares, the continuum of pavement and housing seem to have shortened the distance between White Center and West Seattle. Fauntleroy seems only a stone's throw now. If they are not one district, at least the borders, once vividly defined by my insecurities, are impossible to locate.

I'm just finishing a White Center poem. For years I was never poet enough to do much with White Center. My attempts at poems about my home town seemed blocked by allegiances to memory. That was the trouble: they were *about* White Center. The imagination had no chance in the face of facts.

A long time back, maybe twenty-five years ago, a reviewer in the *Hudson Review* ridiculed William Carlos Williams for saying that one reason a poet wrote was to become a better person. I was fresh out of graduate school, or maybe still there, filled with the New Criticism, and I sided with the reviewer. But Williams was right and I know now what he was talking about. It wasn't some theory of writing as therapy, nor the naive notion that after writing a poem one is any less depraved. It was the certainty that writing is a slow, cumulative way of accepting your life as valid, of accepting yourself over a lifetime, of realizing that your life is important. And it is. It's all you've got. All you ever had for sure.

It may have been time and the attendant losses—Benny, Eddie, Mrs. Baker, a lot of others—and the slow discovery that many of us meet eventually, in our joy as well as our despair, no matter who we are or where we come from, that finally made me realize the relative social values of places are a silly concern. But I like to think writing was a necessary part of that process. I often found the sources of poems in the lonely reaches of the world, the ignored, forlorn, and, to me, beautiful districts of cities, like the West Marginal Way area in Seattle, the sad small towns of Washington and Montana, the villages and countryside of Southern Italy, wherever I imagined life being lived as amateurishly as we had once played basketball.

With its cynical disregard of relative values, the imagination is one hell of a durable democracy. The Bakers, Wilbur, the Tomkins, Betty Bolin, the St. James Lutheran five, Hermann Goering, Groucho Marx and the London Philharmonic might sit comfortably together in the same poem. Arrogant as it sounds, I believe writing poems helped me cure myself of those insufferable snobberies that once stood like dirty glass between me and a world I wanted desperately to confront and be accepted by. If so, some poems must be the best I could find in myself. That's a good feeling to have. As long as they are my best, I don't care how good they are. That makes me one of the luckiest survivors.

The Anxious Fields of Play

BY THE mid-1930s, when I was ten or eleven, baseball had become such an obsession that I imagined ball parks everywhere. In the country, I visualized games in progress on the real grass cattle were eating. In the city as I rode down Fourth Avenue on the bus, the walls of warehouses became outfield fences with dramatic doubles and triples booming off them. Hitting was important in my fantasies. Pitching meant little except as a service necessary for some long drive far beyond the outfielders. I kept the parks small in my mind so home runs wouldn't be too difficult to hit.

The lot across the street from my grandparents' house was vacant, and whenever I could get enough neighborhood friends to join me we'd have a game there. In center field a high board fence bounded the west side of the Noraines' backyard. It was about a hundred feet from the worn spot we called home plate. The right field fence, a good forty feet away at the imagined foul line, ran east and bordered the north side of the Brockermans' yard. "Over the fence," I yelled, "is a home run." "Over the fence," said Mr. Brockerman from his yard, hoping to keep his windows intact, "is out." "It's our game and we can make the rules, and besides, you can't even get a job," I yelled back. It was a cruel remark. The Depression was on and my grandfather was the only man in the neighborhood who had steady work. A few years later, when I was old enough to realize the hopeless state of things for men during the Depression, I wanted to apologize to Mr. Brockerman, but he had long since moved away. No left field fence. Just some trees and the ground of the Burns's yard, looking more trampled than the ferns and grass of the vacant lot.

One evening the men in the neighborhood joined us for a

game. I was so excited, I bubbled. Growing up with my grandparents, I missed the vitality of a young father. I ran about the field, loudly picking all the men for my team. My hopes for a dynasty were shattered when a grownup explained that we might have a better game if we chose even sides. Days after, I trudged about the neighborhood asking the fathers if they would play ball again, but no luck.

When my grandparents had the basement put in, a concrete full-sized basement replacing the small dirt cave where Grandmother had kept her preserves, a pile of gravel was left on the north side of the house. Ours was the only house on that side of the block, and in my mind the woods to the north became a baseball field. The rocks—smooth, round, averaging about the size of a quarter—were perfect for my purpose.

I fashioned a bat by carving a handle on a one-by-four, and I played out entire nine-inning games, throwing the rocks up and swatting them into and over the trees. Third base was a willow tree. Second base was (I knew exactly in my mind) just beyond the honeysuckle and the giant hollow stump that usually held a pool of rainwater inside its slick mossed walls. Many times that pool reflected the world and my face back at me in solitary moments. First base, not really important because I seldom hit rocks that way, was vaguely a clump of alders.

I knew exactly how far a rock had to sail to be a home run. It had to clear the fence I dreamed beyond the woods. My games were always dramatic and ended with a home run, bases loaded, three runs down, two out, the count three and two, bottom of the ninth. How did I manage that? It was easy. I could control my hits well enough to hit three singles to load the bases, because my notion of what constituted a single was flexible. Then I'd select a rock whose size and shape indicated it might sail well, and clobber it. If, for some reason, it didn't sail far enough to be a home run, I simply tried again.

Inning after inning, I swatted rock outs, rock singles, rock doubles, rock triples, and rock home runs. I was the Yankees and also my opponents, the Giants. The only major league ball I heard was the World Series. It was carried on the radio and the Yankees were usually playing. The Yankees also had the most glamorous stars. Sometimes I played out the entire series, all seven games, letting the Giants win three. the score mounted. The lead changed hands. Then the last of the ninth, when Babe Ruth, Lou Gehrig, or Joe DiMaggio broke it up. I don't remember now if Ruth still played with New York when DiMaggio joined the team, but on my Yankees they were teammates.

One game, the dramatic situation in the ninth, a strong wind was blowing, as usual from the south. I tossed a flat round stone, perfect for sailing, and caught it just right. I still can see it climb and feel my disbelief. It soared out over the trees, turned over once, and started to climb like a determined bird. I couldn't have imagined I'd ever hit one that far. It was lovely. It rose and rose. I thought it might never stop riding that high wind north. It crossed the imaginary left field fence before its flight became an aesthetic matter, and it disappeared, a dot, still climbing, somewhere over Rossner's store on the corner of Sixteenth and Barton. I believe that rock traveled about two blocks. Why not? Joe DiMaggio had hit it.

I couldn't see the neighborhood beyond the trees. I simply drove the rocks out over the woods and imagined the rest, though sometimes I heard doubles rattle off the sides and roof of the community hall in center field just beyond the woods. A few years later I realized how dangerous my Yankees had been, spraying stones about the neighborhood. During my absence in World War II, the woods were wiped out by new housing.

One Sunday I left the house to play off somewhere and so was gone when my uncle Lester from Tacoma showed up without warning to see if I wanted to go with him to watch the Seattle Indians play in the Pacific Coast League. When I got home and found I'd missed the chance, I wept bitterly and whined against the fates. I was still whining and sobbing when my uncle returned on his way back home. He must have been touched by my disappointment, because he returned the following Sunday, and this time I was ready. It was kind of him. He saw that I was a bored, lonely boy. Grandfather had few passions outside of the house and the yard, and no interest in baseball.

When I was old enough and had some money, I went to the Sunday doubleheaders alone, catching a bus downtown and transferring to a trolley—an hour-long trip from White

Center. I was there by ten o'clock, when the park opened, and waited for the players to arrive. I collected autographs, of course, and saw several stars on their way to the big leagues, including Ted Williams, who was hitting around .260 with San Diego. I took it all in—hitting practice, infield practice, then the two games. I went filled with anticipation, heart pounding, but I sat, untypically for someone my age, quietly in the stands watching the game. Recently my aunt Dol, Lester's widow, told me that in church I would sit so quietly for a small boy that people remarked on it. I can remember that despite my nervousness and anxiety, I also had moments when I was unusually patient and quiet. I could wait for hours with nothing to do. Given the drabness of life with my grandparents, I had developed ways to entertain myself in my mind.

In 1936, I was a seventh grader and a substitute on the Highland Park softball team. That was something. Seldom did anyone but an eighth grader make the team, even as a sub. "You can beat eggs. You can beat cream. But you can't beat Highland Park's softball team." That was our yell, and the vowel repeat of "beat cream" intrigued me even then. The last game of that season, Mr. Fields, the coach, sent me in to pinch hit. I was twelve and had never been in a league game before. I was excited and frightened and people seemed to swirl—the other players, Mr. Fields, and Miss Shaefer, our other coach. My hero, Buss Mandin, our star pitcher, was watching. The world was watching. The pitcher was no longer another boy; he was a stranger from another universe. The ball came, surely too fast for any mortal to hit, yet as slow as if dreamed. I don't remember swinging. The bat seemed to swing itself and I saw the ball lining over the shortstop hole into left field, a clean single. Mandin, Fields, and Shaefer smiled approval from the sidelines as I held first. I had found a way of gaining the attention and approval of others, and I was not to let it go for nearly thirty years.

In the eighth grade next year, I was the softball team catcher. Ralph Lewin, a short thick powerful boy, was the pitcher. He was good. I was good too, and not afraid of the bat—a consideration at that age. I crouched quite close to the hitter and didn't flinch when he swung. Actually, the closer you squat to the batter, the easier catching is.

One night Ralph and I were at Betty Moore's house. She was the cutest girl in school and somehow I was supposed to be "with her." We were on a sun porch, the three of us, all thirteen years old. Betty's older brother and another boy his age had girls in the darkened front room and were necking. Ralph urged me to kiss Betty, but I was far too scared. He said to me, with disdain, "This is what you do," and he kissed her. I tried to keep my composure and I said, "Oh, is that it?" or something like that, and humiliation flooded my stomach. They went on necking. I had never seen a man kiss a woman before except in the movies, and I'm not putting anyone on when I say that I really thought people kissed only in films. I can never remember being kissed as a child, nor did I ever see any show of affection between my grandparents. I walked out, my face flushed with shame, through the dark living room, where one of the older boys yelled some insult at me, and finally, after years of groping, into the fresh air outside, free and alone. I walked the mile home, degraded and in anguish, and as I cried, my tears created a secondary glow around the street lights. I wanted to be like Ralph Lewin, like Betty Moore's brother, like anybody else. At home, my grandparents were already asleep, and I sat alone, as I did so many times in that still house, and stared into the solitary void I was certain would be my life.

But on the ball field, Ralph and I were social equals. One day we played the alumni, now freshmen and sophomores in high school, and I struck out, fooled badly on a change of pace. The fans laughed. Maybe I couldn't do anything about the humiliation I'd suffered in Betty Moore's house, but I could do something about it on the ball field. I promised myself no one would ever fool me again on a change of pace, and I kept my promise. I developed a technique of hitting late, of starting my swing at the last possible moment to avoid being tricked. Nearly all my hits for the next thirty years were to my off field, right field. Over the years, whenever players asked me why I hit to right and never pulled the ball, I told them a half truth. I said I hit better to right field. That was true. When I hit to left, I tended to grind the ball into the dirt. But I never told them the real reason.

That final year in grammar school we won the championship of our league in an extra-inning game against E. C. Hughes. They had beaten us out of the soccer championship in an overtime game just a few months before and the softball win felt good. I looked to the city play-offs with confidence. In my small world, how could any team be better than ours? Our first play-off game, we were defeated by a team of seven Orientals, two blacks, and a tall Jewish short fielder, by the score of 14 to 0. Despite my working-class background, I was lucky to grow up knowing prejudice was wrong, but I remember thinking then that minority people possessed some sort of magic.

My hitting was my ticket to acceptance. That first summer out of grammar school I spent with my mother in Bremerton, and I joined a softball team. The opening game was played in a pasture, very like the pastures I'd imagined into ball fields years before, and I hit a single, a double, a triple, and two home runs. My standing with the other boys, strangers just a few days before, was insured. The summer was mine.

After that I turned to hardball for several years. In the Park League I began as a pitcher, but one day a shower of triples and home runs convinced me that either second base or the outfield was where I really belonged. The summer I was fourteen I played second base on the Boulevard Park Merchants. All the other players were adults except for my buddy, George Zimmerman, who lived in Boulevard Park and had me try out for the team. I played all the games and collected a lot of hits. I also made the American Legion Team in West Seattle and hit around .350 for the season.

Often a ball game gave me confidence I could find nowhere else. Once, playing center field in a Park League game when I was around fifteen, I memorized the lineup of the opposing team, and in the last inning, score 2 to 1 in our favor and the other team threatening with men on base and two out, I detected a player batting out of turn. The umpire checked and called the batter out.

In high school, though I made the squad all four years, I spent three of them on the bench. I knew the coach, Lloyd Doty, was reluctant not only to cut pitchers but even to try to distinguish between pitchers and players who called themselves pitchers. So I hung in there calling myself a pitcher and became a batting practice ace. Park League experience had taught me three things about my pitching. One, I had exceptional control for a boy; two, I was easy to hit; three, when I was hit, the ball went a hell of a long way. I was indispensable to the morale of the starting hitters. "Just throw your fast ball, Richard," Coach Doty said.

In my senior year, a starting outfielder was caught burglarizing a clothing store and was sent up for a year. I declared myself an outfielder and played every game in right field. I had a miserable season, made errors, failed to hit consistently. My desire for acceptance was so overwhelming in high school that out in the field or at bat I was dizzy with tension and fear of failing in front of the students. I remember I played better when we were away at other schools.

I played semipro ball in the city leagues after that and did well. Just after I turned nineteen, I was called into the service. In the army, the chances to play were few, and I seized them when they came. I remember playing second with some sharp players, one of them a professional, at Logan, Utah, where we held infield drills on the Utah State campus quadrangle. I put everything into it, whipping the final throw of each infield round from second to home in a taut rope that sang through the thin mountain air as the spectators gasped. I remember playing third base in a monastery courtyard at the Army Air Corps rest camp on Capri, while the monks and a Red Cross girl with gorgeous legs looked on. I did not relax on a ball field. I always played my best no matter how makeshift the game.

I was discharged in June of '45, and I immediately joined a semipro team in the city league. It was clear to me by then that I was fouled up sexually and I was drinking more and more. I even played a game drunk and hit a triple far over the right fielder's head. I ended up at third base gagging. The run had made me sick and the manager took me out.

I turned out for the University of Washington team in the spring of '46, and made the squad for a few weeks until I was caught playing intramural softball and cut. That summer I played on another semipro team, but was told to get out by the grim manager after the fourth game, when I made the mistake of trying to joke with him after we'd lost a close one.

That hurt, the sudden hostile and permanent rejection when I was only trying to be friendly. I remember saying goodbye to one of the players, and though I barely knew him, I was close to tears. I felt I was losing something I loved and with my life so void of satisfaction, the loss seemed monumental. The goodbye I was saying to whoever that player was seemed a big goodbye to many things.

I went to school, off and on, majoring in creative writing, but tiring badly after three or four quarters. Then I'd go out and find a menial job somewhere. I worked in warehouses and at a steel mill, then in California at an ammunition magazine. In the summer of '47, I went back to softball, to a team in West Seattle. Several members were old friends from high school, and they were good players. I came to the team after the season started and it took a while before I got into the lineup, but by the end of the season I was the catcher. It felt good, crouching close to the batter as Jimmy Gifford's pitches broke past the batter into my glove for the third strike, and I wheeled the ball down to Ed Schmidt at first base to start the infield throw around.

For the next thirteen years, I played softball in the West Seattle Class A League. The first year we lost the championship to a veteran team, the West Seattle Auto Dealers, in a play-off game. But we had the nucleus of a good team, as well as the camaraderie of young men who had known each other for several years, and in 1948 we became the power of the league. By then, I had studied two quarters with Theodore Roethke and was working on poems at home in the evening, when I wasn't out drinking. I was still living with my grandparents, who were nearing the end. With no sex life, there seemed little reason for me to move out. I was frozen, a perpetual fifteen, but after a bad two or three years, I was playing ball again and loving it. My appetite for acceptance, for the approval of others, was satisfied on the ball fields, if nowhere else.

Ken Gifford, Jim's brother, and one of my high school chums, played third base. John Popich, four or five years younger than Gifford and myself, played shortstop, and his cousin Walt, about my age, played second. Ed Schmidt, also a high school friend, played first. That was the nucleus of the team. When Jim Gifford went to Seattle University to play basketball and pitch softball, Mimo Campagnaro, a strange hypochondriac who threw best on those days he complained of a wrenched back or a devastating headache, became our pitcher. Stinkey Johnson, another high school friend, was the backup pitcher to Mimo. For years, it was as if we were still kids, or so it seemed to one of us.

The last scheduled game of the season in 1948, we found ourselves again playing the West Seattle Auto Dealers. We were tied in the standings for first place, so again the championship was on the line. With two out and the tying run on second in the last of the seventh, I drilled a single up the middle to send the game into extra innings. (Oh, Joe DiMaggio.) Ed Schmidt was managing, and though not a demonstrative man, he couldn't hide his delight in the first-base coaching box. We won in the bottom of the eighth.

I remained after the others went home. Dark clouds were moving in from the southwest. The field seemed lonely and forlorn, abandoned to the dusk. I luxuriated in the memory of the game just completed, and in some odd way I felt at one with the field deserted to the wind. Several times I visited ball fields in the fall and winter and sat alone in the car remembering some game I'd played there, as the rain fell or leaves blew across the empty grounds.

I cultivated a casual, joking attitude on the field to hide the seriousness with which I took each game. But I betrayed that seriousness by showing up earlier than the others and sitting around the park alone, waiting for the equipment to arrive. Whenever players were late, I kept an anxious lookout. (Two more and we'll have nine and won't have to forfeit.) I took that anxiety into the batter's box. I doubt that in those nearly thirty years of ball, I ever batted relaxed. Because hitting was so important, I developed ways of countering my anxiety. I managed to remove any idea of competition from my mind by ignoring the pitcher as a human being until he vanished and only the ball remained. If I was aware of the pitcher as a man, I was finished.

John Popich was just the opposite. He had to hate the opposition. "Let's beat these bastards," he would say without one touch of humor. The son of Yugoslavian immigrants, he grew up in Riverside, where West Marginal Way parallels the Duwamish River, and life for him was an endless fight. Like most of those who grew up in Riverside, he had moved to middle-class West Seattle. I think he suffered conflicts that many children of immigrants do: the society pulling him one way, his loyalty to his heritage pulling him the other. He often spoke with fondness of Yugoslavian dishes his mother prepared. And he insisted, perhaps too much, on poking fun at the Italians on the team—Mimo and his brother Freddie; Robert Rimpini, an outfielder; and Morrie Capaloto, another outfielder, Italian-Jewish by background, who owned a small grocery in Alki. Popich's remarks usually implied the superiority of Yugoslavs. His cousin Walt, from the same area and circumstances, but emotionally far less complicated, suffered little conflict. When Walt spoke of Riverside, which he had left behind for good, it was usually as "those people."

Physically, John was easily the most gifted player on the team—fast, unusually strong, well coordinated. From his shortstop position, he fired accurate cannon shots at Schmidt, who took them easily in his cool, unhurried way as if they were easy tosses. Popich had one failing that prevented him from realizing his potential. He couldn't adjust his aggressive instincts to conditions. One game he flew out every time up, trying to power the ball against a hopelessly stiff wind. With Schmidt's cool, he could have played professional baseball.

One game, at Alki Field, I was run over in a play at home. That was the only play I hated. It is always open season on the catcher, and later, during my last four or five years, I gave up blocking the plate and started tagging runners like a third baseman, flashing in once with my hands and getting out of there. This time, I made the mistake of taking Popich's streaking relay squatting on my haunches. The ball and the runner arrived at the same time and the runner, seeing how vulnerable I was, ran me down. His knee crashed into my head and I rolled back, green stars exploding. I remember lying there on the plate, holding the ball for a moment before my right hand involuntarily relaxed and the ball dribbled out. I was taken out, of course. I had double vision and my right arm ached from a stretched nerve trunk, a neuritis that stayed with me for three months. The run tied the game.

In the last of the seventh, Popich hit the longest home run I've seen in softball. The bases were loaded at the time, and the ball went far over the head of Jack Marshall, a fast young left fielder. It must have landed 150 feet beyond him as he ran back, and he had already been playing deep. I believe it would have cleared many left field fences in baseball parks. With my double vision, I saw two unbelievable drives sailing over two Jack Marshalls, and eight runners scoring.

Popich's home runs were raw power, shots that seemed to take less than a second in flight. Schmidt's were just the opposite. In one game, he unloaded two home runs, and with his classic swing the balls didn't seem hard hit at all. They soared slowly like lazy birds, beautiful to watch, like the rock I'd hit that day long before. Popich batted third, Schmidt fourth, and I followed, swinging the bat as if I was swatting off demons, driving the ball late into right field. Despite our hitting, we were primarily a defensive team. In a typical game, we would grab an early lead, then play flawless defensive ball. Once we got the lead, we seldom added to it. We concentrated on defense as if we considered the game already won. Usually, it was.

Most of the others were married and getting on with their lives. I took the scorebook home and computed averages. When I listened to professional games on the radio, I often lined out a score sheet on a piece of paper, using the blunt back edge of Grandmother's bread knife for a ruler, and scored the entire game sitting alone at the table in the kitchen. I watched my dissolute life passing. Sometimes with anger and resentment that exploded into verbal abuse of friends when I was drunk and filled me with shame the next day, when, terrified I'd end up friendless and alone, I made embarrassed apologies. Sometimes with frustration when I refused to admit my defeat and sought out women, only to find myself unable to conquer my timidity. But mostly with sadness and the intense love of simple compensations like softball and fishing.

One day before a game at Lincoln Park, I had come early as usual, and was sitting in the grass near some boys in their middle teens. They were talking about girls and chewing the tender root ends of grass blades. "Sharon's easy," one of them said. "Jesus, she's easy." He was smiling. Ten years younger than I was, and already they knew more about life than I believed I ever would. I looked away through the trees at the sea. Somewhere out there beyond me was a life of normalcy, and I was certain I would never be a part of it. It was farther than the islands I could see. It was beyond reach. It was a sad moment and I wanted the players to come and the game to begin.

Within a few years we had become a smooth, balanced team. Jim Gifford came back. He was now one of the best throwers in Seattle and could have pitched AA ball. Gordon Urquhart replaced Walt Popich at second base and we formed the best team I've ever played on. Urquhart and I managed the team, or rather I should say Urquhart managed the team on the field and I planned strategy with him over a beer at our sponsor's place, the Blew Eagle Cafe. The strange spelling had occurred during the Depression. Gino, the original owner, first named it the Blue Eagle Cafe, but when the Roosevelt administration launched the National Recovery Act in the early thirties, it adopted as its symbol a blue eagle. Every time a radio announcer said, "Look for the blue eagle," Gino got free advertising. The government insisted he comply with some law by changing the name, but Gino complied only by changing the spelling. The possibilities for obscenity were too good to pass up.

We went through the league undefeated, the first team to do it since the twenties, and that season I played in the most perfectly played game I can remember. Neither side made a mistake. Jim Gifford threw a no-hitter. The opposing pitcher threw a two-hitter. We won late in the game on a triple by our center fielder, Jim Burroughs, and an infield out. I remember it well because it again reflected the way I felt about things in general and my poems in particular. If something was good in itself, well done, it made no difference whether it was important or not, nor whether it had an audience. Here was a game in a Class A softball league at Alki Playfield in a city in the Far West, one of thousands of such games going on all over the country, with practically no one watching, and yet the game itself had been played with a perfection that to me made it important. I was constantly looking for perfection in my poems. It was a handicap really, because in my drive for perfection I rewrote poems completely out of existence. I was blind to all the mistakes I can see there now, but had I seen them then, I would have rewritten again and again until the mistake was gone. And while I didn't realize it then, the reason I had to rewrite so much was that making real changes was so difficult. Each rewrite was almost the same thing over, done with the hope something would change and that, in turn, would trigger other changes that would finally result in a perfect unit of sound. My perfectionism was really a symptom of my stagnation. No matter how I tried, my poems, like my life, were going nowhere. Later I tried to handle this theme in a long poem called "Duwamish Head." That's where the Duwamish is backed up by the sea and no longer seems to flow.

Gordon Urquhart was the most interesting person I played ball with. By lucky accident we found ourselves working together at Boeing and I got to know him well. He surmounted setbacks and adversity with a resiliency I found monumental, and he had a great sense of humor. He had been a marine NCO in Korea in an outfit overrun by the Chinese. He found himself one night standing in the dark, firing wildly as Chinese soldiers in bewildering numbers rushed by all around him. He was hit in the leg and, typical of him, took charge of the survivors he could find the next morning and led them back to safety, hobbling on his wounded leg.

He loved his wife and she died, strangled in an asthmatic seizure while he held her, help on the way too late. I remember the voice over the intercom at work, telling him to call home, and his hurried departure. I offered my awkward condolences a few days later, when he returned. "Yes," he said, "it was a shock." He was most composed and his grief never surfaced, despite his emotional honesty. Later he remarried and went on his indestructible way. An alder. A catfish. Those are my two favorite private nicknames for masters of survival.

Gordon loathed the idea of privileged people, people on top. He used to say sarcastically, "What's happening to your precious Yankees?" when they were losing. He also hated Sugar Ray Robinson, and was outraged when Robinson got a championship fight against Bobo Olson, while Tiger Jones, who had beaten Robinson, was ignored. Of course, I loved Robin-

son and the Yankees because they had class, which, to para-
phrase Henry Reed, in my case I had not got. Like my
grandfather, who identified with Henry Ford, I appreciated
the most successful, especially those who had what I thought
of as style—those who won and looked good doing it. Urquhart
was a winner who identified with the underprivileged, but only
those who tried. (In my poems, I was on the side of the losers
who lived their defeat.)

Urquhart's hatred of privilege was so intense, I think his
own drive for success must have involved some conflict. I even
imagine he may have disliked himself for it. The first time I
met his father, he told me with undisguised bitterness that
Roosevelt had broken him. I didn't get the story clear, but it
seemed to involve large holdings of beef Mr. Urquhart had
had in Montana in the thirties, a situation sure to profit him
considerably until the federal government had made beef
available at low prices or for free to the poor. Something like
that, as I remember. This seemed to have ruined him for good,
because he still dwelled on it with considerable anger despite
the years that had gone by. I remember I was bewildered by
it because my world was so small and immediate that to hate
Roosevelt years after his death seemed a little like being pissed
off at Xerxes.

Whatever Urquhart's relation was with his father, it must
have involved intense attitudes about success and failure. When
Robinson knocked out Gene Fullmer, I was delighted.
Urquhart, of course, was furious and suggested at lunch the
next day that New York money had bought Fullmer to take a
dive. Fullmer was Urquhart: without style or grace, tough and
aggressive, and probably most important, from a remote area
where he could not benefit from the New York publicity cen-
ters. Urquhart had moved to Seattle from eastern Montana.
Like Fullmer, he was a fighter from the moon. Urquhart was
assailing Robinson, when I said, unexpectedly (even I didn't
expect it and had I thought about it probably wouldn't have
said it), "Isn't what you really don't like about him that he is a
success?"

I might have accused him of murder. He was stunned and
flashed into anger. I could have crawled away and died. I
apologized later for the obvious hurt he had felt, but he was

still angry and accepted my apology with something less than graciousness. Some people may think it odd that I would apologize when his anger demonstrated I was probably right. Let them. One of my favorite quotes is Valèry's: "I can't think of anything worse than being right."

Urquhart had little natural ability. He looked terrible in practice. He booted grounder after grounder. Made bad throws. He could never have made any team as good as ours, had we not known how good he was once the game started. I never remember Gordon making an error in a game, and although not a consistent hitter, he seldom failed when it counted. Unlike most softball players, he took his competitive instincts to his job and I've heard he has risen quite high in the Boeing company. I dare say he did it on plenty of hard work and guts, clawing away, refusing to be beaten. He lacked the physical gifts of Popich, the fast reflexes of Ken Gifford, or the cool smoothness of Schmidt. Yet, more than anyone on the team, he was responsible for the best season we had. I find it hard to think of him in a high executive position. He was never good at hiding his feelings, an honesty not usually found in corporate executives. I can't imagine him as cold or manipulative, or anything really but a nice, tough, and resilient man. I remember him vividly because we played ball together. That was our link. We both loved playing, he with his honest intensity, and I with my intensity hidden behind my jokes because I knew if it surfaced it would ruin my ability to play.

Years after I was finally able to have sexual relations with women, I continued to play ball, both in the West Seattle League and in the Boeing League (employees only). Our West Seattle team got old, like that team we had first beaten out for the championship, and we found ourselves coming in second more often than first in the league. I published some painting poems in *Contact,* one of the best of the early West Coast magazines, and for the picture on the cover sent in a photo of myself in a Boeing All-Star softball shirt. I took a kind of perverse delight (still do) in not looking like a poet, and I enjoyed appearing on the cover looking like a jock alongside the pictures of the other contributors, some of them terribly affected shots (face half hidden by smoke in the coffeehouse gloom), when inside the magazine my poems, along with reproductions of the paintings that had triggered them, were by far the artiest items there.

Bob Peterson, the San Francisco poet and now a good friend, was poetry editor. He is also a baseball nut and, I think, entertains fantasies of himself as a star pitcher. When, for the contributors' notes, I sent in my Boeing League-leading batting average of .541, he reduced it to .400. "No one," he said, "would believe .541." "They would if they had seen the pitching," I wrote back. There were younger and much better players on our Boeing team, several of them top players in the city leagues, but they didn't take our games seriously and tried only to see how far they could hit the ball. I was still hitting as intensely as always to right field, no matter how absurd the score or weak the opposition.

A friend named Bill Daly pitched for that Boeing team. Bill made a remark one day to Dick Martin, the third baseman, that had a lot of wisdom: "Dick, I was thinking the other day how much time we've put into this game all these years. What if we'd put that time into work, making a living. We'd probably be rich." Bill also pitched against us in the West Seattle League, and though I knew his stuff well, he struck me out one game. He did it with a drop, not too much on it, that came in high and outside and dipped into the strike zone. I'd seen it all the way, saw it drop into my favorite spot, and I never pulled the trigger. (Goodbye, Joe.) I walked away, the message clear, remembering many times I'd slammed that pitch deep into the right center field gap, had seen the outfielders turned and running as I rounded first on my way to a triple or home run. My reflexes were going and I knew it as I sat down and waited for the inning to end. I didn't feel sad. I didn't feel any sense of loss. I didn't feel humiliated at striking out as I once would have, though I was still intensely trying to avoid it. More than just the reflexes had gone.

The only good sports poem I can remember reading was one called "Cobb Would Have Caught It" by Robert Fitzgerald. Whenever I tried to write about baseball or softball, I found myself thinking about the game itself, and the poem kept turning into a melodramatic sports story with the winning hit coming at the crucial moment. (Oh, Joe DiMaggio. Oh, beautiful rock sailing downwind high over Sixteenth and

Barton.) I was interested in the score, not the words.

In the summer of '72, two of my students were playing softball in Missoula and I started going to the games. I foolishly put my name on the roster one night at the last minute to avoid a forfeit, and before the season was over I played four games, a fat middle-aged man standing in the outfield, being eaten by mosquitoes and wishing he could lose twenty years for an hour and a half. My first time at bat in a serious game (serious because the pitcher was throwing hard), I lined a double over the right fielder's head. Anyone else would have had a home run. I hobbled into second, just as surprised as the spectators. The last game I played, I pulled off a running one-handed catch before a large crowd that went wild. I couldn't believe it when the ball, blurred by sweat and fear, hit my glove and stuck there as I ran full tilt toward the foul line. But now only luck was on my side and luck has a way of running out. I loved those late triumphs, but I could also laugh at them.

I took interest in the whole scene, not just the game. Except for those times I was obliged to play to prevent forfeits, I sat in the stands and took note of the spectators as well as the game, of the players' wives and children, of the players from teams not on the field. One night I watched a player's wife play with a small child. It was beautiful. She was beautiful, a full, warm woman who radiated affection. I imagined myself coming home to her from work tired and putting my head in her lap. Another wife kept score with intense dedication, marking each play in the book, always with the score, inning, and number of outs ready for anyone who would ask. Though she was in her thirties and the mother of three children, her flesh looked soft and virginal, like that of a high school girl.

The player-spectators who interested me were working people of the old cut, posturing, clowning, awkward, self-conscious, never quite accepting themselves, kidding the players in the field with loud, sometimes crude, always good-natured insults. They drank lots of beer. They also turned me through parts of my life I'd neglected for a long time and I suppose I loved them for that.

I thought again about those tiny worlds I'd lived in with far more desperation than I hoped any of them would ever know. I thought of Ingmar Bergman's film *The Naked Night* (sometimes called *Sawdust and Tinsel*), where the degraded protagonist and his wife have finally only each other with whom to face an arrogant, humiliating world. How the crutch we once needed to hobble through life remains in our closet long after our leg has healed. How Gordon Urquhart could fight through his setbacks and his complicated attitudes about life to a kind of success, while my best hope of avoiding defeat was to turn values around with words, to change loss into victory. How John Popich came to the field with his physical gifts, hoping to win the battle he would probably never win. How failures are in many ways successes and how successful people, those who early in life accepted adult values and abandoned the harmless fields of play, are really failures because they never come to know the vital worth of human relationships, even if it takes the lines of a softball field to give them a frame. How, without play, many people sense too often and too immediately their impending doom, After nearly thirty years of writing, I was ready to try a softball poem.

Missoula Softball Tournament

This summer, most friends out of town
and no wind playing flash and dazzle
in the cottonwoods, music of the Clark Fork stale,
I've gone back to the old ways of defeat,
the softball field, familiar dust and thud,
pitcher winging drops and rises, and wives,
the beautiful wives in the stands, basic, used,
screeching runners home, infants unattended
in the dirt. A long triple sails into right center.
Two men on. Shouts from dugout: go, Ron, go.
Life is better run from. Distance to the fence,
both foul lines and dead center, is displayed.

I try to steal the tricky manager's signs.
Is hit-and-run the pulling of the ear?
The ump gives pitchers too much low inside.
Injustice? Fraud? Ancient problems focus
in the heat. Bad hop on routine grounder.

Close play missed by the team you want to win.
Players from the first game, high on beer,
ride players in the field. Their laughter
falls short of the wall. Under lights, the moths
are momentary stars, and wives, the beautiful wives
in the stands, now take the interest they once feigned,
oh, long ago, their marriage just begun, years
of helping husbands feel important just begun,
the scrimping, the anger brought home evenings
from degrading jobs. This poem goes out to them.
Is steal-of-home the touching of the heart?
Last pitch. A soft fly. A can of corn,
the players say. Routine, like mornings,
like the week. They shake hands on the mound.
Nice grab on that shot to left. Good game. Good Game.
Dust rotates in their headlight beams.
The wives, the beautiful wives, are with their men.

Making Certain It Goes On, p. 210.

It struck me as a crude poem and for a while I didn't like
it. It seems to be discussing its own meaning. But one day I
came to believe that the crudeness was right, at least for that
poem.

The summer of '73 I returned again to watch a few games.
It was pleasant saying hello to a lot of nice people, most of
whom ask little from life or from others. A few inquired if I
was going to play again and I told them not a chance, but I
felt a little proud that they had asked. One night a big husky
girl, who played on one of the women's teams in town, brought
a group of handicapped young people to watch one of the
men's games. Some of them seemed retarded, others afflicted
with physical and neurological problems. From all I've written here, I should not have to explain the following villanelle
I finished a few months ago.

The Freaks at Spurgin Road Field

The dim boy claps because the others clap.
The polite word, handicapped, is muttered in the stands.
Isn't it wrong, the way the mind moves back.

One whole day I sit, contrite, dirt, L.A.
Union Station, '46, sweating through last night.
The dim boy claps because the others clap.

Score, 5 to 3. Pitcher fading badly in the heat.
Isn't it wrong to be or not be spastic?
Isn't it wrong, the way the mind moves back.

I'm laughing at a neighbor girl beaten to scream
by a savage father and I'm ashamed to look.
The dim boy claps because the others clap.

The score is always close, the rally always short.
I've left more wreckage than a quake.
Isn't it wrong, the way the mind moves back.

The afflicted never cheer in unison.
Isn't it wrong, the way the mind moves back
to stammering pastures where the picnic should have worked.
The dim boy claps because the others clap.

Making Certain It Goes On, p. 254.

I think when I played softball I was telling the world and myself that futile as my life seemed, I still wanted to live.

How I Never Met Eudora Welty

LOGAN THE Finger and H. Reed Fulton are dead, and
if anyone reading this happens to have attended West Seattle
High School in the 30s and 40s, his sighs of regret should not
appreciably compound the noise pollution problem.

Logan The Finger was the study hall monitor and Logan
The Finger was called Logan The Finger because Logan The
Finger had the thumb and index finger missing from his right
hand. When he signalled you to his desk to give you demerits
for talking to the girl in the next seat, he was not only inviting
you to his desk, he was giving you the finger. A humorless
man, his job was anything but easy. Boys would swing open
the back doors and roll handfulls of steel bearings across the
floor of the huge auditorium room where we held study hall,
and they would rattle off the steel legs of our desks making a
hell of a racket. Sometimes, the students released pigeons in
the study hall. The room had a very high ceiling and there
was no way to get the pigeons out during the day. They would
sit high on the ornamental arch over the stage, and we would
stare at them with some sort of envy for their freedom and
their obliviousness to boredom. Then, someone would tie an
alarm clock onto the curtain cord and snap the blind high up
out of reach where the clock would hang like a bomb until it
went off at the set hour.

Logan The Finger oversaw all this from his chair and desk,
raised on a platform about a foot above the floor. He was
available for help with study problems and I suppose must
have had a broad though no doubt shallow understanding of
a lot of different subjects. I never went to him with a math
problem, math being easy for me then, but students who did

told me he often illustrated his explanations with an example of how you could cheat the Bon Marche department store. My hero of the day was Amos Laudet who crawled commando style on his stomach yards and yards under desks and between student legs, gave Logan The Finger a hot foot and returned to his seat completely undetected by Logan or by the woman in charge of seating assignments, sitting across the room from Logan. I also considered it a tribute to the many students who saw it that they played it cool and Logan never knew what was happening until his foot started to burn.

H. Reed Fulton was the principal. He was also a successful author of boys' books. *Laddie The Great, The Powder Dock Mystery,* and *Moccasin Trail* were his best known works, and West Seattle was probably the only high school in the nation that included H. Reed Fulton on the Recommended Reading List along with Thomas Wolfe, Ernest Hemingway, John dos Passos and John Steinbeck, in the American Literature courses.

H. Reed Fulton had two favorite words, "guts" and "democracy." When he mounted the stage in the auditorium, which was also the study hall, to address the assembly kicking off the new school year, his speech would go something like this: "It was but a scant two weeks ago that I stood on the banks of the Dosewallips river, my creel brimming with trout, and reflected on how it takes guts to live in a democracy. And if you don't have the guts to live in a democracy, then I suggest you find an undemocratic nation where the guts required by a democracy are no longer necessary." And on and on.

The worst thing Logan The Finger could do was send you to see H. Reed Fulton. You might get kicked out of school. Certainly you were in for it one way or another. "Watch out for the lamp," some students warned, those who had been to see Fulton. Logan usually sent you there if you did something he considered wrong but didn't know what punishment it called for. In those days I played the ocarina or sweet potato. Not very well either. I could play "The Organ Grinder's Swing" and that was it. On the first day of the second semester in my freshman year, I was sitting in study hall with nothing to do. No lesson assignments had been given and even if they had, studying was impossible because students were in a long line waiting for seat assignments. People were chatting. The hall was noisy and unorganized, though rest assured Logan The Finger was on the job. With nothing to do, I saw in my assigned seat in the back row and played the ocarina. When I saw Logan approaching, I could tell by his expression he'd heard me and I hid the ocarina under the desk. He looked about, obviously perplexed by the eerie sound he'd heard, then walked over to me and asked if I had been whistling.

"No," I said, exuberantly, naive enough to believe honesty the best policy, "I was playing my ocarina," and I held it up so he could see it. It was too much. Never had he found a student playing an ocarina in study hall and he wrote a note for me to take to Fulton. He was trembling when he wrote it, and I realize now that it must have been the unique nature of the offense that upset him so. Ocarinas in themselves are not that important.

I waited on the bench outside Fulton's office, and I was nervous and frightened. I hated the woman at the desk who asked me to wait there and who smiled at me, sadistically I thought, while I played with my hands.

The first thing H. Reed Fulton did in his office after I sat down across from him was turn the shade on his lamp so that the light poured into my eyes. He took his time while I squinted trying to see him through the glare. And he started very low key. In a quiet calm voice he said, after he'd read the note, "How old are you, Richard?"

"Fourteen," Mr. Fulton.

"Fourteen." Very soft and quiet. He mused on fourteen for a moment. Again soft and quiet, "And do you like this school, Richard?"

"Yes sir, I do."

He jumped up so suddenly I flinched and he screamed at me over the glaring lamp, "Then why don't you have the guts to live up to its democratic ideals?"

He might as well have fired a cannon. I withered on the spot. It was so startling that I don't remember what happened after that, what was said, how long I was there or when I left.

I graduated in 1941 and of course got caught in the war. In 1945 I was out, twenty-one years old, veteran of thirty-five bombing missions and at the University of Washington taking creative writing courses, something I'd looked forward to all through the Army Air Corps, now called the Air Force. I'd started writing when I was nine and writing seemed to be the only thing I'd ever be able or want to do. My teacher was a new man named Grant Redford, a very good short story writing teacher and a sad man who was to commit suicide twenty years later. He was from Montana and had been connected with the old *Rocky Mountain Review*. I think it became the *Western Review* but I'm not sure and I'm not going to look it up. I'm afraid I was never much of a student for Redford. My stories were hopelessly self indulgent, on and on about my personal problems, without form, without development, and without even any good writing. However, I did write humor in those days and had no trouble getting it published in the campus magazine, though I'd hate to see it now. Mostly my writing was used to get myself attention, to satisfy a terrible streak of narcissism, and it wasn't until I concentrated all my efforts on poems that I was to realize the only real reward of writing, that special way you feel just when you've done something you like. That's far more satisfying than seeing your name in print, good reviews, flattery or applause after a reading. And more enduring.

The Northwest Writers Conference was scheduled for the summer of 1946 and Grant Redford was one of the organizers. I felt then that artists, writers, jazz musicians were touched with a strange kind of magic and that if you could make contact with one some of the magic would rub off on you. I remember climbing some sawhorses in 1942 in the old Trianon Ballroom in Seattle, just to stand against the tiered bandstand next to an old Chicago jazz trombone player named Floyd O'Brien who was playing with Bob Crosby's Bobcats. I was balanced on a sawhorse within two or three feet of this magic man when he turned to me and said, "Shit, it's hot in here." I thought then how wonderful it was that this great musician, touched as he was by some gift from heaven, would make such a down-to-earth statement. So when I heard Eudora Welty was coming to the Northwest Writers Conference, nothing would do but that I get to talk to her.

I approached Redford and explained my problem. I wouldn't pay the ten dollar conference fee unless I got to talk alone with Eudora Welty. Redford promised to look into it for me. What a chance this seemed. Miss Welty might give some magic advice that would open my soul. Maybe she would say in a burst of insight (didn't all great writers have equally great bursts of insight?), "I can tell, Mr. Hugo, that you'll be a fine writer some day." Or maybe she'd advise me to go to Australia to broaden my base of experience. I would not have gone, but I would have considered it.

Had I ever met her I'm sure she would have said, though no doubt more graciously, what Roethke said two or three years later, "Get your fat ass to work." But I never did meet her. It turned out that she was in much demand and Redford couldn't guarantee a private audience with her though he could insure an audience with a very successful author, H. Reed Fulton. Ten dollars seemed high.

Grandfather's Car

IN 1929, Grandfather bought his first car, a brand new model A Ford. He turned sixty that August and I would turn six in December. Grandfather had a garage built in the front yard. It stood ahead of the house and just off to the side. Only a few feet separated the corner of the house from the corner of the garage. The pie cherry tree in the front yard drooped over the garage and, in the summer when the branches were heavy with cherries, those on the south half of the tree lay limp across the garage roof.

Grandmother's carnation beds grew between the dirt path and the house, and across the path, behind the garage, my grandparents grew string beans and sweet peas. Next to the garage was a lovely bed of pansies and forget-me-nots. They were always in cool shade since the garage blocked the sun until afternoon, and after that, the house blocked it.

The garage was forbidden territory. Grandfather kept it locked at all times, except when he unlocked and slipped through the side door to nip at the whiskey bottle he kept in the nail keg, or when he unlocked the main doors to take the car out. If he was going for only a few minutes, he carefully locked the doors even though it meant he had to leave the car to open them again when he returned. Grandfather also kept his fishing tackle in the garage.

When I was in psychoanalysis long years later, I told my doctor about the whiskey Grandfather kept in the garage, and he said my grandfather had once been a heavy drinker and that there had been terrible scenes with grandmother about his drinking. I protested. I had lived with my grandparents since I was twenty months old and I had never seen grandfather drunk nor had I witnessed any scenes. "It happened before you were born," the doctor said. A few days later my imagination told me with sudden and startling clarity that the doctor was right.

No remembered scenes about his drinking, but a vaguely remembered one about mine. It must have been about the time Grandfather bought the car, because I believe I was five. He was feeding me his home brew in the dank dirt cellar. I imagine him smiling, but that can't be memory. Then I was upstairs sitting on a stool in the kitchen. Then I was falling off the stool onto the floor. Grandmother realized I was drunk and there were words I don't remember, but I have the faint sense they were spoken in anger.

The closest I saw Grandfather to being drunk was when I was twelve. Grandmother's brother, Charles Alber and a younger couple, named Armbruster, came from Michigan to visit. I'd never seen Grandfather so animated. Normally he was, around me at least, silent, glum, whistling softly to himself as he piled wood against the north side of the house or turned spadeful after spadeful of ryegrass and dirt over in the early spring to ready the garden for planting, while I watched silently.

Grandfather had never met Fred Armbruster but he had known his father, and seeing those people from the farming communities around Ypsilanti and Ann Arbor where he had lived until he was fifty-one awakened some old enthusiasm in him I wasn't used to. He talked much more than I'd ever heard him, and he asked questions about many people back there. Once I asked him if he ever wanted to go back to Michigan and he said in his usual blunt manner, "The weather's no damn good there."

While Uncle Charlie Alber and the Armbrusters were there, the Seattle Gas Company, Grandfather's employer, held its annual picnic. As I recall, it was the only time Grandfather ever went to the company picnic. It was held at Shady Beach, a resort on the north shore of Lake Washington, and I'm sure if the visitors from Michigan had not been there we would not have gone. A boyhood chum, George Zimmerman, joined us and he piled into the Model A with my grandparents and me and we rode the twenty-five miles or so to the picnic, the people from Michigan following in their car.

George and I had great fun riding the water toboggans down the curly chute and spraying out onto the lake where, as our momentum gave out, we sank into the clear water.

Unlike most Pacific Northwest lakes, the bottom at Shady Beach remained shallow for several hundred feet instead of dropping off fast into water darkened by depth, and because the bottom was white sand the shallowness was deceptive.

Grandfather sat at one of the picnic tables with the other grown ups, laughing and talking. It was the only time I can recall when he seemed happy for an extended period. When George and I went to the table to see the grownups about something, Grandfather spit tobacco juice on my bare leg and roared with glee. He seemed so fun loving and high spirited that I assume he was feeling his booze. I remember looking at him surprised as his tobacco juice ran down my leg and I remember his face burning with crude if not cruel laughter.

The day ended badly. A 21-year-old red-headed man ran onto the long dock and halfway out, having come so far and with the water looking like it might be twenty feet deep, he dove in head first and broke his neck. He lay moaning on the dock while men stood around and debated the best way to carry him in. Ideas ranged from putting him on one of the toboggans to making a stretcher using "a coat and two lean saplings." Finally, the ambulance howling its arrival, the men carried him bodily up the dock. No one even supported his head. The next day I read about the young man's death in the papers and, for weeks after, George Zimmerman and I wondered at how ineffectual grown men were in a crisis. We both blamed the stupidity of adults for the young man's death.

Grandfather never drove over thirty-five. When he encountered an even slower driver, which was seldom, he passed the man cautiously and later explained that he had "busted on around him," momentarily pleased with his role as demon of the road. Though Grandfather's car brought some mobility to our drab lives, he and my grandmother remained stay-at-homes. He used the car mainly to go to work at the ugly gas plant at the north end of Lake Union. My grandmother continued to walk to White Center to shop, though we bought little there since the garden provided all our vegetables and at least once a week we killed one of the chickens in the coop in the backyard.

When we went on a picnic, we went to Lincoln Park. It was a little over a mile away, a beautiful long park that runs on a cliff up above Puget Sound. The trees there are huge and the grasses rich and flowers bloom in loud clusters.

A couple of times Grandfather took all of us, including Aunt Sarah and Cousin Warren, who lived close by, to the Duwamish slough to fish for porgies. It was less than two miles away and lay at the bottom of Boeing Hill and in the murky water we could usually catch all the fish we wanted. Each trip, Grandfather stopped at a small service station on 9th Avenue, S.W., to buy some gas and, since I had been begging, a candy bar for me. The bar was called Chicken Dinner and I had it devoured long before we were headed down the long hill to the slough. A few years later I started walking to the slough with friends from White Center.

Our big trip each year was to Lake Meridian where we spent at least one week of Grandfather's vacation. It was about thirty miles away, a major adventure for us. What a lovely lake in those days. Although a fairly sizable resort lay at the southeast corner of the lake, the rest of the shore was more pastoral than usual for the Pacific Northwest. A few old, charming farm houses stood far apart on the shores, and the land slanted and rolled into the water without hurry. Instead of the usual thick forests of evergreens, the shore was decked with willows, alders and grass.

We stayed across the lake from the big resort in a smaller resort, if you could call it a resort at all. The only facilities there were the cabins we rented, the boats, a short dock, a picnic table or two, and a couple of swings. I loved the fresh odor of the lake, the mist rising in morning when Grandfather and I left in the boat to fish, the play of cloud reflection and light off the water, the sunfish that grouped over their sand nests in the shallow water under the dock.

Cousin Warren, Aunt Sarah and, before her divorce, Uncle Carleton, often went with us. Warren would go with Grandpa and me down the lake in the early morning to a cove where we anchored and stillfished over the side of the boat, using angleworms for bait. Although we fished for anything that would bite, catfish, bass, perch, crappie, we usually caught

perch. That was years before the Washington State Game
Department began their rehabilitation programs, killing the
spiny rays and catfish (called "undesirable" in the Game
Department literature) and replanting the lakes with trout.
Grandfather went after many of the same fish he had gone
after in Michigan. So much of my early Pacific Northwest fishing is what is now regarded as midwest fishing.

Grandfather had an outrageous pole. It was bamboo and
came in several sections. Assembled, it was so long that one
day, using half of it, Grandfather fished my baseball glove off
the fairly high roof of the house where I'd thrown it trying to
dislodge a baseball from the rain gutter. I think it was an old
catfish pole he'd used in Michigan. It seemed to hang forty
feet over the lake. Warren and I kidded Grandfather about
it, but Grandfather sat silently set in his ways and our remarks
bounced off his hide without leaving a dent.

With all that leverage, whenever Grandfather got a bite,
he would rear back and tear the fish out of the lake by the
roots. The fish would explode into the air and I would imagine a look of amazement on its face. I used a steel telescopic
rod, about eight feet long and I played the fish who, I was
certain, preferred that civilized battle of wits. My fish were
not amazed. They had been defeated in a fair fight and knew
it.

Grandfather was agonizingly patient. When the fish weren't
biting, he refused to move the boat to another spot. He sat
silently, watching his line and responding to my pleas with an
occasional grunt. I felt that if you could see your line, it meant
the fish could see you and that's why they wouldn't bite. They
would bite only if the day was cloudy, the surface of the lake
was ruffled by wind blurring the bottom, the lake was so deep
you couldn't see the bottom, or the water itself was murky.
Even today I don't care to fish ultraclear water. Once when I
had been staring far too long at my worm and the fishless
bottom of the lake, I said, "Please, Grandpa. Let's move. I
don't like to see my bait." "Then look the other way," Grandfather snorted.

Once I found a dead baby perch floating beside the boat.
I scooped it up and put it on my hook in place of the worm.

In a few minutes I caught the biggest perch any of us ever caught in Lake Meridian. The resort owner, a farmer who had lived on the lake for years, said it was the biggest perch he had ever seen, and Grandfather beamed. "By gosh," he told the others, "Dick got a whopper."

Grandfather loved to fish Lake Meridian I'm sure, but he seemed old doing it, silent, glum, withdrawn. I never saw him again as youthful and loud as he had been that day at Shady Beach. Years later, struggling with sexual timidity and believing time is not on our side ever, I tried a poem about Lake Meridian.

Meridian

When I came here first the lake was full,
coves formed slowly and land rolled
into the water with arcs expected of birds
and the middle seemed raised from the shores.

To keep the lake a size, the rate of rain
played to the speed of vapor
and the absorbing silt. I saw the faint tides,
and clouds faded first in the water.

Ales and doctors and dispersing girls
paced the shoreline changed by slides
that left no trace. High Slavic lakes
will be erased by fill dirt and collapsing stone,

and every perch go cannibal in coves
where the moon is thorny on altering floors.
I come only when cold claims the senile,
and water rolls to the shores like surly ground.

Making Certain It Goes On, p. 15.

That poem must be twenty-five years old at least. Reading it now, I think Meridian represented a world of order and pleasure that cracked as I grew older.

The trips to Meridian aside, my grandparents worked hard at the grim life in their small world. At one point in my analysis, the doctor remarked that for them, "there was only harshness and the soil."

I overheard grandmother tell someone about Grandfather's terrible temper. This, like the excessive drinking the doctor had imagined, was unknown to me. I heard Grandmother say, perhaps to a neighbor, that years ago their chickens were being killed. Although we had chickens in the backyard, I assumed she was talking about Michigan. One day, according to Grandmother, Grandfather found their cat in the coop and had nailed it halfway up the wire with a blow of a two by four as the cat was trying frantically to escape. While the cat hung there on the fence, Grandfather beat it to bone, guts and blood. I remember I found it hard to believe.

While I couldn't imagine Grandfather violent, I was aware that he was naive. One day, two men came to the house to sell siding. They sat in the front room and talked for a long time. I can't recall how old I was but remember I didn't like the men though they were pleasant. They talked Grandfather into signing something and a few days later my grandparents were upset by something that came in the mail. "Do you have the paper you signed?" Grandmother asked. "Yes," he said loud with defiant certainty and got the paper and read it. I have no idea what that business was about or what the outcome was, but I remember thinking he should not have signed anything when those two men asked him.

I remember Cousin Eileen asked me if I knew what a lawsuit was. She was around twelve and I was six or seven at the time. She lived with us off and on. Her mother had died when she was six. Grandfather put on his only suit and a tie and looking uncomfortable as he always did when dressed up, he drove off in his model A. Eileen tried to explain that he was on his way to court, that someone was suing him for fourteen dollars, but I was too young to understand, though the amount sticks in my mind.

Grandfather held a menial job at the Seattle Gas Company. I think he guarded the parking lot at one time. He was ignorant, having only a grammar school education and having been a tenant farmer most of his life in Michigan. Once Eileen told me he was studying for an exam so he could get a better job at the plant. Later she told me he had flunked the exam. And once, though I don't think it was connected to anything specific, on one of her visits, my mother remarked with some disdain, "Your Grandfather was never much good at making money."

Grandfather had his heroes, Henry Ford and Jim Jeffries. "Old Henry Ford showed them," he would say in a rare demonstrative moment. Or, "If Johnson (Jack) had fought Jim Jeffries in his prime, that nigger wouldn't have lasted as long as a snowball in hell." When he spoke he usually said something he'd said many times before. The bit about Jack Johnson and Jim Jeffries stands out because it and my grandmother's claim that Catholics were storing arsenals in the basements of their churches, were the only two utterances of prejudice I remember hearing in the house. Once I asked Grandfather about blacks, only "blacks" was insulting to Negroes in those days so I'm sure I said "colored" or "Negro." Grandfather said he had known a Negro in Michigan and he had been a damn good man.

When Grandfather wasn't working or sitting in the chair in the kitchen staring at the floor, he was reading the Saturday Evening Post and chewing tobacco. He kept a bucket of water beside him and he would spit into the pail. The water got darker and darker over the weeks until finally he threw the tobacco-black liquid on the garden and refilled the pail with fresh water. Usually he read in the kitchen. Sometimes he took his magazine and spit pail to the living room where he sat in one of the two ugly brown velveteen chairs. We lived in the kitchen so much it seemed odd to see him in the front room.

When I wanted some candy, I'd go to him to ask for a nickel. He always kept reading, taking no notice of me as I asked him over and over, "Grandpa, please give me a nickel, please." I had to keep on and on, begging and whining just to get him to respond. He would refuse at first, but if I begged long enough he'd finally give in.

I bought penny candy at MacCameron's drugstore in White

Center and then ate it in bed while I read a mystery, usually one serialized in the *Saturday Evening Post*. My grandparents went to bed very early, often before nine and I would be up alone in the house. I didn't dare play the radio very loud if at all, and by the age of nine, out of boredom, I was putting words on paper at the table in the small dining room off the kitchen.

Every year for many years I bought two plugs of chewing tobacco for Grandfather on his birthday. I never had them gift wrapped and I didn't buy a card. I just handed them to him and said "Happy Birthday, Grandpa." He seemed pleased and would grunt some clumsy thanks.

It seems strange, but he played the violin. I don't remember it well. He kept the violin in the cellar and once in a while he would bring it up and play. He played only a few tunes. I remember one of his favorites was "Red Wing," another, "Pop, Goes The Weasel." He kept time by stamping his foot. After he didn't play anymore, I used to see the violin case in the basement, lodged above one of the beams, and I would take it down and open it and look at the violin.

Mr. Windler was a foul tempered man, and at times a brutal one. Once he took me fishing with his family. That was a kind act. I was lonely and bored much of the time and entertained myself with private games I played in the woods on either side of the house. Mr. Windler, his wife, his oldest child, Mary, Bobby, who was my age, and Jimmy, the baby, and I went to Cedar River. Bobby Windler had a butterfly collection, and he could be seen about the neighborhood often with his net grabbing new specimens which he pinned to the cloth boards. Grandfather didn't approve. The idea of a boy with net chasing butterflies struck him as unmanly. Grandfather called Bobby "Butterfly Windler" with some disdain.

At Cedar River, I found Mr. Windler at one time in the afternoon fishing a still, clear backwash. Obviously, fish were not there. If they had been we could have seen them. "I don't think there's any fish there, Mr. Windler," I yelled on my way downstream. "Why the water's connected to the river," he said harshly, "Can't you see?" I decided he was insensitive, as were all people who couldn't look at water and imagine where the fish were.

I never could like Mr. Windler. He had a purple face and seemed always to be in a rage or on the verge of one. He was mean to his children, especially Bobby and Mary who were step-children. He also took a dislike to me at some point. Once when I was passing his house with my BB rifle he suddenly appeared on his front porch and began haranging me about some awful thing I was supposed to have done with my gun. I remember it was a false accusation but he went on and on. "They should take it away from you," he screamed. "I told you you'd get in trouble with that gun." I kept walking quietly home but I wanted to say, "Oh fuck you, you redfaced son of a bitch. Just fuck you."

I was in our kitchen one day at the sink. It must have been a warm day because the back door was open. Grandfather was in the front room, reading the *Saturday Evening Post,* and Grandmother was there too. When I heard the knock at the back door I stepped to my left to see who it was. It was Mr. Windler, and he immediately started yelling at me. He accused me of something that wasn't true, and his voice swelled in anger and accusation. He said I was a rotten influence on the other children in the neighborhood. I looked into the front room, thinking maybe help would come. My grandparents couldn't help but hear. Grandfather kept reading as if nothing was happening and Grandmother looked at the floor. I was left alone to face this raging man and I was too small and frightened to answer him. He quit and started to move off, then stepped back and shouted, "And another thing." In desperation, frustration and rage, I slammed the door in his face.

Bob Bunce was only a bit older than I was. The Bunces lived on 16th, just a block west of our place. Mr. Bunce was a humorless man and a well-dressed one. I don't know what he did for a living, but it did not involve his hands. Their house was a nice one for that neighborhood, relatively new, with a large well-kept lawn and big cherry trees. I used to play football with Bob in his yard once in a while.

Mr. Bunce always made me feel uncomfortable. Once I

watched him play Bob ping pong. When he announced the score I'd repeat it, as small boys are prone to do. "Keep quiet, will you," he said, and the way he said it made me feel cheap and dirty. We still had the old outhouse at my grandparents, and one day after a football game in Bob's backyard I asked to use their bathroom. A few days later, Bob told me his father didn't want me to use their bathroom anymore. Because I wasn't used to bathrooms, I hadn't flushed it the last time.

A few years later, I heard Bob had died. The circumstances are vague. I remember he was working on a mountain lookout but I can't remember if that had anything to do with his death. I was still quite young when it happened and I remember the news seemed bewildering because I had planned someday to apologize to Bob for my grandparents and to tell him I wished I could grow up like him in a middle class home and learn some manners.

Bob had a younger sister, whose name may have been Jean, though I'm not sure. We had some mutual friends and shortly after I graduated from high school, I found myself in the Bunce home talking to Mr. Bunce once again after all those years. He looked the same. Rigid, fixed mouth. Still composed. Still humorless. And still making me feel uncomfortable. Years later I came to believe he was a bourgeois, someone who wanted the emotional advantage. Grandfather was no bourgeois, he was simply and understandably boorish.

Grandfather owned a .45 revolver. He bought it when I was still a boy and he kept it in a holster that hung on my grandparents' bed. He only used it twice.

One morning I stepped onto the back porch just in time to see a potato plant topple over at the rear of the garden, out between the chicken coop and the pear tree. A few moments later, another plant fell over. What a strange sight. I stepped quietly on the dirt path toward the rear of the garden. A gopher was gnawing at a potato stalk. Then the plant fell and the gopher moved to the next one.

I slipped back to the house and ran in to tell Grandpa. Grandfather sneaked along the path with his .45 until he spotted the gopher, by now gnawing away at his fifth plant, and blasted it. That was the only time he ever shot the gun. Normally, he protected the garden by catching gophers in traps.

One day a Jehovah's Witness showed at the front door. Only strangers came to the front door, since our friends all knew we used only the back of the house to come and go. The Jehovah's Witnesses were holding a convention in White Center. I remember hundreds of people marching into the small community, a bedraggled bunch, sad and always in my memory in tatters. Representatives were making the rounds of the neighborhoods trying to win converts. The man at the door insisted Grandfather listen to a record of their leader. He intended playing the record on a hand-cranked player he carried. Grandfather said he didn't want to hear their leader. The man insisted. Their voices rose in anger. Finally, fed up, Grandfather rushed to the bedroom and came back with the .45 and chased the man out of the yard.

After the full-sized cement basement was in, I used it for a playground. On my roller skates I played imaginary hockey games, though the stick and puck were real enough. I would rush the imaginary goal on the wall and flick the puck with a snap of the wrist. I used back hand shots, long slap shots and close in trick shots. I raised a lot of dust brushing my hockey stick across the floor.

One afternoon, after a violent prolonged session of hockey, I came upstairs where Grandfather informed me that I could skate in the basement but I could not play hockey anymore. I was furious. I hated anyone breaking into the private games I'd developed to break the boredom. We argued and the argument became a fight. Finally, tears of frustration blurring my vision, I screamed at him that I'd skate all right, I'd skate until the dust was so goddam thick it would never settle.

He chased me into my bedroom and forced my head down against the bed with his hands. "God damn you," he said, his voice hissing with anger, "You'll look for another roosting place." That was an old threat, one he'd used since I could remember. And that man who, according to my grandmother, had once beat a cat to pulp with a two-by-four, couldn't even bring himself to hit me. He could only press my head into the soft bed and hurl the same old threat of dispossession.

For no reason I can guess, I was elected treasurer of the senior class, class of '41, West Seattle High School. I didn't want the office and didn't run. Someone nominated me and I ended up with the most votes.

Being a class officer, I was one of the first to receive my diploma in the ceremonies at the civic auditorium. My grandparents took me there in the Model A. I realize now that my graduation meant something to them, although they never understood my going to college, least of all majoring in creative writing.

Many of the students planned a drunk in Everett that night, thirty miles north of Seattle. In the parking lot they were yelling, "See you in Everett." I was in the back seat of the Model A, headed home. Except for the home brew Grandfather had urged on me when I was little, and some Port wine I sneaked at Aunt Sarah's one day, I had never done any drinking. I sat silent in the back seat of the car and stared straight ahead.

Suddenly I was ashamed of everything, of the Model A, my grandparents, myself, my not going to Everett, my lack of maturity at feeling the shame, my inability to summon any dignity. It was unbearable and I lay down on the floor of the car so the students wouldn't see me as we inched out of the parking lot. I don't think my grandparents took any notice. Years later in the analysis I recounted this. The doctor said the shame went back to a much earlier experience or series of experiences, that I was playing out a sort of emotional déjà vu. We never discovered what that first shame was.

I bought my first car in 1941, a Model A Ford, a convertible. On one of his visits, my stepfather tried to teach me to drive. He was impatient with my timidity at the wheel, and the confusion I felt trying to coordinate the clutch with the accelerator. He took to yelling at me and that destroyed what little confidence I had. Then of course he was only around for a short time with his fairly new Plymouth. So when I bought the Model A I didn't know how to drive. I didn't bother asking Grandfather to teach me.

I was a menace. Within a few days after I started my amateur touring about the streets of Seattle, I had a wreck, came around a corner far too fast and piled into the rear fender of a car waiting at a stop sign. The driver was a woman, and she was quite decent about it. Later, when I called her home to make arrangements to pay her, her husband answered the phone and when I asked for her, he snarled distrustfully, "Who wants her?" I didn't understand his suspicion, but later, when I realized he thought some potential lover had been calling, in a sad way I was amused. The idea that I could be mistaken as a sexual threat in the world of men seemed absurd.

Within a few weeks I'd taught myself well enough to get a license. I still wasn't very good. One day a chum from high school, Ken Gifford, who years later would be a teammate on a long lived softball team, put his fingers in my eyes waving an enthusiastic hello to a friend named Mike Mitchell, who happened to be walking down First Avenue. Blinded and confused, I ran into a car that had just double parked. My insurance I thought, would cover the cost of the dented fender. But the insurance company claimed I had given them a wrong address on my application and as a result hadn't received a notice of cancellation they'd sent a few days before the accident. I doubted I'd given them the wrong address, since I'd had only one all my life, but I was too naive to do anything but accept their story. Later, Uncle Lester, who spent decades in insurance in Tacoma, told me I should have turned the matter over to the State Insurance Commissioner. From what I've since heard about state regulatory agencies, I'm not sure Uncle Lester wasn't being naive himself.

My grandparents celebrated their Golden Wedding anniversary in 1942. They went as dressed up as I'd ever seen them to the St. James Lutheran Church in White Center for the ceremony. They were remarried as part of the festivities, and they sat in the social room in the church basement while people congratulated them and made speeches. Except for their clothes, they looked very much the way they looked at home sitting in the two straight-back wood chairs, their backs to the windows in the kitchen. They were silent and said nothing, each with a life that no one knew going on somewhere inside. Sometimes they looked at the floor the way they did at home. Grandfather looked uncomfortable at times, at other times sad, old and tired. They didn't speak to each other.

Shortly after that, Grandmother broke her leg. Rather, her leg broke, snapped as she stepped off a curb in downtown Seattle to get on a bus that had not pulled fully over before stopping. She collapsed in the street. The bus driver, a man named Charlie Meadows, lived in our neighborhood and knew grandmother. He closed the doors and drove off leaving her helpless on the cement.

Nights I went to bed sober right after the war, bad dreams exploded me awake. Even a slight sound would bring me wide awake up from the bed. A car horn in the streets made me flinch and jump as I walked perfectly safe along the sidewalk. I had moved back in with my grandparents and continued living there as if the war represented only an interruption in a life that would know no change.

If anything, the war must have reinforced my unconscious resistance to growing up and leaving home. It was the first time I had been away from home for any length of time, and on my one foray out into the big world I had nearly been killed several times. Had I had some successful sexual encounters with women, I think things might have been different. As it was, I tried to recapture the past. I even played cowboys and Indians with a little boy who lived across the street. The woods to the south of the house had not yet been wiped out by new houses, and I played out childhood games there.

Grandfather let me use his car and once I tried fishing the Duwamish slough. I drove the old Model A to the slough using the same route we had used when I was a child. I regretted that the old service station was no longer in operation as I passed the abandoned building and rusting pumps, that I could not stop there and buy gas and a Chicken Dinner candy bar. I sat on the grassy bank of the slough where I'd sit so many times as a boy and eagerly threw my line in. It must have been almost ten years since I'd fished there. No bites. Not one.

A machine shop now stood across the slough and a brief field beyond the water. I hadn't been fishing an hour when three machinists came out of the shop and laughed at me for fishing in such an absurd place. They gestured toward me in ridicule and I wanted to yell at them: please understand, I used to fish here years ago. I'm trying to recapture. . . . I was embarrassed by my sentimental attempts to ignore the changes that had taken place. The machinists were right. It was a silly place to fish.

Since Grandpa always kept the garage locked, he left the key in the ignition, though that was a recent habit. Since I found the key in the ignition when I took the car, illogically I left it there when I parked. The car was stolen one night in West Seattle. I was sitting in a café with some friends and could see the car parked a half block up the street. As I talked I looked away for a few moments. When I looked back the car was gone.

The West Seattle police station was only a block away and we went there immediately. The desk cop was a bitter, hostile old man, slow to give us attention. We tried to explain that the car had just been taken, that if he got the report on the radio they might be able to catch the thief in the act. But he arrogantly took his time, obviously annoyed that we'd bothered him about such a trivial matter as an old car.

My grandparents were in bed when I got home. By now they went to bed around eight. Grandfather was nearing retirement but he still had to drive to work early in the morning. I woke him and gave him the sad news. "Christ," he said. The next morning and for several mornings he had to get up at 4:30 to catch the bus. I loathed myself for the discomfort my stupidity and carelessness had brought the tired, old man. I thought that if I quit school, and got a job and gave them all my money, maybe that would make up for it.

A week later the car still hadn't been found. Grandfather went to see Stu Hillborn who attended the Lutheran Church, and who was a cop. Hillborn checked and the car was not even on the missing list. The old cop in West Seattle never even reported it. In a few days the car was recovered.

It was recovered on VJ day in fact. I was playing semi-pro baseball and was waiting at Lower Woodland Field for other plays to show up. I came early to things, especially baseball games. When our manager showed up, he told us the Naval Air Station team we were scheduled to play wasn't coming. The war was over and almost everyone on the base at Sand Point had gone AWOL. I ended up at someone's house in West Seattle drinking a poison called Martin's Scotch Type Whiskey. I still remember that word "type" on the label.

I woke up dreadfully hung over and two detectives were in my bedroom. Grandmother had let them in and I stood up bleary eyed in my shorts when they asked me to. The boy arrested with the car—he had been pushing it because it was out of gas—had told the police the car had been given to him by a tall slender blond man. I didn't even come close. If the boy was taking a wild shot to get off the hook, he couldn't have made a worse guess.

They drove me downtown to the jail. The girl working at the desk had gone to high school with me, and with one disturbed glance and no words she asked the detectives if I'd been caught at something but they shook their heads. I suppose unshaven and hung over I looked like a suspect for something. The girl seemed relieved I wasn't in trouble and, though we really didn't know each other very well, I found her concern touching.

I wanted to be angry at the thief, mostly on behalf of Grandfather who had been getting up so early all those days. It was impossible. They brought in a pale 15-year-old boy who looked as criminal as Julie Andrews. Had we ever seen each other? We hadn't. I took great pleasure that morning bringing the car back home.

Because I didn't have a car, and because Grandfather was understandably against letting me use his now, I sometimes asked him to drive me to the playfields where my baseball team was scheduled to play. Our games were in the late afternoon, long after Grandfather was home from work. One day we drifted over and bounced off the curb with a jolt. "What the hell was that?" he asked. I told him he'd run into the curb. "Jesus," he said. I knew his senses were failing and his driving days numbered. Another time, going down long, steep Boeing Hill, the brakes failed. I saw grandfather pressing the pedal and saw we weren't slowing. We were sure to run the stop sign at the bottom of the hill where other cars in the cross traffic on West Marginal Way were pulling out after stopping. "Can't you stop," I yelled. "No," he said still pressing his foot to the floor. I grabbed the handbrake just in time. Had he been alone I was sure he would not have thought that fast and I feared he would kill himself if he didn't stop driving.

I bought a car, another Model A. I still harbored bad feelings toward Charlie Meadows for having left my grandmother lying in the street in downtown Seattle. And I'd been riding the busses and trolleys to the University for some time. Service was slow and over the months (in the case of Meadows, over the years) I'd built up a fierce hatred of the Seattle Transit System. One Sunday around 8 A.M. I was arrested, dead drunk, trying to run trackless trolleys off the road with my Model A.

When they threw me in the tank, my face smashed against the cold stone floor and I started to weep with fear and frustration. I kept saying "Please" to no one in particular. The floor only was cold. The jail was horribly overheated, a series of cells, all opened, with tiered cots constructed with iron strips. No mattresses. Down at the end of the corridor that fronted the cells was a dirty porcelain toilet bowl with no seat.

As my head began to clear, I found the prisoners to be a hostile lot for the most part. One who was not hostile was a sad, demented derelict who said to no one in particular, "I found a home here." He seemed to be warming a can of food on the radiator, and I got the impression he was always in this wretched place and happy to be there. One man was being held for murdering his wife. He said grim things that might have been lines from a play or a movie script, things like, "Tomorrow we'll all see the judge. Then we'll find out if we have any life left, or if our life has been broken for good, never to be repaired." One young man was in for fighting. He snarled at the others and stared out the window. As, out of fear, I tried desperately to make contact with one then another prisoner, and failed, I began to think: I can't be like these men. I can't be part of a world where people care nothing for each other.

I tried to sleep on the interlaced iron bands but couldn't. Once the windowless main door had slammed shut, it was impossible to make contact with anyone outside the jail. Hours went by. You could not get the jailors attention by pounding on the door. The door was so thick, he wouldn't hear. Finally, the jailor brought some food, an ugly looking bean dish, and I begged him to let me make a phone call. He told me to shut up and threatened to beat me if I didn't. It occurred to me that nothing could stop them from keeping me there forever. I would finally learn to be as unfriendly as the others just to get along in that grim, dirty world where day crawled through the stifling air.

I was called around 11 that night. I'd finally fallen asleep and I stood up groggy when the aging jailor called my name. He took me to a phone outside and gave me a number. "Call this number and tell him your bail." I dialed and a nasty voice asked me what my bail was. When I told him, he said, "That'll cost you twenty." While we waited for the bondsman, the jailor started talking about how much he did for the prisoners and how much it cost him to do these favors. I didn't know what favors he was talking about, since it had been impossible to contact him from the jail through the solid wall and window-less thick door. Then I realized the man was asking me to give him money. A few hours ago he had refused to let me make a phone call and had threatened me with assault, and now he was asking me for money. I was too frightened to refuse but had no money with me. When they gave me my possessions downstairs I had just 20 dollars to give to the bondsman. Later, the bondsman told me he gave five of my twenty to the jailor, a kickback for giving me the number to call. Everyone who got out of jail was in effect paying the jailor.

I found a plainclothes detective and borrowed five dollars to get my car back. He was the most unhurried man I've ever seen. When he handed me the money he said, "I never do this, but you look less like a criminal than anyone I've ever seen in here." The next day, I returned and paid the detective. Then I found the jailor and gave him two dollars. I doubt that anyone had ever returned to give him money and he was startled by my innocence. Of course, I was so frightened by the experience and so naive I imagined that, if I didn't leave everyone there happy with me, they could for no reason put me back in jail.

I lost my driver's license in the trial. The Veterans Administration sent down a silver-tongued character witness named Rose who extolled my war record, my thirty-five missions, my citations. The court was impressed but just barely. During my weekend drunk, I'd smashed my fender against a stone driveway marker at the home of one Herbert Kimsey who happened to be Seattle Chief of Police. The police tried to tie my dented fender to a hit-and-run accident in another part of town, but that was soon dropped when I told the court how the dent came to be there. My story was too wild to have been made up. Rose gave such a warm speech on my behalf that following the trial, the witnesses against me, the arresting officers, shook my hand and told me how sorry they were. Later I learned that had the Veterans Administration advised me to plead innocent instead of guilty, I would not have lost my license.

My grandparents didn't understand why I went to school on the G.I. Bill instead of getting a job. In his remaining years, I suppose Grandfather had hoped not to be saddled with an immature freeloader. Someone who paid no rent, who came and went as he pleased, who had no girl friends, who drank way too much and too often. Grandfather made little effort to hide his disdain of me.

One day at the table, in response to something Grandmother had said about a young man who attended the Lutheran Church and had grabbed off a nice wife, I said that I'd like to grab one off too but didn't seem to be able to. Grandfather snorted, "You don't grab them in the right places, I guess." And I thought with terrible bitterness, "No. Old man, I don't because I'm sick and frightened and bewildered and masturbate at twenty-two and probably will all my life and you are to blame, you and your old car and this old house and the terrible things that have happened to me here, and so I have to suffer your goddam insults because I'm a cripple and can't live anywhere else." But I kept quiet because I needed one place I could stay for certain. It made little difference. We hardly spoke anymore.

One December I told Grandfather I wanted a book of Emily Dickinson's poems for my birthday. Roethke had spoken of Emily Dickinson when he talked about slant rhyme, and I was eager to read any poet who might be able to help me. Sure enough, on my birthday I got the *Selected Poems of Emily Dickinson*. What a surprise. Where had he found the book? Surely not in White Center. No store there would carry it, or any poetry for that matter. And Grandpa never went downtown. Maybe Aunt Sarah had found a copy when she was shopping downtown.

Grandfather signed the book on the title page, right under "Emily Dickinson" and above "with an introduction by Conrad Aiken." In a shaky hand, he wrote "from Grandpa." Today, when I look at the book, I'm reminded that there are many kinds of recluses.

After Grandmother died in December, 1949, Aunt Sarah cooked for us at night after spending all day in the dry goods store in White Center where she'd worked for thirty years. Talking to Aunt Sarah one day Grandfather said of Grandmother, "Why, she told me she was going to die." His voice caught slightly when he said that. It was the only time I saw him even close to tears.

He had been slightly lame since I could remember. His legs seemed cramped when he walked and he moved slowly and awkwardly. Some of his trouble had been a double hernia he carried for years. He wore a truss and finally he had an operation. He recovered all right but he still limped. For years he had not been able to get in and out of a rowboat.

I discovered Phantom Lake sometime after the war. I don't remember how. It was quite close to Seattle, across Lake

Washington and Mercer Island and just beyond the community of Bellevue, a new suburb that was becoming popular, a
place for the upper middle class to settle.

When I first found the lake, a German immigrant who
lived in a dignified white farmhouse rented boats to fisher-
men. The lake was ringed with brush and trees except for a
patch of bare shore here and there, and only one other farmhouse was on the lake. The water was murky and the lake was
filled with monster perch and crappie, the biggest I'd ever
seen. Had Grandfather been younger or less lame, I would
have taken him there.

My first trip there, I took a big catch of huge perch and
brought them home. The size of those green-yellow fish broke
down Grandfather's glum countenance. His eyes shone at the
sight and he immediately set to cleaning them, something I'd
hoped he'd do as I hate to clean fish that need scaling. Grandfather loved to eat perch. From the time I was a little boy, I'd
heard him say, "Perch are the best eating fish there is."

After Grandmother died and I'd moved out, I still brought
Grandfather fish now and then from Phantom Lake. I'd go
out alone and enjoy the charm of the strange murky water
that reflected clouds so vividly, the thick willows that hugged
the shoreline, the unusual size of the fish. Most of all, I loved
bringing those big perch back to the home that was now the
only old house on a block of new, modest houses. I had the
Model A now. He had given it to me when he realized he was
too old to drive. I still had it when I married in August of
1951.

One day I brought my wife and a couple of friends to see
Grandfather. He sat in one of the velveteen chairs in the living room, looking sadly at the floor as we tried to draw him
out. When we got on the subject of fishing, he began to stir.
Before long, our friends, also a young married couple, had
him talking about fishing trips he'd taken as a young man in
Michigan. He spoke warmly of a trip he'd taken to a lake where
they had caught hundreds of bluegill, and his eyes shone at
the memory and he smiled.

On the way home, my wife and the couple talked about
what a wonderful old man he was, how warm he became when

he opened up. I had some terrible sense of failure. Why hadn't I ever brought him out like that? Why had we had so little contact over all those years? I felt close to him at moments, fishing at Lake Meridian or when we walked to Mr. Husted's barber shop to get our hair cuts, but I could never remember talking to him for any length of time. Maybe we had talked when he was sixty and I was five and we drank beer together in the cellar. It seemed we had all gotten used to living a life inside. Strangers saw us better than we saw ourselves.

My wife and I nicknamed the Model A Sam, and finally I sold it to a librarian we both knew. Somewhere in that period was a note I remember. Someone had taken it down from a phone call that came in while I was away from my desk at work. "I want Sam." I let it go for 35 dollars but I never got the money. When I let the librarian have the car, he said he'd pay me in a few days. I suppose he just forgot, because he was reasonably honest. I didn't follow up. Not getting the money seemed appropriate and after months had gone by it ceased to matter.

I still drove out to the house now and then. I'd bought a 1939 Plymouth, a beat-up old clunk but, because I'd never owned any car except a Model A and because my sense of time was shaky, in my innocent way I thought of it as a new car.

The last time I saw Grandfather alive he was in bed at home suffering from cancer of the gall bladder. I stood over him and he looked at me only briefly and said, "I don't feel very damn good." That was the last thing he said to me. A man of few words to the very end. Days later, it was in February 1953, Aunt Sarah called me at Boeing and told me he was dead.

I cried heavy tears at his funeral. I hadn't cried at Grandmother's funeral because I feared that if I started I could never stop. Now I let go and my wife's fingers dug into my arm to give me support. They buried him next to Grandmother in the cemetary.

I'd done four poems based on Grandmother over the years following my grandparents' death, and I felt obligated to do one about Grandfather several years after he was gone.

The Other Grave

Long and smelling good, the cemetery grass
could be a kiss. You failed a field
of Ypsilanti wheat. Below your stone
you never try to touch her there beside you.
I used to blame your failure on the moon.

When old, you needed words like "lake."
"Lake" I'd say. Your eyes began to farm.
Horses took you and a friend where coves
were wonderful with bass—bluegills
clowning for your rind below the log.
Catfish ran five pounds. See my picture.
See my mustache then. Any photo fades.
You remain in yellow with your catch.

I'd like to sing you, point each word
about you up and shoot. Wasn't gold
too easy for your maps, or love
too simple for your brilliant arms?
I said a British wind was in your face—
only blue the undertaker planned.
The tunes you hummed were so unknown
I told a dog you were a fine composer.

Why am I afraid or sorry you are dead?
My hands paid contraband to be this still.
My mouth rotted with the truth
to be as tough as wheat before your stone.

Making Certain It Goes On, p. 89.

Were he alive he would not understand the poem and we would remain to each other mutual failures. And a few years after his death I found myself on the analyst's couch, trying not to say what with all my sobbing and strangulating fear and shame I couldn't stop from coming to utterance, "And by God, I showed them. I showed them, doctor. I didn't move away, I stayed in that house and I watched them die and finally they were gone." And even though the statement was factually

untrue, the doctor said matter of factly, "Yes, you had survived."

My wife and I continued to fish Phantom Lake. It was so
close we could go there on a moment's whim. Most of the
people who came to fish the lake were blacks. They seemed
proud, private people, very warm and friendly. "How you
doing?" they'd yell as they rowed by. An aging Swede immigrant fished there, the best crappie fisherman I've seen. No
matter what the time of day, he managed to bring in a huge
catch of black and silver crappie.

Someone started to sell lots around the shore. A new house
appeared at the far end of the lake. Then another. Bellevue
was growing. As more modern homes appeared, the owners
pressured the German farmer to stop renting boats. He resisted
and was still renting boats the last time we went there, but the
future was clear. It was no longer fun to fish there under the
staring windows of people on the rise who resented us. The
fish were getting smaller and, though perhaps I imagined it,
the water seemed to be getting clearer. We stopped going there.

I saw Grandfather's car for the last time by chance. By
then I owned a 1948 Ford, a car only six or seven years old.
But I wasn't driving that day, I was riding in someone else's
car coming home from work. We were headed north on 4th
Avenue, then Seattle's main north-south arterial street, and
we had just passed the old railroad depots at Jackson street.
The next street is Main, and we were crossing it when I looked
to the right up the slight hill beyond 5th and there was the
old car parked. Several of the buildings in the block were
abandoned. One had been a grocery but now housed some
gypsies who had hung curtains across the large storefront
windows. An old Japanese grocery operated in that block, and
there was a rather good, modest Japanese restaurant.

Most model A's look alike, but I could not have been mistaken. I'd lived with that car for about twenty-five years and
would have known it anywhere. I saw it so suddenly and so
briefly that I had no time to call back the sometimes warm but
more often sad past it represented. I wondered who owned it
now and what it was doing in that odd part of town, on that

dingy drab street. I remember I thought irrelevantly that Grandpa had never had a Japanese meal in his life, only the plain meat and potatoes he'd known on the farms in Michigan.

If I had been warned or could have stopped for a few minutes, had some time to prepare, I would have indulged myself. I would have tried to dream back a lot of moments and relive them without shame, fear or anger. And I would have abandoned any idea of separating the sentimentality I'd inherited and knew was crippling from the honest affection for life I didn't ever want to lose. If I found I couldn't weep, I would have waited and remembered until I could because I believe some things and some moments deserve our tears. But there was no time for anything except the surprise I felt seeing Sam so unexpectedly and in such an unlikely place. Then it was gone and we were moving north into the modern chrome traffic of downtown.

The White Line

I'VE SEEN around 2500 movies I suppose. That's not a bad estimate, counting the ones on TV. I'm a selfish sort of buff. I prefer to go to the first showing on Sunday, usually at noon in most cities, when few people are there and I can lose myself to the dark of the theatre, and the picture. I like to go alone. When I was drinking heavily as I did for many years, I was usually hungover at movies and found it easy to cry at the ending, no matter how gross or corny it was.

Some movies I've seen several times: *The Bank Dick, Never Give A Sucker An Even Break, Frankenstein, Dracula, Duck Soup, A Night At The Opera, The Blue Angel.* I never fail to be shaken by Emil Janning's suffering in *The Blue Angel.* What an audience I am. Easily taken in. By nature not very critical and most receptive. Was there ever more hilarious obliviousness than Leon Errol's in *Never Give A Sucker An Even Break,* when he stops to rest halfway up the absurd mountain, unaware of the gorilla a few feet away? I best not get started on favorite moments.

I got going to movies early, around 1930 or 31, and I saw both *Dracula* and *Frankenstein* first run. By first run, I mean the first time they came to George Shrigley's White Center Theatre in White Center, Washington. That took a little time after they opened in downtown Seattle. Say a year. George Shrigley's theatre had one rest room. It was just to the right of the screen, a small cubicle with a single toilet bowl. When you opened the door, the light inside fell across your face letting the audience know who was going where. One night a woman used the john, the only time I ever remember it happening, and though I was just a boy or perhaps because of it, I imagined how embarrassed she felt as the light revealed her to the crowd.

George Shrigley had a wide white line painted across the

single aisle. Children had to sit below the line so they wouldn't disturb the grownups watching the movie. Since we were noisy, and since we sat between the adults and the screen, Shrigley kept the volume high so the dialogue and music could climb over our screams and laughter and reach the rear of the house. Once in a while one of us would try to move above the white line, but the usherette kept close tabs on us and would hustle whoever it was back below the mark.

But for all that, George Shrigley's White Center Theatre was paradise. I would do anything to go there. Beg for money. Whine for money. Try to find a grocer kind enough to give me deposit money for pop bottles I scrounged. Those grocers weren't easy to come by in the Depression. Shrigley's was two blocks away, but it seemed worlds from the drab house where my grandparents sat quietly in the evening, seldom speaking, waiting for nine o'clock to come so they could go to bed. They had gotten into the habit of going to bed and arising early when they had been tenant farmers in Michigan before they moved west, and they had accepted hard work and boredom as norms long ago.

Not me. To me the norm was what those people were doing up on the screen. I mentioned being more or less uncritical and it struck me recently that one reason I believed everything I saw on the screen was simply that since someone had taken pictures of it, it must have happened. How our dull home could have used the Marx Brothers. "Waiter, do you have any stewed prunes?" "Yes sir." "Then give them a little black coffee, that will sober them up." Oh, how Ralph Schau and I howled at that. I was nuts about Ken Maynard. In fact, I was Ken Maynard, especially when the kids in the neighborhood played cowboy. And my horse was beautiful, whether it was his or one I made up when I tired of his.

My grandparents saw two movies in their lives. *Heidi*, starring Shirley Temple, and *Tugboat Annie* with Marie Dressler and Wallace Beery. *Heidi* was Grandmother's favorite novel, she said. I doubt that she ever read another. Reading was hard for her. She had only finished four grades of grammar school, and to understand the words she had to move her lips when she read. Grandfather had finished all eight grades of grammar school and read the *Tugboat Annie* stories in the *Saturday Evening Post.* They were taken to see *Tugboat Annie* in downtown Seattle, but they went by themselves to see *Heidi* in White Center. I remember how odd it seemed when they left to go out for the evening. They left the house seldom at night. Grandfather went to work at his menial job at the Seattle Gas Company and came home. Grandmother walked to White Center to shop, usually for meat and bread. We grew our own vegetables and had milk delivered. I remember Grandfather coming home caked with coal dust from some awful job he'd done that day, tired and depressed. Not so long ago I saw *Our Daily Bread,* and at the end, when the women and children are cheering and applauding the men as they bend their backs to the noble task of digging a ditch, I thought, "Oh, kiss off, King Vidor."

I have my favorite movie of course. It's called *Man On A Tight Rope,* directed by Elia Kazan in 1952. For the next few paragraphs I'm going to play the role of movie critic. (If Stanley Kauffman is reading this, I'll thank him to stop.) I've seen the movie about twenty-five times, more than any other, and I'm not ashamed to admit that I cry every time I see it, and I haven't had a drink in years.

It's a corny film, I suppose, but that doesn't bother me. All art is corny or it isn't art, a thing some modern poets seem to forget. The theme is simple and an old one: people versus system. In this case, the people are circus performers, not very good ones, and the system is the Communist bureaucracy of Czechoslovakia. The protagonist, Cernik (Frederic March), the director of the circus and prior to its confiscation by the State, its owner, plans to break out from behind the "iron curtain," to cross into the western sector with his circus mostly intact. The border becomes a kind of symbolic line separating the will from the imagination, the world of serious organizational adult responsibility from the paradise of childhood play. The only Communist official (Adolph Menjou) who realizes what Cernik is up to, thanks to his own active imagination, is himself done in by the system he has served with his considerable intellectual gifts.

There are weaknesses in the script that would turn off a

viewer of any sophistication but they don't bother me. A certain patness of plot: the stranger (Cameron Mitchell) is a newcomer to the circus and the object of Cernik's daughter's (Terry Moore) love. He is suspected by Cernick of being the informer (they know there is one) who rats to the government, and he just happens to be a deserter from the American Army who has acquired skills in his army training that can be used in the escape attempt. Some of the dialogue as written is too said: there's a dreadful sequence between Cernik and Barovik, the head of a rival circus, in which they stage a fight to convince the Communist authorities that they hate each other. Barovik does hate Cernik and tells him so but announces that they are both circus people and have a common enemy, the government. And one cliché is right out of those awful World War II masterpieces: a lion tamer, brave in the cage and frightened in life, suddenly rushes out onto the bridge and fires wildly at the Communist border guards making it possible to free Cernik's wagon that is stuck on the bridge, and tow it across to safety. The lion tamer is a sitting duck and falls to the guards' fire, the eternal coward who found courage long enough to sacrifice himself for the others.

But for all that, I love the movie so much that I judge people by their reactions to it. If you don't like it, chances are I wouldn't like you. The cutting and timing are so effective, the music played badly by the third rate band (the circus is third rate in all respects) so touching, that the climax never fails to stir me. I still tighten from the suspense as the circus approaches the border under the guise of giving a free show to the troops, as the elephants, acrobats and clowns pass under the eyes of the ominous guard towers. And I still, and hope always will, find the courage of small unheroic people moving. Cernik dies at the end. He is wounded before the final parade to the border begins, by the real informer, the foreman of the tent crew (Richard Boone), who calls the tent crew the "real workers." In Boone's big scene, where he accuses Cernik of treason, he is torn by loyalty to the State and loyalty to a friend he has known for twenty years, torn to a point of strangled inarticulation.

With Cernik dead, but the circus across the border, more

or less intact as he'd hoped, his wife (Gloria Grahame) takes charge and orders the circus to go on. Laughing children appear over a hill, and she tosses a life-size ragdoll dancing partner to one of the clowns who hesitates in his sadness, then realizes he can only do one thing, and starts to dance. In the last shot, the circus is still parading and playing along an empty road in an uninhabited countryside.

There are superb moments. A lyrical sequence early in the film, shot mostly from high above, where the lovers (Moore-Mitchell) engage in sexual play as they drift down a lovely sparkling stream, oblivious to all but each other. The first interrogation of Cernik in a repressive basement-like corridor-like room with a low ceiling, where a tyrannical petty official (who is later obsequious with his superior) questions Cernik and then fines him for failure to incorporate State-recommended material in his act. A secret meeting of the circus inner circle where the knife thrower (Pat Henning) confronts Cernik with his procrastination. A scene at the border where Cernik and two others case the layout for the escape and glance longingly at the mountains of Bavaria. Perhaps most effective of all is the sad way the playful music ("Chattanooga Choo Choo" repeats in the movie) is performed by the amateurish musicians. More than anything in the film, that music attests to the poor odds facing not only the tacky circus but humanity itself.

I still find the progression mystifying. I remember every scene but, as often as I've seen the movie, I'm still surprised by what comes next. It's as if the editor himself is playing games with us, though the sequence seems as inevitable as a Mozart symphony each time. It may be that to remember the details as vividly as I do, but not the sequence, is my own unconscious tribute to the film.

Frederic March has had bad notices from time to time and he can be wooden in certain roles. His Willy Loman was unfortunate. He is wondrously effective as Cernik. Perhaps that wooden quality is just what is needed to portray a man who, pushed to the brink, must be finally and fatally resolute though by nature he is fluid and warm. (Cernik also performs as a clown in the circus.) Appropriately, his face shows no struggle when he rescinds his dismissal of the insane French woman bareback rider moments after he has fired her at the insistence of State officials. Her behaviour in public is erratic and is seen as an embarrassment and a threat to public order by the regime.

The captain of the Communist border guards is a kind of slob, but a sympathetic one who wants to enjoy life as much as possible in a world that seems to advocate the serious and the bleak as ideals. In one scene he is eating lunch, his face hedonistically close to a bowl of soup. In another, he is getting a rubdown. His official duties, even answering a telephone, are boring annoyances, intrusions in his search for comfort. He comes out hastily putting on his uniform when the circus approaches the border check point. He laughs at the diversionary antics of the dwarf. When the escape is complete he stares across the border at Cernik's mother, once "the strongest woman in Europe." She stares back and in her face is defiance and rigid hatred. In his, sadness, admiration, even envy. He turns away and gesturing at a huge placard photo of a high official, knocked askew in the fracas, barks, "Straighten that sign." He is most people, trying to make out as best he can in a world he has little to do with making, wishing he could cross that border into the land of healthy irreverence.

Gloria Grahame is the epitome of a kind of woman liberationists loathe, and with good reason. She is a bitch who rides Cernik without mercy for his failure to stand up to the Government officials, and who tries to make out with the lion tamer. After Cernik knocks her on her ass with a vicious sock on the kisser, she says tenderly, "You should have done that years ago." Later, she is seen polishing his boots. I doubt anyone played the masochist better than Grahame. But women liberationists would be all for her at the end when she is firmly in charge of the circus. Her strength is every bit as believable as the lion tamer's heroics were not. And though she refers to the dead Cernik when she orders the circus to go on, her strength seems to come from herself, not from her relation with Cernik. Perhaps Robert Sherwood, who wrote the script, didn't intend it that way but that's the way Grahame plays it.

One thing impressive about the film is the power of personal loyalty that runs through it. That loyalty is taken for granted, except in the unfortunate sequence between Cernik and Barovik where, in a lapse of writing, it is too said. It is true that the knife thrower declares his loyalty to Cernik, but Pat Henning is so good in the part the declaration doesn't seem like an intrusion. Besides, it is included as part of the criticism of Cernik's failure to act and could be considered crude diplomacy. Barovik's statement is one of those speeches that no matter how true becomes false when put into words: "I really love my wife." The people are loyal to Cernik because he is all they have to be loyal to. They are freaks, outcasts, forlorns, and the bond they feel is something like the bond of persecuted minorities. Because the loyalty remains understood by virtue of the tricky circumstances of human relationships and not utterances, by something less defined but more real than the hard physical labor shared by members of the tent crew—a labor that the traitor-foreman tries with words to will into a basis for loyalty—the final act of courage against bad odds is understandable and believable.

When the movie first opened it got good reviews but was not a hit. I saw it in Seattle where it played as a second feature to a poorly produced Betty Grable musical. People of both left and right political persuasion didn't like it for reasons probably not so different from the reasons Governments don't like rundown circuses or Nixon distrusted the arts. When *The Old Man And The Sea* appeared, an Eisenhower cabinet member wondered aloud why anyone would want to read about an old man who is a failure.

For poets the film should be special. Like Cernik, poets cross that border, often at some risk, to reach that land where usual moral judgments are suspended and we can play to the child in all of us. Our poems may be serious, but we get them playing in that region over there that has little to do with making a living or obeying laws, and like the circus, we often end up doing it alone for our gratification. Sooner or later we face some form of tyranny. In some nations the tyranny is governmental. In ours, it tends to be more social, but just as real, and often far more insidious. Unless you are still young, if you are a poet you know some people hate you for it. If you don't know it you are too damned insensitive to be writing. What's more, some of them who hate you can, like the tent crew foreman, have known you a long time and may even be friends.

Recently Auden's poetry has been attacked by critics, and while I like Auden, I understand their objections to his poems. But I find it hard to think those critics would deny the psychological rightness of Auden when he says:

If a poet meets an illiterate peasant, they may not be able to say much to each other, but if they both meet a public official, they share the same feeling of suspicion; neither will trust one further than he can throw a grand piano. If they enter a government building, both share the same feeling of apprehension; perhaps they will never get out again. Whatever the cultural differences between them, both sniff in any official world the smell of an unreality in which persons are treated as statistics. The peasant may play cards in the evening while the poet writes verses, but there is one political principle to which they both suscribe, namely, that among the half dozen or so things for which a man of honor should be prepared, if necessary, to die, the right to play, the right to frivolity, is not the least.

> *The Dyer's Hand* (© Vintage Books Edition, 1962), pp. 88–89.
> Reprinted by permission of Random House, Inc.

Given the bad habits of time, we could not have stayed forever below the white line in George Shrigley's White Center Theatre. But we were better off there than we realized and were fools to want to cross too soon into the adult section. We had no way of knowing how complete we were down front, hopelessly committed to the flow of horses and men and the music that swelled to resolutions we would never know outside in the light of day.

Grandparents' house in White Center, Washington.

Aged two and a half.

About four.

"Stinky" Johnson and Hugo.

From left: Hugo, Grandfather Monk, Cousin Warren, Grandmother Monk, Mother (Esther Hugo).

Hope to Win a
War Gets Thin

(—"Tretitoli, Where the Bomb

Group Was")

Catch 22, Addendum

ONCE IN a while a friend will ask me what I think of *Catch* 22. When I'm asked I feel faintly uncomfortable because, being a writer and having been a bombardier in the 15th Air Force in Italy, I suspect my answer is supposed to carry some extra weight and I don't like bearing the responsibility of the expert critic. My admiration for those who do is considerable.

I enjoyed the book, and I'm sure I would have enjoyed it without my background of experience, but given that, Heller brought memories pouring back, some painful, some delightful, and all of them welcome because bad or good they are mine.

The bombers in *Catch* 22 are mediums in the 12th Air Force, and the airfield is located in Corsica. Rome, readily accessible in the novel, is subdued by war, slightly sinister, but a relief from the boredom of the airfield. Under the squalor, life still pulsates. Women and booze can be had.

Our bomber was the B 24, a heavy bomber, the flying pregnant water buffalo we called it. We flew fewer and longer missions, and we flew at high altitude. And we were located near Cerignola, which is not Rome, in drab, hostile Puglia.

If modern war is a "giant slapstick" as Karl Shapiro said somewhere, is really a spectacle of men and whole nations gone bananas—and I think it is even when a war is as close to being "justified" as was World War II—then I suppose no one has captured that insanity better than Heller, at least not since Byron's hilarious description of battle in "Don Juan."

Funny as *Catch* 22 is, it is more sad than funny. Accuracy wouldn't have it another way, and Heller is much more accurate than a stranger to the experiences that initiated the novel could imagine. After the misery, despair, boredom and fear are modified or erased by years, the sadness remains, a gnawing constant. My favorite book about the war remains *The Gal-*

lary by John Horne Burns because, despite its dated style, it confined itself to the essentials of suffering and fear, most of all to a sadness undiluted by sociological or political idealism. When someone is trying to kill you, you try to stay alive. The side you happen to be on makes little difference, and even if it did, you had little or no control over it to start with. Idealism is a luxury most poor people can't afford. I wish this weren't true.

Some critics have objected to Milo Minderbinder bombing his own airfield. Psychologically it's a rare weak point in the book. When men are as terrified as Yossarian is, they are dangerous. Milo would have shot on the spot because funny as war can be, the men involved are often deadly serious. One story that made the rounds in Italy was about a line sergeant (a sergeant who worked on the flight line on the field) who was finally caught after ten B24's had exploded on takeoff over a period of several weeks. The sergeant, the story went, had been getting 1000 dollars a plane and 100 dollars a man from the Germans, a total of 2000 dollars an explosion. He was tried, convicted and executed within a half hour after he was caught. His immediate superior, a lieutenant, had put a .45 to the sergeant's head and pulled the trigger a minute or two after the sentence was read. I don't know if the story was true or not but I never met anyone who didn't believe it.

Aside from objections to the Minderbinder bombing, *Catch 22* seems most accurate when it is screwiest. I clowned my way through the war as best I could, and so did others. What else could a sane person do. If we were sane. The events were out of control. Yossarian is a sane man in a world gone ape. Even rational scientific laws are suspended. Planes disappear into clouds without a trace, and mystical as that may sound to someone who wasn't there, it is true.

Yossarian can accept this mad world and fly more and more missions as the quota increases until finally the odds run out and he is killed. He can escape it by telling lies, by saying the madness is really sanity, and giving glowing reports to high level Washington officials about perverted and degenerate men. Or he can run away.

In a stretched sense, some of us did all three. The quotas

of missions were not increased arbitrarily in the 15th Air Force and I doubt they were in the 12th. I presume this was a dramatic device employed by Heller to good purpose. And you could get out of flying anytime you wanted to. All you had to do was ground yourself and lose your flight pay. Flying was voluntary in World War II, and if you quit, the command had no recourse except idle threats. It was the Cathcart in you that made you go on, that part of you that wanted the approval of others, that couldn't risk social censure. I flew because others were flying and I couldn't have faced their scorn. And the missions increased too, not in real numbers, but in the size those numbers became when compounded by fear. The final mission may be only one, but that one was a million. The fictionalized facts in *Catch 22* were psychological realities, and that's the worst kind.

Yet my hero of those days was a man from Texas named Marshall who, after a series of crashes and dangerous missions, finally had his plane so badly shot up over Vienna one day that almost every system in the plane malfunctioned. He managed to fly the ship by holding the stick deep into the pit of his stomach which would normally put the nose straight up. Even then he lost altitude and managed to stagger over the Yougoslavia border where he and his crew bailed out.

Aided by the Partisans, he came back about a month later, white as tile, and announced that he would never fly again. For a while some superior officers threatened him but he held fast. When he said never, he meant it. They couldn't even fly him to Naples to take the boat back home. They had to haul him across Italy in a truck. I remember standing in the Puglia mud and watching him wave goodbye cheerful and resolute, the only man in the back of the truck. I was so young it never occurred to me that I admired a man for doing what I feared to do because if I did no one would admire me.

I accepted without question a world where events defied explanation. Planes that disappeared from formations without anyone remembering what had happened to them. The huge orange rectangular mass, like a geometric fish flopping or maybe a billowing bedsheet on the bank of the Danube at Weiner Neustadt. The train at Szeged exploding into a lovely fireworks display with rockets and flares zooming out over the buildings from the marshalling yard. Fear on the ground. From altitude sheer spectacle. We had fears of our own. I remember once a friend criticized a long bombing mission poem I'd written because he said I showed no awareness I was bombing people, and in a rare burst of intellectual superiority I said that's exactly the point. We were not bombing people. Towns looked as real as maps. Bomb impacts were minute puffs of silent smoke. The first time I saw "the enemy" was after I returned to America where German POWs were waiting on us in the mess hall at Camp Patrick Henry, Virginia. Somehow they didn't look like the enemy.

I ran away too. I drank heavily. I hitchhiked into Cerignola to find something to do though I knew nothing was there. I wanted to feel in town and out of war. I hitchhiked to Foggia and played Benny Goodman and Tommy Dorsey records in the USO club. Those records seemed terribly important. I had to hitchhike over thirty miles one way to hear them. In one way or another others were running away too. Bombardiers were denied the lead position on their last mission. They had a habit of dropping the bombs a few miles short of the flak area to insure a safe return.

I think the reason we accepted the madness was that we didn't know it was there, or if we did we didn't care. The more missions you flew, the narrower became your concerns until finally all you really cared about was your own survival. I remember our pilot, Lt. Howard (NMI) Steinberg, telling me a Jewish joke once about a young man who couldn't wait to get into combat. He volunteered eagerly for the infantry and all through the training he grumbled impatiently and expressed his dissatisfaction with a system that delayed him from confrontation with the enemy. Finally he got to North Africa and was facing the Germans. His first taste of combat was a prolonged devastating German artillery attack, and when it finally stopped he stood up and yelled in Yiddish, "My God. A man can get killed out here."

That's no joke. I had volunteered for the Army Air Corps for the cheapest kind of romantic personal reasons. I felt weak and inadequate, and foolishly thought facing and surviving danger would give me spiritual depth and a courageous dimension I lacked and desperately wanted. "I went hunting wild after the wildest beauty in the world." And when, like the Jewish soldier in Steinberg's joke, I woke up one day, around my fifteenth mission, and realized I could be killed, things were never the same. I was not mocked by "the steady running of the hour." I was terrorized by it.

It wasn't the reality of the war alone but what your imagination did with it. You had nothing but time, mocking hours, in which to dwell, and you dwelled on being killed. Your imagination expanded your chances of dying hopelessly beyond statistical chance.

Any dreadful story I heard I would play back over and over to myself. Like the story about the flyers who bailed out over Munich to be marched naked into the center of the city before screaming mobs and then beaten to death. I could see it vividly, by day in my mind and at night in dreams. And the panic in my belly was physiologically real. Every morning explosive diarrhea and phlegmatic choking. When lucky I avoided the bizarre dreams by drinking myself into insensibility. One bombardier carried liquor in the plane and started drinking at 14,000 feet on the let down, as soon as he could safely remove his oxygen mask. And when we picked up an Axis Sally broadcast, either in the air or at the base, I could no longer laugh off her threats. She was out to kill me and I knew she could do it.

It would be unfair to infer I was typical. Most of the flyers, while fearful, handled their fears better than I could. They had gone to war with less illusions than I had, and they were simply more stable to begin with.

Yossarian was mature enough to have a kind of honor despite his fear, and the old Italian in the whorehouse was old enough to have none. He would have told the lies Cathcart wanted him to, and so would I but for far less sophisticated reasons. The Italian knew it made no difference. Worried as I was about myself I would never have seen the truth about Cathcart. Fear stopped me from seeing the most obvious madness, let alone distinguishing right from wrong.

I didn't question it when some idiot in Air Force Headquarters hatched the idea that when the entire airforce was bombing the primary target, we could divert the German's attention by sending a lone bomber to another target on what was called a "nuisance raid." We never asked how one plane could divert the attention of a nation from 1500 hundred planes, especially when those 1500 planes were several hundred miles from the one plane. And no one asked just what in the hell "German's attention" really meant anyway. As if a nation has the organic senses of a man. We were giving Austria our famous eye fake.

When these "nuisance raids" started, no one in our squadron was getting any medals or citations, except, of course, for the automatic ones like the Air Medal which was given after five missions with an oak leaf cluster added after each successive ten. Medals were awarded on the basis of a written report submitted by the squadron intelligence officer. What you actually did had little effect. But what the report said you did, and how it said it made all the difference.

Our squadron intelligence officer was a man named Barudi or Buradi, something like that, a nice, mild, honest man as I remember. I think he had been a physicist teaching at Kentucky or Virginia. Whatever his talents, he couldn't write and no one was getting medals. You could have hung by your heels from the bomb bay and shot down ME 109's with bow and arrow and the report issued from the squadron would have made it sound drab routine.

Barudi (I'll call him) took a month's leave around the time the nuisance raids were starting and his replacement was a big, fat, cigar chomping American blowhard. What nation could have provided him so readily? He was everything Europeans lampoon in the American. He talked in a loud coarse voice and was unaffected by anything, dismayed by nothing. And he could write. He could pour bullshit onto paper as easily as he could pour it into the air.

And in the entire Air Force, against odds of around 1500 to one, we, Lt. Howard (NMI) Steinberg and crew, were selected to run a nuisance raid on Innsbruck while the rest of the Air Force was bombing Vienna. Not going to Vienna where the Germans had over 300 flak guns was fine. On the other hand, even with Anthony Cartwright, our English immigrant tail gunner who had eight Zeros in the South Pacific and three ME 109's with us to his credit, going it alone over Austria wasn't inviting. In those days a bomber alone was virtually a sure target for a fighter.

Two navigators were on the flight deck behind the pilots. One, who I think was named Moody, operated a radar set that could scan the earth through the cloud cover below. The other operated what we called a G Box, a radar set that gave navigational fixes from impulses sent from fixed tower positions in allied-held territory. Our crew navigator, Ryan O'Brien, was in the nose turret just forward and above me doing pilotage navigation, taking fixes whenever the clouds parted and he could see recognizable check points.

Once I had pulled the cotter pins from the bomb fuses, usually when we were climbing from 9000 to 11,000 feet, allowing the bombs to arm as they fell, I had nothing to do until we reached the target. The trip north was usual. Uneventful. The long ponderous climbing, the boring roar of the engines, the way the earth below gradually lost all vertical contour and flattened out as it wavered and fell back. Sometimes I pretended to sleep, tried to sleep, and often to show others how courageous I was I told them I slept.

I'll have to explain, I hope clearly and briefly, what happened on a radar mission. The radar navigator could see the town reproduced on the radar scope, though the bombardier could see only the clouds below. The town would appear about the size of a quarter, depending of course on the size of the town, and while we were avowed to be concentrating on a particular strategic target, say the railroad marshalling yards at the south edge of the city, in reality we weren't fooling anybody. The chances of hitting even the town were only fair.

I would operate the bombsight just as if I could see the target, only the radar operator would act as my eyes by reading the information from the radar scope to me over the intercom. I would kill course, that is fly the plane directly toward the target without drifting off course, by cranking corrections into the course knobs on the sight in response to the radar navigator's orders, "Left, Bombardier. Right, Bombardier." And I would kill rate, that is adjust the bomb sight so that the rate of a motor driven index toward a stationary index was corresponding to the rate of approach of the plane to the target. I did this by adjusting position of the stationary index on the bombsight in response to the radar navigator's announcements of approach angles to the target, "Sixty-five degrees. Sixty-degrees." When he said "fifty-five," the movable index should be moving exactly past fifty-five on the bomb sight. The indices were also electrical contacts, and when they met they sent an electrical impulse to the bomb racks and the bombs dropped.

Everything was set. I had the bomb bay doors open. My panel lights were on. The voice of the navigator was clear. I adjusted the stationary index, which really adjusted the rate of the moving index until the moving index was crawling up the dial on the sight at exactly the announced rate of approach.

The first thing that went wrong was my throat mike went out. This happened about two minutes before bombs away, so although I could hear the radar navigator I couldn't answer him. When the movable index touched the stationary index, the panel lights indicating the bombs in the racks failed to go out, meaning the bombs hadn't fallen. I hit the salvo handle and still the lights burned. I hit it again. Nothing. Meanwhile, the radar navigator was saying over and over in my ear, "Bombardier, drop the bombs. Bombardier, drop the bombs."

There we were, flying through clouds 25,000 feet over Innsbruck with a load of bombs, I couldn't drop the bombs and I couldn't tell anybody I couldn't drop the bombs. Getting rid of the bombs was the important part of the mission to flyers because, not only did it remove a terrible danger, it meant you had another mission to your credit and were that closer to going home, and it made the plane lighter, faster. When the bombs fell out you could feel the plane jump like a horse, suddenly freed of all that weight. And you would peel off, if you were in a flak area, and take advantage of that speed as you went down and out, away from the black bursts that were threatening your life, the plane screaming from speed, the wings vibrating from the strain.

This day there was no flak. Still the urgency of getting the bombs out was there, and by now it seemed like everyone in the plane was yelling at me to drop the bombs. I was so frustrated I beat my gloved fists against the plexiglass bubbled windows in the nose. I attacked the salvo handle like a savage. I swore, prayed, swore, begged and swore to no one in particular. The racks were frozen and the bombs were stuck, and I couldn't tell anyone.

I stood up with my head in the astro dome, one foot on either ammo can that held the ammo for the nose turret guns, and I looked back through the dome and the pilot's windshield at Steinberg. I suppose a case can be made for man's ability to speak with his eyes, though I suspect the whole facial expression is involved in wordless communication. If eyes alone can talk, they can probably say, "I love you" or "You turn me on, let's shack up" or "You're boring me" or "I hate your guts." But try with eyes alone to say, "The bomb racks are frozen and my throat mike has malfunctioned." Steinberg and I stared helplessly at each other over the tops of our oxygen masks through two layers of glass.

I hooked onto a walk-around oxygen bottle, took my parachute and started back through the narrow passageway to the flight deck. Unattached from the electrical heating system, I immediately felt the terrible cold, around −70°. When I finally reached the pilots, I tore off my mask and yelled explanations at Steinberg over the engine scream.

Steinberg yelled back that the only thing we could do was toggle the bombs out one by one by prying a screwdriver against the release arm of each bomb shackle. We had tried the pilot's emergency bomb release cord and that was frozen too.

I took the screwdriver, had the engineer close the bomb bay doors, and walked out the catwalk to the bomb racks. Then I wedged myself between the racks, rapped a mugger's grip around the left rack with my left arm, and signalled the engineer to open the doors. As the doors rolled open, the blast of air into the bomb bay shocked my eyes. I'd had to leave my parachute behind because the space between the racks was too narrow, and I was standing in that roaring rush of air, one arm tight around the shackle, on about ten inches width of catwalk, five miles above the earth.

That sounds brave, I suppose. Oddly, I felt no fear of the height or the situation, and I think for several reasons. One was simply that I was young and had no real sense of what I was doing. Another is that, while I'm quite frightened of heights, I had no sense of height because five miles without reference ceases to be distance and becomes a vague void. Then static distance, looking down the side of a skyscraper (I'm always intimidated when I'm in New York) is far different than being propelled by engines. In a sense, the engines keep you from falling because they are holding you up.

Just as I reached for the first bomb shackle with the screwdriver, the bombs fell out.

All this time we had been circling aimlessly through clouds, but I suppose more or less in the Innsbruck area. Our navigator, O'Brien, had come back from the nose turret and, with much more strength than anyone else in the plane, had finally pulled the pilot's bomb release cord free.

I watched the bombs going down, converging as they seemed to into one mass. Just then the clouds parted and I watched that hunk of component explosives falling farther and farther away toward a bleak, blue black uninhabited region of the Alps. Before the bombs landed, the clouds snapped shut. We had no idea of exactly where we were. There's a possibility we were over Switzerland, which is less then fifty miles away from Innsbruck, a meagre distance when you are at high altitude, flying. I'm sure of one thing. We had contributed nothing to the war effort. Those bombs fell where there were no towns, no farms, no roads.

When we returned to the base, the big blowhard was waiting to interrogate us, as the squadron intelligence officer did after each mission. We told him everything in detail. He listened. Chewed his cigar and when we were through, said in his coarse booming voice, "I'll see to it you boys get the DFC for this." Someone, I wish it had been me said, "For what? The mission was all fucked up." "Never you mind," the loud fat man said.

A month later, Barudi was back but the blowhard had done his work. A line of flyers at least two city blocks long stood in a field and received medals from a general flown in for the occasion. I hate to risk a detail sounding this apocryphal, but the general actually took the medals he pinned to our chests from a cigar box held by a colonel. And so the officers (enlisted men were given few citations) of Lt. Howard (NMI) Steinberg's crew were given the DFC for bombing some remote mountains, maybe in Switzerland.

Yossarian couldn't help but fall in love with the chaplain at first sight because in the chaplain he recognized himself, a sane man caught up in a world controlled by ugly creeps. The chaplain, like Yossarian, is bewildered and ineffectual. A good man can offer the world the gift of his good impulses and in war they are ignored or rejected.

And I hope Heller would have treated that big blowhard with generosity and love too. Wherever I've gone in institutions, I've met a few men like the blowhard. In industry. In universities. In the military. They are easy to make fun of but not so easily dismissed. They seemed to know, to have always known, that most organized human endeavor, waging war or building cities or citing men for bravery, is essentially bullshit. Many of them don't know they know this, but they know it all the same. Sociology isn't my strong point, but I hope many of them learned it watching Marx Brothers movies.

And like the blowhard, their answer to bullshit is more bullshit. And they get things done not because they believe in them but because they don't. Laws. Rules. These are created to occupy people. The healthy cynics cut through it all, booming and laughing and chomping cigars the whole way.

And I don't think I'd like people whose code of ethics is so rigid they'd be critical of the lies in that written report on the Innsbruck nuisance raid, lies that rang like nature's deepest truth "—despite intensive damage to their aircraft by enemy flak and fighters . . . ," ". . . persevered through a series of frustrating malfunctions to lay their bombs squarely on the target." Not when a few months later those medals and citations meant discharge points, meant a lot of us were finally getting out and going home.

Ci Vediamo

I'LL TELL you some stories. I won't press the point, but I hope these stories demonstrate some of the problems involved in writing. Problems of how memory and the imagination modify and transform experience, problems of stances you might have to take or drop to order language into a poem. Some of that heavy stuff.

In World War II I was a bombardier based in Italy. I was on the American side, but let me assure you the history books are right. We won. If you had seen me bomb, you might have doubts.

I was the world's worst. One day I missed not only the target in the Brenner Pass, but the entire Brenner Pass itself, thirteen miles wide at that point. My fear made hard concentration difficult and I didn't trust the equipment. I would glance over the bomb sight as we approached the target, having made the siting and adjustments, and think: that doesn't look right. The sight must be crazy.

In 1963 I went back. It was not easy. I was almost forty. My wife and I quit good jobs in Seattle and went to Italy to live for a year on savings. Once our savings were gone we would be broke and jobless. That worried me. I'd never had much confidence in my ability to find a job. If it hadn't been for my wife's courageous resolve, I could not have made the break. I tried for a grant—a Guggenheim, I think—but no luck.

Some friends urged us to go. Some people I worked with at the aircraft factory found it hard to understand what I was doing. One colleague asked me seriously why I was going to a land with all that violence. What violence? Imagine living in the United States and thinking Italy violent.

I really didn't know why I was going. When people asked, the only answer I could find was: I just want to see it again.

I came to one Italy in 1944 and another in 1963. The 1963 Italy was filled with sparkling fountains, shiny little cars that honked and darted through well-kept streets, energetic young men and beautiful well-dressed young women, huge neon signs that said CIT and CAMPARI and CINZANO in bright blue or red or green.

The 1944 Italy I remembered brown and gray and lifeless. Every city, every small town reeked. No young men in the towns and no cattle in the fields. The war had taken the men and the Germans had taken the cattle. That was the Italy I expected to find when I came back. I hate to admit it, but that was the Italy I wanted to find. I fell in love with a sad land, and I wanted it sad one more time.

I must confess to a perverse side of self. I give and give to beggars, but there is in me something that feeds on the now of things. Of course I want it all better, want poverty gone forever from the world. But I also have the urge to say, "stay destitute three more days, just until I finish my poem." I'm ashamed of that in me.

There were good reasons for loving the sad early Italy. The best reason being Italy was earth. The sky became more and more frightening as I neared my thirty-fifth bombing mission. If I made thirty-five I would go home. In the air I could disappear forever in one flash, fall to my death when my chute failed to open, or fall in my open chute to a German mob that would beat me to death as they had others. In the sky there seemed as many quick ways to die as there were thermols and flak bursts jolting the plane. I could age on earth, die slowly enough to make some final, corny speech—I'm a going, partner—the way they did in the old movies. On earth, you can say goodbye.

My first memory of Italy is a stone wall, about three feet high, grape vines and a soft evening sky, a blue I'd not seen before. The wall and vines were close to the tent where our bomber crew spent one night on the outskirts of a town called Goia. I never saw Goia again. The next day we flew to the base where we would live for the next eight months. It took us eight months to fly thirty-five missions because the winter turned bad in 1944, and we lost a month of good flying weather in the fall when our squadron was assigned to fly gasoline to a British Spitfire base in Lyon.

The closest town of any size was Cerignola, eleven miles away. I still can't say it very well. I find it hard to make the "gn" sound in Italian. This was the province Puglia (Apulia), on the Adriatic side, perhaps forty miles inland below the spur.

I found out later that Cerignola had a bad reputation in Italy. Some Italians considered it an unfriendly if not dangerous town. American G.I.s were to be off the streets by five in the afternoon. There were rumors of stabbings and robberies. I doubt they were true. If anything, we were the hostile ones, bitter at finding ourselves stuck in that lonely, austere land, caught up in a war we had nothing to do with starting. Since we never saw the enemy as we passed five miles above him on the bomb run, we imagined the Italians were enemies. Of course, until late in 1943 they had been, though often not very willing ones. If you are frightened and resentful, it's easier if you have a defined enemy. On bad days, the Italians were our enemies.

The closest large city was Foggia, about thirty miles west. To get there, you had to go through Cerignola. I used to hitchhike to Foggia, and sit in the Red Cross alone, drinking coffee, eating cookies and listening to records. I played two over and over on the little player, Benny Goodman's "Don't Be That Way," and Tommy Dorsey's "Song of India." I often hitchhiked those thirty miles just to hear Lawrence Brown's trombone passage on the Goodman, or Bunny Berrigan's trumpet solo on the Dorsey. After hearing the records many times, I would hitchhike back to the base across the drab, flat countryside.

The British had bases in the area and I was fascinated by the British. One day in Foggia, I found a little hotel bar. The only other people there were the bartender and three English G.I.s "I say," one of them said in an accent I found delicious, "will you ever forget your feelings when it was announced that Hitler had attacked Russia?" "Oh, I say. Wasn't that the grossest miscalculation," another answered. "Yes," the third said, "if it hadn't been for that, we would have been for it."

I've never forgotten that exchange. They seemed worldly to me, their view wide and deep.

Hitchhiking back from Foggia one day, I was given a ride in a British command car. I saw the colonel in the back seat lean forward and tell the driver to stop. The colonel was so poised, polite and charming, I asked him if he were a member of the aristocracy and he said he was. He was an Earl. He asked me many questions about our missions and I told him everything he wanted to know. I didn't care that it was classified information. Enough close flak bursts had convinced me the Germans knew our altitude. Besides, I am loose-tongued by nature. Had I been captured, long before the Gestapo brought those blow torches and pliers to my cell, I would have been known as Blabbermouth Hugo.

The Colonel reminded me very much of the actor, Herbert Marshall. I envied his composure, his gentility and easy good manners. Although in no way did he register amazement or disapproval, I imagined he found it strange that a nervous, overtalkative, boorish boy could be an American officer. I had the impression he found me interesting but decided that was simply his aristocratic training—always let the serfs know you have a keen interest in their lives. I hoped that some day I'd perfect my own composure and detachment. I wanted very much to be like the Earl, or Herbert Marshall.

Bob Mills, a pleasant, civilized young man, had attended Stanford University for a year or two. A bombardier, he had grown a long, handsome black mustache and his warm, fluid personality got him elected president of the squadron officers' club. He was given 500 dollars in lire and the task of buying more liquor for the club. He was also assigned a jeep and he asked me to go along with him to Barletta on the Adriatic coast where the liquor was produced and sold.

Among other dangers our imaginations had created was the danger of bandits and we took our .45 automatics. I had my gun (piece, if you're still G.I.) stuffed in my right trench-coat pocket and I felt a bit like Humphrey Bogart sitting there in the jeep as the olive trees and grass and magpies passed by.

Mills drove, the huge wad of lire tucked away on him some-where. It was a good way to break the boredom, bouncing through the Italian countryside.

Though, like most G.I.s, I couldn't hit a cow with a .45 if I was holding her teat, the bulge and weight of the gun in my pocket gave me a sense of security. It is one thing to kneel, helpless, in the nose of a bomber jolted by bursts of flak fired five miles away by men whose names you will never know and whose faces you will never see. You trust to luck. You are not about to master your fate.

But this was the earth and the gun was real. The bandits who came pouring out of those hills would be real and I would shoot them. I and Bob Mills and Humphrey Bogart in our trenchcoats. We would blast them with our .45s and they couldn't help but see our faces set in resolve, our glittering eyes.

We rolled into Barletta in about two hours, maybe less. The children picked us up and ran after us filling the day with sisters for sale and pleas for cigarettes and candy. There must have been thirty already by the time we stopped at the distillery (perhaps not the right word) and more were run-ning toward us. And great good soldier that I was, when I stepped out of the jeep my gun fell from my pocket and crashed to the stone street. I bent down to pick it up and when I raised up the street was empty. Not a sound. Not a child anywhere. I stood in the eerie emptiness of that silent street and did not then comprehend what fear the war had put in those chil-dren. I wondered why they weren't fascinated by the gun as, I was sure, American children would have been.

You'll notice that the men I wanted to be are strong men, men in control. Humphrey Bogart. Herbert Marshall. Each in his own way, tough. My urge to be someone adequate didn't change after the war. When I gave up fiction as a bad job and settled back into poems for good, I seemed to use the poems to create some adequate self. A sissy in life, I would be tough in the poem. An example:

Index

The sun is caked on vertical tan stone
where eagles blink and sweat above

the night begun already in the town.
The river's startling forks, the gong
that drives the evening through the pass
remind the saint who rings the local chime
he will be olive sometime like a slave.

Screams implied by eyes of winded eagles
and wind are searing future in the stone.
The cliff peels off in years of preaching water
and the cliff remains. The saint is red
to know how many teeth are in the foam,
the latent fame of either river bed
where trout are betting that the saint is brown.

Flakes of eagle eggshells bomb the chapel
and the village ears of sanctuary dumb.
In a steaming room, behind a stack
of sandbagged books, the saint retreats
where idols catch a fever from his frown.
The saint is counting clicks of eagle love.
The river jumps to nail a meaty wren.

And April girls enlarge through layers
of snow water, twitching fish and weeds
and memories of afternoons with gills.
If a real saint says that he could never
see a fiend, tell that saint to be here,
throat in hand, any Friday noon—
delirious eagles breed to tease the river.

Making Certain It Goes On, p. 73.

I don't even understand that one any more. Once I did,
though, or I wouldn't have published it. (I have a smattering
of integrity, thank you.) Note how definite the voice is. How
strong the command to the self tries to be. How the poem
urges the man in it to accept reality in all its cruelty and dif-
fuseness. And I even took a private pride in the difficulty of
the poem. I wasn't afraid of anything. No sir. You don't
understand my poems? Screw off, Jack. But in real life, be my
friend. Like me. Like me.

I went to Cerignola far more often than to Foggia. It was smaller but closer. All restaurants were off limits in Italy during the war and there were few places to go in Cerignola. The Red Cross, of course, but they didn't have swing records. When I went to Cerignola, I usually got drunk in a little makeshift bar. The girl who waited tables was short, stocky and stacked. The love starved G.I.'s watched her as she brought the *spumante* to the tables. They taught her to whip her hand along her hip as if she were a cowboy making a fast draw. Every time she did it, pointed her finger at us and depressed her thumb hammer, the soldiers howled.

The bar had a band, trumpet, accordion and drums. The trumpeter's best number was "Stardust" and he played it often while the G.I.s rolled their eyes and exclaimed. I sat alone and drank *spumante,* listened to the music, watched the girl's ripe behind bulge her dress and wondered what the raucous enlisted men would think if they knew how self-conscious I was. Not because I was the only officer there, but because I was too timid to approach a woman and feared a lifetime of sexual deprivation. I laughed when I knew it was expected and made a point now and then of the attraction I felt for the girl. I could not have had her even if she had consented, but I wanted her and I could let the world know that.

My first time in the Cerignola area had been from August, 1944 through March, 1945. It was April when I saw it again, April 1964. The countryside was green with grain and the weather pleasantly warm. Cerignola seemed bigger. A nice looking hotel operated next to the building that had been the local Red Cross. A door or two from the hotel was where the bar had been, with the finger-pistol packing *mama mia* waitress. I wasn't sure now which door it was. Shops were open for business. People of all ages were in the streets. No children begged us for cigarettes or candy, or offered their sisters for sale. The streets seemed unusually wide, and I noticed iron grillwork on balconies of recent apartment buildings.

Foreigners seldom visit Cerignola and we were curiosities. I got into a discussion with some young men and suddenly realized we were circled by at least a hundred onlookers. "Who,"

I shouted involuntarily in English, "are all these people?" and they moved off slowly as if they understood from the volume of my voice that I didn't want my every word a public matter. A comic looking old man stared and stared at my wife, his lower lip quivering as if he were about to break into tears of resentment. In a tobacco shop, a man went into rapture when he found I could speak Italian, wretched as my Italian is, all three hundred words of it. Everywhere we walked, people trailed us. The owner of a delicatessen said he remembered me. I was the soldier who got into a fight with another soldier over a dog. No, I wasn't.

I wanted to find two places. One was the squadron area where we had lived for eight months, and the group head-quarters nearby. The other was a field somewhere south of a town called Spinazzola. What kind of a field? Just a field, with tall grass, slanted uphill from the road. An empty field.

To go anywhere on our own in Italy during the war, we hitchhiked. What a discouraging time, standing beside a dirt road as truck after truck went by, empty, the drivers staring past us down the road. Some drivers laughed as they passed. They were bitter, resentful at finding themselves in this drab land with little to break the boredom but some awful Italian booze. They expressed their frustration by refusing us rides. Some even slowed down and we would run to the truck only to have it pull away from us. That was the driver's idea of fun. And we turned bitter at them and made obscene gestures when we were sure they weren't giving us a ride. We stood with our thumbs out and the trucks went by for hours. After a while, even the road seemed bitter. We swore at the drivers under skies I remember the color of winter. I've never been able to tolerate those British war novels that see war as an adhesive force binding us all together in our common cause.

Once I hitchhiked a long way to see a friend. We had been in training together for over a year in the States. I was well along with my missions and feeling the strain. Each flight seemed tougher as my imagination worked overtime on the danger during the long periods of bad weather when we were grounded. I don't know how many rides it took to get to my friend's base, but when I finally arrived we chatted about old friends in training, who had been killed, who got to stay in the States. I'd made arrangements to be away from the base for a night, and stayed over. The next morning I started home. I picked up a ride early in an ammo truck. It was hooded, something like a covered wagon. I yelled "Cerignola" at the driver, he yelled what I heard as "Cerignola" back, and I piled in. The opening in the back was small, and I only glimpsed the landscape as we bounced along the miles. When I got out, I was in a town I'd never seen, miles off-course. Some American fliers were walking about, and I saw one I'd known slightly in training. He told me I was in Spinazzola. Where was Cerignola? He didn't know. Lord, I was lost in the Italian countryside. What if I didn't get back? Would I be court-martialed? I bought a carton of cigarettes in a small PX and started out of town.

Spinazzola is a hill town, and I walked out of it down a long dirt road lined with shade trees. The road ran out before me through hills of grass, and I walked a long time. What if I was scheduled to fly tomorrow and wasn't there? I thumbed the army vehicles that came by and none stopped. I considered lying down in the road to stop someone, but that was no thought to have in those days. Someone might just run over me and keep going. "You should have seen me flatten that fly boy lootenant."

After I'd walked for well over an hour, I sat down to rest by a field of grass. I was tired, dreamy, the way we get without enough sleep, and I watched the wind move in waves of light across the grass. The field slanted and the wind moved uphill across it, wave after wave. The music and motion hypnotized me. The longer the grasses moved, the more passive I became. Had I walked this road when I was a child? Something seemed familiar. I didn't care about getting back to the base now. I didn't care about the war. I was not a part of it anymore. Trucks went by and I didn't even turn to watch them, let alone thumb a ride. Let them go. I would sit here forever and watch the grass bend in the wind and the war would end without me and I would not go home, ever. Years later in psychoanalysis I would recount this, and the doctor would explain it as a moment of surrender, when my system could no longer take the fear and the pressure and I gave up. If that's how to lose a war, we were wrong to have ever won one. Years after the war, I would try to do that day justice in a poem and would fail miserably. I wouldn't even spell Spinazzola right, and my editor wouldn't catch it.

Centuries Near Spinnazola

This is where the day went slack.
It could have been digestion or the line
of elms, the wind relaxed and flowing
and the sea gone out of sight.
This is where the day and I surrendered
as if the air
were suddenly my paramour.

It is far from any home. A white
farm tiny from a dead ten miles
of prairie, gleamed. I stood on grass
and saw the bombers cluster,
and drone the feeble purpose of a giant.

Men rehearsed terror at Sardis
And Xerxes beat the sea.

And prior to the first domestic dog,
a king of marble, copper gods,
I must have stood like that and heard
the cars roar down the road,
the ammo wagon and the truck,
must have turned my back on them
to see the stroke of grass on grass
on grass across the miles of roll,
the travel of my fever now, my urge
to hurt or love released and flowing.

A public yes to war. A Greek will die
and clog the pass to wreck our strategy.
There will be a time for towns to burn
and one more sea to flog into a pond.

Making Certain It Goes On, p. 29.

I got a ride shortly after I left the field of waving grass and in a short time was on foot on the outskirts of Canosa. I knew where I was now. Canosa was off-limits, so I couldn't pass through. I had to skirt the town, across barren farm land and, halfway across the field no one had planted for years, I met a woman, perhaps thirty, and her daughter, maybe eight. The woman was dark and beautiful, her face strong, handsome, and brown, her eyes and hair the same heavy black. She wanted me to sell her a pack of cigarettes from the carton I'd bought in Spinazzola and I refused. I still don't know why I didn't give her the carton. What the hell, I could get more. That day haunted me, came back unexpected when I sat in a class, or later when I was at work in the aircraft company, or when I fished or drank in a tavern, came back welcome to remind me how harmonious and peaceful we can feel, came back unwelcome to remind me how we learn little from our positive experiences, how we slip back too easily into this ungenerous world of denial and possession. I've made far worse mistakes than refusing that woman cigarettes, but no mistake came back so often. After being bitten by a dog or stoned by Italian boys, my lack of generosity could have been understandable. But after the field of grass?. . . .

Do you understand? I'm not sure I do. I had to find the field again. I had to find Spinazzola and retrace that day. If you need a reason, say I am a silly man.

We talked money in the streets of Cerignola, and in a matter of minutes we had a car, a driver, two assistant drivers, all young men, and we were shooting off at far too fast a speed toward Canosa. I wondered if it would be there, Spinazzola, the road leading out, the field of grass. At least some of it was true: there, to our right as we neared Canosa was the field where I'd made the mistake. Was that woman still lovely? Probably not. Probably fat and lined. Italians let themselves get old as if time were a natural thing. In Canosa, an old man in a horse-drawn wagon blocked the road. Our young driver and his assistants screamed *"cornut"* as he mumbled bitterly at them and his balky horse.

A few miles later, Spinazzola came to us, riding high on a hilltop and glowing white and gray like a tourist come-on brochure. I always have the same feeling when I see those hill towns: I'll go there and never leave. Yet, from this vantage I couldn't remember it. Did I have the name wrong? Maybe there were two Spinazzolas. But in the town, I recognized it immediately.

My wife and I walked about Spinazzola. Down at the end of the town we found the old dirt road lined with windbreak trees leading downhill away into the uninhabited countryside below. And there, near where the road led out of town, was an old *cantina*. Inside, marvelous, old crude wood tables and benches, warm dim comforting light, a friendly old man who offered us *fagiuoli*. But we wanted only wine. Wine, and the feeling one gets in a *cantina*, like you want every friend you ever had to be there with you.

I hope the *cantine* never die in Italy, but I'm sure they are being replaced by the plastic bars with the ugly expensive chrome coffee machines, the ridiculous pastries that look unique and all taste alike, and the awful excuses for liquor that look like various colored skin astringents sitting in bottles some decadent child designed. We sat there and drank wine, and the *cantina* became very much like that field of grass I still had to find.

I found it. It was a lot further than I'd remembered and I was surprised I'd walked so far that day nearly twenty years before. It must have been five miles out of town. I saw it just for a moment as we sped by in the car and I didn't ask the driver to stop. I didn't even mention it to my wife at the time, and that was unusual because we were fond of sharing our intimate affections for places. Back in Cerignola, I told her I'd seen it. It was still there and long ago something, important only to me, had really happened. Whatever it was, I didn't accept completely the psychoanalyst's explanation of it. It obviously had much truth to it, but it was maybe too pat. Whatever, by now I was old enough to know explanations are usually wrong. We never quite understand and we can't quite explain.

Spinazzola: Quella Cantina La

A field of wind gave license for defeat.
I can't explain. The grass bent. The wind

seemed full of men but without hate or fame.
I was farther than that farm where the road
slants off to nowhere, and the field I'm sure
is in this wine or that man's voice. The man
and this canteen were also here
twenty years ago and just as old.

Hate for me was dirt until I woke up
five miles over Villach in a smoke
that shook my tongue. Here, by accident,
the wrong truck, I came back to the world.
This canteen is home-old. A man can walk
the road outside without a song or gun.
I can't explain the wind. The field is east
toward the Adriatic from my wine.

I'd walked from cruel soil to a trout
for love but never from a bad sky
to a field of wind I can't explain.
The drone of bombers going home
made the weather warm. My uniform
turned foreign where the olive trees
throw silver to each other down the hill.

Olive leaves were silver I could spend.
Say wind I can't explain. That field is vital
and the Adriatic warm. Don't our real friends
tell us when we fail? Don't honest fields
reveal us in their winds? Planes and men
once tumbled but the war went on absurd.
I can't explain the wine. This crude bench
and rough table and that flaking plaster—
most of all the long nights make this home.

Home's always been a long way from a friend.
I mix up things, the town, the wind, the war.
I can't explain the drone. Bombers seemed
to scream toward the target, on the let-down
hum. My memory is weak from bombs.

Say I dropped them bad with shaking sight.
Call me German and my enemy the air.

Clouds are definite types. High ones, cirrus.
Cumulus, big fluffy kind, and if the rain,
also nimbus. Don't fly into them.
I can't explain. Somewhere in a gray ball
wind is killing. I forgot the stratus
high and thin. I forget my field
of wind, out there east between
the Adriatic and my second glass of wine.

I'll find the field. I'll go feeble down
the road strung gray like spoiled wine
in the sky. A sky too clear of cloud
is fatal. Trust the nimbus. Trust dark clouds
to rain. I can't explain the sun. The man
will serve me wine until a bomber fleet
lost twenty years comes droning home.
I can't explain. Outside, on the road
that leaves the town reluctantly,
way out the road's a field of wind.

Making Certain It Goes On, p. 124.

One down and one to go. Now we would find the air base.
Then, my past safely reclaimed, we would become tourists
again and move on to Lecce and the baroque churches.

I'd already seen Vincenzo Lattaruolo in the streets of Cerignola the day before. It was a hard face to miss, homely, rough,
humane. With his big broken nose and his coarse features, he
would be a natural as a character actor in films. We needed a
driver to help us find the airfield, and he offered his services.

When he had been a young boy, maybe ten or eleven, Vincenzo had worked at one of the American air bases. I asked
about Pete, also a native of Cerignola, who had worked at
ours. Vincenzo said Pete had gone north to Milan to work in
the factories. Vincenzo picked up a friend, who turned out to
be the driver, and we went out to find the site of the 825th
Squadron, 484th Bomb Group.

It wasn't easy. For two days we ran about the grain covered countryside and we found the site of many squadrons
but not the 825th. It didn't help when I mentioned it had
been located the same place as the group headquarters, and
by the third day I was getting discouraged. There had been
many squadrons in that region called Tretitoli. Then I
remembered the three whores in the pumphouse.

Three whores had set up shop in a pumphouse about a
quarter of a mile from a squadron and had operated there
for weeks. When the command discovered them, clued by the
sudden breakout of VD in the men, it took photos before
throwing them out, and pasted the pictures in placards which
were posted on the squadron bulletin board. The caption read
"The Pumphouse Trio" in big printed letters. Then under
the photo of the three wretched-looking creatures, a sarcastic
diatribe congratulated the American G.I. on his taste in women.
The poor prostitutes looked so scroungy, I imagined one might
contact VD just looking at the photo.

Italians seem to remember subjects of gossip no matter
how old, and Vincenzo picked up as I told him and the driver
about the whores. The word for pumphouse was beyond me,
but *torre d'acqua* was good enough.

Soon we were approaching the site. The farm buildings
we had used for group headquarters and the squadron mess
hall were still intact. My wife knew we had found it, and she
murmured, "Oh, dear," and started to cry softly. I never
understood how she knew. I'd never described it to her, nor
had I given any sign of recognition.

There they were. The squadron mess hall on the corner.
The courtyard that had been our outdoor theater where Joe
Louis, the only celebrity to visit us, walked through the crowd
of G.I.s yelling, "Hey, Joe. Want to fight?," and stood on the
stage, his huge hands reaching nearly to his knees because his
powerful shoulders were so slanted. The group intelligence
building. The group commander's upstairs quarters, and below
it the briefing room where we would sit very early in the
morning and stare at the red ribbon on the map leading to
the target. Silence when the ribbon led to Vienna and back,
(would we get back?), or to Munich, or Linz. Joking if it was a

"milk run." More often than not we heard our fearful silence as we stared at the map and listened to the briefing.

The other buildings were gone, the squadron headquarters, the squadron intelligence building, the sheet metal quonset hut movie house and theater. Remember the marvelous Italian magician? The Italian Jazz band that played famous American numbers and had the solos memorized note for note? Even the drum solo was Krupa, no variation from the original. The movie *Bombardier*, when Pat O'Brien said, "General, you'll see the day when the pilot is only a taxi driver paid to carry the bombardier over the target," and the riot that threatened to start when the pilots in the audience, who worked themselves to exhaustion flying formation for eight and nine hours each mission, began to scream while the bombardiers cheered? What was the name of that even worse movie where Noah Beery, Jr., home with wounds and recuperating on the sands of Santa Monica with Martha O'Driscoll, said with solemnity and resolve, "I can't wait to get another crack at them," and we yelled "Shit," and "Fuck you," and "Oh, my naked ass!" And wasn't that a good build? Martha O'Driscoll's? We whistled and stomped when she came on the screen in her bathing suit.

Beautiful fields of grain now and recently constructed farmhouses nearby, a part of the *Mezzogiorno* program. I showed my wife where our tent had been, and I remembered a subnormal farm boy who brought eggs to sell. We teased him a lot. One of us would say, "New York." And he would say, "New York fineesh." He thought American cities had been levelled by bombing, and we found his ignorance funny.

Maybe because the day was bright, the grain a warm green in the wind, and the ground hard, I remembered Captain Simmons, the squadron supply officer who didn't provide us with enough blankets, and the cold, wet winter of 1944–45 when we shuddered at night trying to escape into sleep from the cold. I wrote Grandmother and asked for a sleeping bag and she sent one. In 1964 I still had it, somewhere among our belongings back home. Simmons didn't seem to do much but make excuses and bullshit a lot and hate Italians.

A young G.I., maybe nineteen (I was twenty), knocked up

a farm girl who lived near the base. Her father demanded the boy marry her and the boy wanted to, but Simmons intervened. "I'm not going to stand by and see that nice kid throw his life away on a goddamn eye-tie." Simmons and some others had gone to the farm to "reason" with the father. I don't know how they communicated with no common language, but Simmons bragged about knocking "the old bastard" around when he insisted on the wedding. "All that son-of-a-bitch wants is to marry his daughter off to an American so they can get in on some of our money," Simmons explained with no self doubt. A long time later, I knew enough about the southern Italian peasant and the power of religion in that life to realize what a sad business it had been. On bad days, Italians were our enemies.

And it was here where the grain now grew that Squadron Commander Joel O. Moe of North Dakota knocked on each tent door one afternoon and drunkenly announced that he would demonstrate the correct way to slide into third base. No grain then. Only unrelieved mud. And in his fresh uniform, while we stood in front of our tents, Major Joel O. Moe came running down the sloppy road between the two tent rows and hit the mud in what must remain baseball's longest and filthiest slide, and we applauded and called him safe.

The mess hall was now a school operated by two nuns who had been little girls in Cerignola during the war. Had they begged me once for candy and cigarettes? They gave us *strega* and cookies and we spent a warm hour there. Later I would try to do the experience justice.

Tretitoli, Where the Bomb Group Was

Windy hunks of light, not prop wash, bend
the green grain no one tried to grow
twenty years ago. Two nuns run a school
where flyers cursed the endless marmalade
and Spam, or choked their powdered eggs
down throats Ploesti tightened in their dreams.
Always phlegm before the engines warmed
and always the private gesture of luck—

touching a bomb, saying the name of a face
spun in without a sound at Odertol.

Hope to win a war gets thin when nuns
pour *strega* in a room where dirty songs
about the chaplain boomed. Recent land reform
gave dirt to the forlorn. That new farm
stands where I would stand in the afternoon
alone and stare across those unfarmed miles
and plan to walk them to the yellow town
away from war, disguised in shepherd black.
That pumphouse hid three whores for weeks
until disease began to show.

Now, no roar. No one sweats the sky out
late in day. No trace of squadron huts
and stone block walls supporting tents.
Those grim jokes. The missions flown
counted on the plane in cartoon bombs.
Always wide awake toward the end
when the man came saying time to fly,
awake from dreams complete with mobs,
thick clubs and slamming syllables of hun
I couldn't understand, trapped behind
cracked glass somewhere deep in Munich
I have never seen, waiting for their teeth
to snip me from the drunken songs of men.

We drive off. Children wait for class.
Grain is pale where truck pools were,
parked planes leaked oil or bombs were piled.
The runway's just a guess. I'd say, there.
Beyond the pumphouse and restricted whores
where nuns and shepherds try to soar by running,
arms stuck out for wings against the air,
and wind is lit in squadrons by the grain.

Making Certain It Goes On, p. 120.

Not good enough. I should have given it more time. The last six lines in the third stanza refer to a recurring nightmare I suffered the last weeks before we left for home. That face spun in at Odertol was a young man named Sofio from Chicago, a bombardier, eager to be friends. His pilot's name was Martin, and the crew seemed doomed from the first. They crashed once on take-off and survived. Another time, separated from the formation in a plane crippled by flak damage, they were hopped by three ME 109 fighters and would not have lived had not four P-51 fighters from the only Negro fighter squadron in the theatre of operations shown up to rescue them. Only two of the American planes bothered to attack the Germans. The other two hung back in reserve above a cloud. The blacks were hot pilots and two were enough to route the Messerschmidts. We watched it from the formation.

Because I was a warm, friendly man, (still am, I guess), I was sometimes mistaken for a homosexual. Sofio was warm and friendly, too, and years later when I remembered this, I caught myself wondering if he had been homosexual. I was too sexually naive to consider those matters when I was twenty. Whatever his sexual leanings, he was a likeable young man. He died at Odertol near the Polish border, nailed by centrifugal force to the interior of a B-24 that would never pull out of the tight spin down five miles of sky. I remember the Messerschmidts shooting into the bomber even after it was hopelessly locked in the spin. I remember my terror that day, the unbelievable number of German fighters that struck during the eight minutes we were left unprotected by our own fighters on the bomb run because those who took us up there for the long haul had to turn back to avoid running short of fuel, and my certainty we would be killed. We had crashed only a week before—miraculously the full load of gas and bombs hadn't ignited. That was our first mission following the crash and it was hardly one to rebuild our confidence. I was so frightened that day that the sight of Martin and crew spinning into oblivion remained immediate and vivid long after the fear was in the past. It is still vivid. Sofio. Why did I think of him that day in 1963 in Tretitoli? I didn't know him well.

Maybe because in a world of men he remained, like me, a boy, and I sensed that. Like me, he had not developed the cold exterior expected of men in those times.

Our losses were terrible. The wing must have lost at least thirty per cent, the highest we suffered that late in the war. And no publicity because it happened on December 17, 1944, the same day the Battle of the Bulge began.

One German fighter had come into the formation and instead of shooting and pouring through had put the nose up, like putting on the brakes, and hung in full view like a hesitant bird. Our tail gunner, Tony Cartwright, said it was like a target in a shooting gallery. He, no doubt with help from other gunners in our six-ship box, blew it apart. He speculated that the pilot was a woman given the timidity of the unexpected and fatal maneuver. We had heard rumors that German women were flying fighters that late in the war. We gave each other congratulations on the ground, loud, wild, laughing congratulations for being alive. We did not mourn those who hadn't come back. We were too happy to have made it ourselves.

I remembered the dark green man from the gunnery shed who had to be flown to Bari for hospitalization. Our co-pilot flew him there. The man was dark green because his wife had sent him a "Dear John" letter; he could do nothing about his loss but dwell on it until it was too much and he blew his stomach open with a .45 he had just repaired.

I remembered that only a day or two after we arrived we were called to a meeting of officers in Squadron Headquarters where we heard the Squadron commander deliver an incoherent speech about formation flying. He ended this chaotic diatribe by assuring us that he was a good guy and if any of us would just have a drink with him we'd realize just how good a guy he was. A week later he was sent home, a mental casualty of the war.

I remembered a co-pilot from Tennessee who came into our tent and sobbed because his crew had crashed trying to land in Vis and some were dead. He had stayed behind and claimed that if he'd been there to help the pilot, it would not have happened. And I remembered his pilot when he came back weeks later, his face so disfigured I barely recognized him.

And Charlie Marshall. Sweet, bull-shitting Charlie Marshall from Texas. He had some bad luck, a couple of crashes and other narrow escapes. The Germans shot his plane up bad one day over Vienna. By holding the stick back as far as he could he managed to stagger over Yugoslavia and bail everyone out. He came back limping and pale two weeks later, having been rescued by Tito's partisans. His leg was injured in the jump, but he was pale from the slivovitz the partisans forced on him morning to night. He also had had a frightful time talking the partisans out of shooting his co-pilot. Since the co-pilot's name was Gross and since he didn't drink, the partisans suspected he was not an American.

All flying was voluntary. You could quit whenever you wanted and all you lost was your flight pay. We didn't quit because of social pressure, fear of what others would think, and the fear of ending up in the combat ground forces, although that was a remote possibility. Charlie Marshall had had it and he quit. "Hugo," he said to me, "For every man there's a limit. There are pilots with 30,000 hours in the air. They haven't reached their limit. Maybe they never will. But for old Charlie Marshall, it's nineteen hundred and twenty-six hours." He had acquired about 1,700 hours as an instructor before he was transferred to combat.

They threatened Charlie with court martial, but he knew his rights and held firm. Finally, they offered to fly him to Naples where he could catch a boat home. "You're not flying Charlie Marshall anywhere," he assured them. How I admired his resolve. Finally, they had to drive him across Italy in a truck. We watched him wave from the truck when it pulled out. He was grinning and very much alive, and I had the feeling he would be very much alive for a long time.

Nothing would do but that we lunch at the home of the driver, Vincenzo's friend. It was a house I'd passed many times on the edge of Cerignola 20 years before. Now: screaming children silenced by screaming parents. Tripe and wine. A long afternoon. Why did you come back? I don't know. Are

you still flying? No. No. That was just the war. I'm a poet now.
No. Not famous at all. Just one book published. Another taken.
Rich? Hardly. What did I do in America? Worked in an aircraft factory. And what do you do? What we can. Drivers
sometimes. Drivers, today. No. I will not go back to the aircraft factory. When our money is gone we must go home and
find jobs. Yes. Cerignola is much better now. No beggars. No
bad odors. Lots of young men. Lots of grain in the fields. And
it is all beautiful now, all much better now. That back there,
that war. That was a terrible time. *Troppo tensione. Troppo miseria. Troppo fame.*

Vincenzo drove us back to the hotel. Could we stay longer?
No, we were taking a bus that afternoon to Bari. I was feeling
the wine as we rode through the wide streets of Cerignola.

Reputation? I came from a town with a bad reputation
too, just like the reputation Cerignola had in Puglia. What the
hell does it mean? Look at the warm, friendly time we had
had at lunch, the long afternoon of hospitality. How do nice
people get in a war? People like Sofio or Charlie Marshall?
How does anyone? Could this be the place we ridiculed and
sometimes feared and came to with hard feelings, yelling at
children who begged us for food, trying to scare them away?
Troppo miseria is right. That's what the Neopolitan cabbies say
about Naples and that's what I say about the whole damned
world. And what the hell can we do about it but hope we are
born again, next time better. I didn't know how good the poem
would be but it would be honest and I would like it because it
wouldn't be any tougher than the human heart needs to be.

April in Cerignola

This is Puglia and cruel. The sun is mean
all summer and the *tramontana*
whips the feeble four months into March.
It was far too tense. Off the streets by five.
Flyers screaming begging children off
and flyers stabbed. The only beauty
is the iron grillwork, and neither that
nor spring was here when I was young.

It used to be my town. The closest one
for bomb-bomb boys to buy *spumanti* in.
It reeked like all the towns. Italian men
were gone. The women locked themselves in dark
behind the walls, the bullet holes patched now.
Dogs could sense the madness and went mute.
The streets were mute despite the cry
of children: give me cigarette. But always flat—
the land in all directions and the time.

I was desolate, too, and so survived.
I had a secret wish, to bring much food
and feed you through the war. I wished
you also dead. All roads lead to none.
You're too far from the Adriatic
to get good wind. Harsh heat and roaring cold
are built in like abandonment each year.
And every day, these mean streets open
knowing there's no money and no fun.

So why return? You tell me I'm the only one
came back, and you're amazed
I haven't seen Milan. I came in August
and went home in March, with no chance
to experience the miles of tall grain
jittering in wind, and olive trees
alive from recent rain. You're still my town.
The men returned. The women opened doors.
The hungry lived and grew, had children
they can feed. Most of all, the streets are wide,
lead nowhere, and dying in your weather
takes a lifetime of surviving last year's war.

Making Certain It Goes On, p. 118.

At the hotel when we got out, Vincenzo did too. He said,
"Of all the Americans here during the war, you're the only
one who ever returned." He started to sob and he suddenly
embraced me and said, *"Come mio fratello."* His crying became

more violent and I turned, vaguely embarrassed, and started up the stairs, his choked sobs trailing me from the street. "Oh, hell," I thought, "I'll never be Humphrey Bogart or Herbert Marshall," and I sat down on the stairs and had a good cry too.

My wife sat understanding beside me while I blubbered, matched Vincenzo Lattaruolo sob for strangulated sob, though he was hidden from me beyond the closed door, and I never saw him again. I still wasn't sure why I'd come back, but I felt it must be the best reason in the world.

At officers' club, with a member of the bombardier crew.

Bombardier crew; Hugo is second from left, front row.

They walked away.

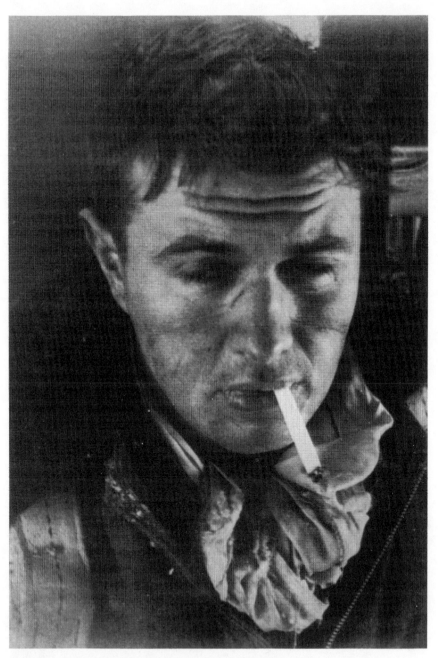

Italy: after a bombing mission.

The Milltown

Union Bar

You Could Love Here

MY LIFE was turning to shit. My marriage was breaking up. I was drinking, unable to control my outbursts of anger and my fears that I had become too difficult to live with. What's worse, I was too blurred to know my wife was about to leave me.

We had come to Montana almost directly from Italy. At the age of forty, I was about to start teaching. I knew nothing about Montana, had only been there once, nearly twenty years before had passed through on a troop train. I remember stopping somewhere, and lovely coeds from a college I could see on a hill across the valley handed each of us a basket containing fruit, candy, and magazines. It seemed idyllic that day, the fresh young girls, the innocent looking school in the distance. It seemed like some America that G.I.s imagined overseas in a World War II movie. I don't know where it was. I've never seen that place again. Or if I have, I didn't recognize it.

I was frightened. I'd never taught and didn't know if I could do it. Dean Robert Coonrod of the College of Arts and Sciences, first person I met at the University, said, "The letter from Sol Katz did it." The implication was clear. I nearly didn't get the job. Good old Sol Katz.

When you are as insecure as I was that fall of 1964, everything, including Coonrod's remark, seems important, takes on some extra dimension it shouldn't. Good things and bad things. And nearly everything happening was bad. My wife and I had grown apart in Italy. The fault was mine. I couldn't hold myself together that far from friends, that uncertain of ever finding employment again. I drank too much, sullen the last two months, walked the streets of Florence in a hopeless state of depression that bordered on psychotic withdrawal.

Bad things. Warren Carrier, my new boss, the new chairman of the English Department, said, "By the way, you're Leslie

Fiedler's replacement." Jesus, God. Leslie Fiedler's replacement! One of the most famous teachers in the nation. I hadn't read a book in years. Except for books of poems. I'd never been much of a reader and didn't feel capable of analyzing anything I'd read. I was certain I'd fail.

I made the mistake of trying to teach the survey lit course as I thought someone should teach it. Hard as I worked, I'd overlooked the dictionary as a source, and one day I got hung up on the phrase, "Fierce tiger fell." A student with pointed sarcasm and obvious disdain read the possible meanings of "fell" from the dictionary aloud in front of the class. He had no idea how very close he came to driving me out of the academic world for good. I was about to apologize to the class, to explain that I wasn't qualified, was sorry I'd wasted their time, and walk out. My teaching career came that close to lasting about three weeks.

The house we intended to rent in Missoula was still occupied and typically we found a funny rundown apartment in a place called Milltown. It was in an old frame apartment building run by Goldie and Chuck Towne. Within a week Chuck Towne died. Goldie pounded on our door at 5 AM, yelling that something was wrong. He was almost gone when we got to him. I called an ambulance and tried mouth-to-mouth. I remember I had the irrelevant thought that this was the only time I'd ever kissed a man and he was dead.

There was a long, dreadful scene in the Missoula railroad station when my wife left for good. We sat and cried for hours. We had been close and it was over. The Missoula railroad station is so cheerless, you'd weep there saying goodbye to Hitler. Then she was gone and I was walking alone down Higgins Avenue, for some reason unusually aware of my shoes each step I took. Then, I was sitting in a bar near the station, tears pouring down my face, and the bartender sophisticated enough to say nothing. He'd seen drunks cry before.

I was naive about English departments and didn't understant the animosity of some of the staff. I didn't know that some professors hate you for being a poet. (Not only do I understand that very well now, I can walk into any English department and in a very short time tell you exactly who those professors are. When it comes to spotting *them,* I'm as sensitive as a candlefish.) Every rude remark, every disdainful look was magnified by my situation and my insecurities. I was on the verge of going under and I didn't know where to turn. I was drinking so heavily that my voice caught and betrayed my shaky emotional state in class. Sometimes I broke into tears.

There were kindnesses, too, and they magnified themselves. Carrier telling me he understood what I was going through and that he had enormous faith in me as a human being. Walter Brown, the Chaucerian, and his wife Mackey, having me over several times for dinner. The late Vedder Gilbert, always the gentleman, offering help in small but generous and important ways. And John Herrmann, then director of creative writing, sensing one day that I far too upset to meet classes and sending me home, telling me not to worry, that he would cover for me.

I moved into the house in Missoula alone when it vacated. I made it clear that students were welcome, that there would always be a drink or a beer when they came by. Since the house was across the street from the school and since students were favorably disposed to free liquor, I guaranteed myself company during this lonely, empty time.

But of all good saving things from that time, one place and one group of people, one man and one woman. Across a small dirt roadway from Goldie Towne's apartments was a frame bar, the Union Milltown Bar. As I write this, I remember how I felt in those days and I hope you heard the trumpets when I put the name of that bar on the page. Trumpets, too, for Harold Herndon, the first man I met in Montana, the owner of the Union Milltown Bar.

A girl was tending bar the first time I walked in. There was one customer, and a man I took to be another who came to me, put out his hand and said, "I'm Harold Herndon. I run this bar. I'm glad you came in." He could not have picked a better time and I could not have picked a better bar. I fell in love with Harold Herndon and that bar from the very first.

Everything seemed right. The animal heads on the wall—goat and ram under plexiglass domes; the habit of the bartender to buy every fourth or fifth drink; the clientele—workers from the Bonner Mill, the railroad and the woods; the funny old tongue-in-groove lumber walls; the strange, not really good but for that bar perfect, paintings of western scenes and events—buffalo hunts, a lynching, and one man alone waving hello to anyone who might be there across the void of the uninhabited plains—oh, aren't we all, buddy, aren't we just fucking all? And isn't this the right bar, this warm, homely bar where people know that waving to be the human condition, and know it better than anyone any place else knows it?

Harold is a short man, stocky, slightly and humorously sarcastic. His face looks like that of an ex-boxer, his nose broken, his jaw firm. He sees the world as the comedy it is and, when he was about to tell me something funny about one of the customers, he preceded his story with a little laugh, a sort of half-smile, half-laugh that signalled his good-humored vision of the world was at work again. For the most part, he enjoyed the people who came in.

Harold had spent some time in an orphanage. I couldn't miss the hard life behind his eyes, the sadness. But I couldn't miss his strength either. There's something durable about him. He is a survivor, an alder tree, a catfish. Sometimes, usually when he is worried about money, his view of his fellow man gets grim. He becomes distrustful, feels people have taken advantage of him. And they have because he has been generous with them for a long time. Harold might run a tab for several weeks for a truck driver and never ask for money. Then, when feeling the pinch, usually because he'd borrowed money from a bank to "improve" the bar (I begged Harold for years to leave that beautiful place alone), he would demand that the truck driver pay him back. Often there would be a scene since Harold in his bad moments, forgets diplomacy.

Despite the kindness of Carrier, Herrmann, Gilbert and Brown, and the supportive company of Norman Meinke and Dave Smith, I did not feel I belonged in the English Department at the University. I was going back to an existence I'd known years before. I'd come from plain, naive working class (even peasant class) people, the kind of people who came into that bar, and it was in that bar I felt at home. With my wife gone, and seemingly much of my life a meaningless failure, I felt free to drink just as much as I wanted to—and that was a lot.

I suppose I felt the need to be with people who had their feet on the ground. Harold, depsite his occasional flights of fancy about the bar, his dreams of turning the bar into a major enterprise, had his feet on the ground. Harold is also an engineer with the railroad and, when I first knew him, a train had derailed miles west of Missoula in the mountains. The engineer had been fired. When I asked Harold about it, he said, "Oh, shit. He was drunk." I needed those simple, factual explanations of things. They seemed very important. A down-to-earth attitude I could anchor on.

In those days a wall of tongue-in-groove lumber chopped the room off right where the bar ended. An old furnace stood against the wall. It heated the bar in the winter and the wall gave the bar a snug, comfortable feeling. To go to the bathroom, one had to go through a hinged door in the wall and make his way across a cold room furnished with booths that were seldom used. One thing I loved about the bar was that often I was the only customer, and for some reason being alone there was a good feeling.

Harold was pleased I was a poet. I think I was the first poet he ever met. One day he said, "Say. You like to write poems about ghost towns. You ought to go to Garnet."

"Where is Garnet?" I asked.

"Just go to Bearmouth and turn left." What a beautiful line. The certainty of place, the certainty that we are not lost, the certainty that the world and our lives have checkpoints with names and definite directions we can follow, the certainty.

And so the Milltown Union Bar became a home. Though I lived in Missoula, I headed east to Milltown every chance I had. I drank there so much that the telephone number was kept on file, along with my home phone number, in the English Department.

The first few months I found myself doing hateful things. For no real reason one night I became angry with a sad, embittered little mill worker named Johnson, and I started to yell at him. No real reason as I say. Just a lot of personal anger spilling over because the man bored me. "What did that guy say to you?" Esther the bartender asked. I told her I was sorry. He hadn't really said anything. In the years ahead I went out of my way to be friendly with that grizzled little man who had so little to show for his life. He was a regular and I saw him often.

But gradually I became a good heavy drinker. I took my favorite stool, drank to closing time, left quite smashed but without making a social mistake and drove home without incident. Over and over. From my favorite stool I could see myself in the mirror behind the bar. That was the man I must accept, the one I must make peace with, that big sad face in the mirror. Forty years old. Then another December 21. Forty-one years old. I'd probably never have another woman.

Though I'd had what I guess were good sexual relations with my wife, once she was gone, I was faced with my lack of experience. I had found my sexual adjustment with her and, in the thirteen years we were together, I had cheated but once, and that had been virtually inadvertent (I wasn't looking for anything at the time) and a dismal failure. In the bar of a small restaurant in Missoula, called The Shack, I tried to pick up the bartender one night. She was from Dillon, an attractive enough woman, but my conversation turned her cold. It came to me that I didn't know how to do this, I was making a fool of myself, and I left half a drink on the bar and went home.

No. The Milltown Union Bar was where I belonged, alone or with Harold, or with Jennie his wife who often tended bar, or with Gene Jarvis from the mill who howled with animal pleasure when he felt his booze, or with Guy Weimer with his loud declamatory way of conversing with you and the whole bar at the same time ("Jesus Christ! The Goddam fishing isn't worth a shit this year."), or with friendless Johnson who mumbled the very little he had to say. But mostly alone. The sky could pour east forever.

Fred Miller is a man people like when they see him. He is very good looking, a bit like Tyrone Power, but he has built into his face the look of a mildly mischievious boy who, like W. S. Merwin, is making it through life without the need or desire to use his intelligence, thank you. When you see Fred

Miller, you feel better about things. When you talk to Fred Miller, you feel better about things. That Fred Miller is so instantly likeable, probably saved his life.

Fred tended bar now and then for Harold. One cold night during a hard winter a mill worker named Scott came into the Milltown Union Bar. It was late, after 1:00 PM, and the only other person in the bar was Fred's wife. Scott ordered a beer and exchanged a few words with Fred. As Fred turned to the cash register, Scott said, "You're a nice guy, Fred." Those were surely the most important words Fred has ever heard. When he turned back to give Scott the change, Scott was pointing a pistol at him.

Fred gave Scott the money, about 140 dollars, and Scott took off in his car while Fred called the cops. Scott raced to Missoula and headed south on Higgins Avenue. The broadcast had gone out and a Missoula policeman named Doug Chase heard it up Pattee Canyon where he was parked. When Scott's car, which seemed to fit the description, approached, Chase stopped it and radioed back to the station. He was instructed to wait for help which was on the way.

Doug Chase is probably the nicest cop in town, maybe in any town. He spends much time talking to school children because his role on the police force involves public relations work. Like a lot of nice people, he tends to trust humanity. He ignored his instructions and walked towards Scott's car, and Scott shot him in the stomach and took off up Pattee Canyon. The road brought Scott to the Clark Fork River where there was no bridge. In the zero weather, ice and snow, Scott swam the river. He was back in the Milltown area where he had started.

Fred was home by now, and when he heard over the radio that Scott had shot a cop, he realized Scott had been quite capable of pulling the trigger earlier in the bar. Fred imagined that Scott knew where he, Fred, lived, and he sat rigid in his kitchen with a shotgun waiting for Scott to come through the door. Though Fred's fear had obviously excited his imagination, and blurred his logic, in fact, Scott was close. Fred lived near the river where Scott had crossed in the freezing night.

At four that morning, Scott phoned the police from the

Bonner Railroad station, a small building a quarter of a mile to the east of the bar on the tracks that pass close to the bar. He was freezing to death, he said, and would they come to get him. That night he slept soundly in the warm jail. The next day he didn't ask how Doug Chase was doing in the hospital.

One of the troubles with Freshmen in the comp class, I found, is that they feel they have little to write about. I got Carrier to authorize 50 dollars for Fred to talk to my class. That should give them all something to think about. Fred never showed. When I asked him why he hadn't—it seemed such an easy 50 dollars for less than an hour—he said he was too shy to talk in front of an audience.

Bill Stafford talks about the bonuses of life, things life gives us that trigger and fit into poems. I was drinking at the Milltown one afternoon when a crusty old man approached. He had been living in a cabin out somewhere in the remote countryside and the cabin had burned down leaving him homeless. Harold gave the man free lodging upstairs over the bar. Like many Montanans, the man, who had never seen me before, immediately started talking about his personal life. In Montana, many people assume that with the scarce population, 735,000 people in a state bigger in area than any except California, Texas, and Alaska, loneliness is the norm and when you meet someone else you have license to speak intimately simply because you are two people in a lonely, nearly uninhabited landscape. This luckless man whom Harold had befriended gave me one of Stafford's bonuses, a great opening line for a poem. The first thing he said was "Harold knew I'd been burned out in the valley." It was too good. I never could do a thing with it. I mentioned this to a class at the University of Washington years later and a young poet named Jim Matsui picked up the line and used it in a poem.

One night I was the only customer, sinking into the soft warm light of my new home, and feeling the soft warmth of the cold stinging bourbon, when two young men walked in, one in his late twenties, the other in his mid thirties. Dale Paulsen was bartending.

The older man was fat and had a long, large nose that ran out of rigidity toward the tip. It wobbled and looked false. He sat one stool away from me and started to talk. He was terribly funny. The younger man played the electric slot machine.

The fat man broke us up, Dale and me. It seemed impossible that he couldn't have made it as a professional comedian. Not only was his patter hilarious, he was inherently funny as the great comics are. Perhaps it was his looks, his girth, and that unusual nose. Neither of us had ever seen the men before. During a lull the fat man asked me the direction to Drummond and how far it was. The young man hit the slot machine for 12 dollars in free games and Dale paid him off out of the register.

Then the younger man sat with us while the older man played the machine, which was down the bar toward the door. The younger man was more conventional looking. He had a round face and dark hair. His conversation was usual too. The fat man lost about five dollars to the electric slot machine.

They traded places again. Now the fat man really turned it on. What a funny man and how odd that anyone this entertaining would come to this out-of-the-way bar. It was as if a traveling show had gotten off course. The young man hit the machine again, this time for 27 dollars, and Dale paid him and they left. The next day Harold found the hole drilled in the machine, where the young man had inserted the thin steel rod that kept free games already won from subtracting while they were being played on the machine.

"They asked the way to Drummond," I told Harold after he muttered things about relative inteligences of bartenders he had employed.

"Sure," Harold said glumly, "and the bastards laughed all the way to Great Falls."

I tried other bars of course and enjoyed them, but never like the Milltown. That was love, love of home, love of the possibility that even if my life would never again change for the better, at least there, in that unpretentious watering hole that trembled when the Vista Dome North Coast Limited roared by, I could live inside myself warm in fantasies, or chat with honest people who were neither afraid nor ashamed of their responses to life. It wasn't the worst way to be.

Often friends went there with me, Dave and Annick Smith, Jim Welch, and later, Lois Welch. Alone or with friends, the charm of the place seldom failed me.

I wish the following had happened in the Milltown because it and that bar deserve each other. But it happened at the Double Front, in Missoula, owned by Harold's brother Gene. That bar is gone now. Gene sold his liquor license and retained only the restaurant where he sells chicken and shrimp.

It was there that one night drinking alone I felt a hand on my face and whirled around, angry. It was an old woman next to me. She said, "Don't be mad, Mister. I just wanted to touch your face." I fell all over myself covering up, told her it was alright, that I understood.

I was in love less than two years after I started going to the Milltown, and I don't mean with just the bar. I was smack in the middle of a love affair and I was happy. But, although I intended to ask the woman to marry me, two children and all, I still couldn't shake the remorse of my divorce. I got that February, 1966. It was a breeze, I charged desertion and my wife in Seattle didn't respond or contest. So on February 10, 1966 at 1:56 PM an old judge signed the decree and said, "You are no longer obligated to this person," and I wanted to say, "How in the hell do you know, you old fart?" But I thanked him, took note of the time because it seemed like a dramatic moment in my life, and went outside and sat on a bench and cried for awhile. I was never very good at letting things go.

No offense to my wife, now ex-wife, but that affair in '65–'66 was easily the best sex I'd had or would have for several years after. I couldn't believe how passionate it was nor how very easy it seemed each morning when she would drop by on her way to school—she was a graduate student—and we would spend an hour in the sack. I'd never been that good before. My timidity vanished completely.

But I was hard at the booze. Not that she was a model of sobriety. And I still held much affection for my ex-wife. My sentimentality wouldn't vanish despite the sexual satisfaction. What the hell, nearly fourteen years of a marriage where we had been unusually intimate and close even for man and wife, fourteen years of helping each other like man and wife, brother and sister, over some very rough terrain, those years didn't just go away even if I was very much in love now. It was love but it came at the wrong time and I blew it.

I got too drunk too often. I slobbered about my sad moments I had known in my marriage, leaving my lover to feel that I still loved my wife. I made too many demands when I got drunk, a sort of test I was putting my new love through to see if she really loved me because, after all those hours staring in the mirror at the Milltown, I still hadn't decided if that was the face of a man who could be loved. Finally, she took off when school was out in the spring of '66 and I spent the most depressing summer of my life.

Where had she gone? No word. I sat in the Milltown day after warm day, sullen, certain now that the face in the mirror was that of a man who deserved no love, and who would find none. It would have been easier if school had been in session. I had come to love teaching. It was the only job I'd ever had that I took seriously, and the affection I felt for students, and often could feel coming back in the classroom, was a salvation in those days. But this was summer and I had nothing to do but drink and stare at that loveless man in the glass.

When my ex-lover came back married in September, everyone knew about it but me. Finally, a grad student named Lahey came to my house and told me. My first reaction was to make an Alka Seltzer and drink it—my hand shook when I raised the glass—and to announce bitterly that I would never get entangled with another woman as long as I lived.

The next two weeks were ridiculous, but only in retrospect. I locked myself in the house for eight days because I broke into sobbing so suddenly and so frequently, I feared being in public. I wrote silly letters to friends and even people I didn't know. I declared a desire to die in my sleep. Richard Howard wrote back and said, correctly, that he thought I was fooling myself. David Wagoner did too and added, "What would W. C. Fields say to all this?"

It wasn't the loss of the woman, I realized afterward, that drove me to such absurd behavior. It was the fear that I was losing everything, that given my shrimpy sexual history, my timidity with most women, the ease with which I could return to my fantasies, there was a very good chance I would never have a woman again. That even if I could have, I might very well revert to an old self, the man who invited rejection and then retreated to his "cave of sorrow" to stare out jealously at the world of assumed normalcy.

I was bitter. For a short while I thought I'd kill her. How silly can you get? Then, a long period of resolve. It seemed that I had been treated rotten by women all my life. And it seemed that at my age I had to admit that either I was some-one who deserved it or I wasn't, that I was either a shit or a good man. And if I was a good man, why then screw them. If there were to be any tears from now on, they would not be mine. All this infantile reasoning required sustenance with booze, of course. I wrote a poem called "The Lady in Kicking Horse Reservoir." That was as close to direct vengeance as I'd come. Earlier that year, after she had first disappeared for the summer, I wrote a poem called "Degrees of Gray in Philips-burg," anticipating the struggle I might have to go through, anticipating that I might never experience kisses like hers for years to come. "The last good kiss/you had was years ago." If a poet is supposed to suffer for his art, I felt I deserved at least the Nobel Prize.

By now Harold had the back wall torn out, the furnace replaced by a new one buried under the building, and the old booths replaced by new booths and plastic tables with chairs. This was the first big improvement. I fought Harold, though not significantly since it was his bar, on every one of them. "Stop," I pleaded. "Don't improve anything. This is a won-derful bar just as it is." But Harold is a determined man. "I'll get the overflow crowd from East Missoula if I fix this place up," he announced.

She came back to school without her husband who would visit when he could. His work kept him in Wyoming and she wanted to finish her degree. The day she came to see me we were in the middle of a melodramatic conversation when Kenneth Hanson called from Portland to tell me he'd won the

Lamont Prize. It was good news and it was good coming in
from the outside.

The Milltown Union Bar
for Harold Herndon

(Laundromat & Café)
You could love here, not the lovely goat
in plexiglass nor the elk shot
in the middle of a joke, but honest drunks,
crossed swords above the bar, three men hung
in the bad painting, others riding off
on the phony green horizon. The owner,
fresh from orphan wars, loves too
but bad as you. He keeps improving things
but can't cut the bodies down.

You need never leave. Money or a story
brings you booze. The elk is grinning
and the goat says go so tenderly
you hear him through the glass. If you weep
deer heads weep. Sing and the orphange
announces plans for your release. A train
goes by and ditches jump. You were nothing
going in and now you kiss your hand.

When mills shut down, when the worst drunk
says finally I'm stone, three men still hang
painted badly from a leafless tree, you
one of them, brains tied behind your back,
swinging for your sin. Or you swing
with goats and elk. Doors of orphanages
finally swing out and here you open in.

Making Certain It Goes On, p. 166.

Those Days I Was and Wasn't Wallace Stevens

I BECAME Wallace Stevens in 1951. I had no idea how, if I was truly A Poet, I'd be able to survive the Boeing Company where I started to work that year. In those days I believed what a poet did for a living was important. After all, we poets are sensitive, aren't we? And can't the wrong job kill our creative powers?

But there was Wallace Stevens, his long years in the business world, his dedication to writing so private it seemed he told no one where he worked that he wrote poems. Could I be him? Could I be that tough, that resolved to go on alone when all around me were people who didn't know or care?

Of course there were differences, and not just in our poems where, alas, the differences were obvious. There were also obvious differences in position, the vice president of a large insurance firm, me grade ten storekeeper in an even larger boom and bust industry. Fortunately, my fantasies didn't allow for distinctions. I had to survive so I became Wallace Stevens. Well, an unreasonable facsimile. If I published a poem I would bring the magazine to work and show it to others. I wasn't selective. I showed it to those I thought would be interested, and I showed it to those who had no interest but whose admiration I wanted. For all my failure to be Wallace Stevens in practice, anywhere except inside in some ridiculous region of the mind, I still benefited from my admiration of him and of his work. When Stevens wasn't being an ideal, he was a poet. One poem, "Owl's Clover," I would read aloud over and over to turn on, or as we used to say, to find inspiration. That poem worked for me—the language excited me again and again to write. Later Stevens would reject that poem from his *Collected Poems* as being too rhetorical and I would realize I wasn't a very good reader of Stevens. I preferred "Two at Norfolk" and "Dry Loaf" to "The Emperor of Ice Cream," "Sunday Morning" and "The Snow Man." Whatever my shortcomings at being or reading Stevens, he was there one more time when I needed him.

Now I was forty and for the first time a teacher in a university, the University of Montana. I'd been away from school sixteen years and had forgotten whatever it was I thought I'd learned. After high school, I'd never been a voracious reader, and for some reason I forget much of what I read, just as I remember much of what I hear and see. I felt unqualified to teach anything but writing, and I wasn't sure I could teach that. The renowned teacher, Leslie Fiedler, was on leave from Montana that year. Imagine my confidence when my boss told me I was Fiedler's replacement.

The first quarter I was given an upper division course in a survey of poetry. I worked hard at preparation but, with my marriage breaking up and my excessive drinking, it was a shaky time, too shaky to make up for sixteen years overnight.

Midway through the course a student savagely pointed up my incompetence in front of the class. I had already admitted to that, hoping, I suppose, to avoid what was now happening. I thought if I said it first they'd show some mercy when I demonstrated how true it was. Following the attack by the student, which was both telling and humiliating, I hesitated hours in the next moment. My impulse was to walk out forever, back to Seattle and the aircraft business where I suspected I belonged. I still don't know why I didn't obey that impulse.

The next quarter I was given a course, upper division, in modern poetry. I started with Byron's "Don Juan," which I consider a modern poem. I blew it. I couldn't think of anything to say about "Don Juan" except how damned funny it is. Then I remembered the most brilliant lecture I'd heard, or rather I remembered hearing it. Jackson Mathews had

delivered that lecture at the University of Washington, on
Valèry's "Graveyard By the Sea." I believed the more difficult
the poem the better off I'd be. We could struggle through it
together, and I'd be assured the class didn't understand the
poem any better than I did. We would be on equal terms. I
looked up Mathews' essay on the poem that had appeared in
Poetry and had been the foundation of that brilliant lecture. I
took on Valèry. I blew that. My intellect wasn't up to it—I was
just too dulled by the years away from school, by lots of fishing and drinking and softball and very little reading.

Then I rediscovered "The Comedian as the Letter C." Not
only that, but by very good luck, I discovered a book by a man
named Fuchs called *The Comic Spirit of Wallace Stevens*. But
even without the Fuchs book I found I understood what Stevens was talking about. Years before that poem had both
attracted and bewildered me. But in those sixteen years I'd
gone on writing poems. Hadn't I, like Crispin, like a lot of
poets, tried on this role and that in order to write, believing
some choice was involved in the pose that seemed necessary
to get the words down? Hadn't I written many times as if "the
mask" was an act instead of a serious psychological manifes-
tation? Didn't I know by now that we don't will who we'd like
to be, that who we'd like to be is tied irrevocably to who we
are? Isn't posturing easier in real life than in a poem? Was it
possible we actually take OFF the mask when we write? I was
tingling with possibilities. What I couldn't get Fuchs did. That
quarter in one lecture I became a teacher.

The next quarter or maybe later, I tried "The Man With
The Blue Guitar," and did ok, but not as good as an MA student in literature who did his thesis on the poem. My boss
called me in. He said that only two guys in the department
understood "The Man With The Blue Guitar," and that he
was too busy. I had to be the student's thesis advisor. It was
the only academic thesis I ever advised. Since then I've settled
in to teaching only creative writing except for one "literature
type" course a year. But that day in my boss' office I became
an academic, and while others may ridicule that term, I was
proud. I joined a group that includes a lot of people I admire.

So it was Wallace Stevens along with my boss and his faith

in me that kept me in teaching. My boss, Warren Carrier, now chancellor at the Platteville branch of the University of Wisconsin, even sat in on one of my lectures on the "Comedian As The Letter C." Afterward, he said with no motive other than being helpful, "You slipped up on that one passage. That's the mask becoming the man." When Stevens and Fuchs didn't turn on the lights, Carrier did.

My enthusiasm for Stevens has diminished over the years though lines and poems he wrote still haunt me. It isn't that Stevens is any less these days. He may be more. It's just that as I've gotten older my naive admiration and even adulation of other poets has given way to a genuine appreciation of them as mortals who went on writing. That's no mean matter. I suppose getting older is running out of others you'd like to be.

With his life and his poems Wallace Stevens told me to keep writing. He also told me to keep teaching. None of that was necessary but I didn't know that. Even the photo of him that appears on the dust jackets of his books seemed an inspiration. He sits there still, suit, vest and tie, benevolent, pompous, dignified and, if you look real close, not taking any of it seriously. Something in his face, in the attitude of his bulky frame, suggests that the welcome clown we know from his poems lived deep inside him. Just a rundown of his titles tells us that somewhere in Wallace Stevens was the entertainer. Some angels are very necessary. Some angels don't even know they're angels.

Some Kind of Perfection

I SELDOM talk about reading as an influence for a couple of reasons. One is that I remember what I see and hear far more vividly than I remember what I read. The other is that in a sense we've all been influenced by the same poets, either by the masters directly, or indirectly by poets already influenced by the masters. But a few influences from reading I don't share with others.

I remember four books in our house. The Bible which my grandmother read, moving her lips to form the words so she could comprehend them—she'd only had four years of schooling and could not read without moving her lips. She could write but used no capitals, no punctuation, and she spelled with a rudimentary crudeness that my mother and I used to laugh about, though not with cruelty I hope.

The other books were *Heidi*, Zane Grey's *Rainbow Trail*, and a children's book called *Peter Rabbit and the Big Brown Bear*. Grandmother often announced that *Heidi* was her favorite novel. She read it over and over. I would never read it.

But I read the Zane Grey several times, and it seems I must have read the Peter Rabbit book hundreds of times. Every so often, a chapter of the Peter Rabbit book started out with a poem, a rhymed quatrain, as I recall, ABCB. I delighted in those poems and would read each aloud as I came to it, taking special pleasure in the rhyme.

Somewhere in that book, which I've not seen in decades, toward the end of a chapter, Peter Rabbit is caught in a blizzard. His situation is desperate, snow piling fast and harsh winds blowing. He must find shelter. Then he spots far across a field, a light shining, and he makes his way across the wide meadow through the swirl of snow and the driving gale, finally arriving nearly spent at the entrance of the dwelling, which is really a cave house complete with door and windows. Peter, with a final effort, throws open the door and collapses inside on the warm floor, safe at last from the elements.

The next chapter started with a poem. The owner of the cave house, who turns out to be the big brown bear, is speaking. It went something like this:

> What are you doing inside of my house?
> You knocked all the snow off your feet with your jump.
> Why don't you knock before you come in?
> I've a notion to cut off your head with a saw.

The first time I read it I felt let down. "Jump" does not rhyme with "saw," as anyone can plainly hear. After all, the poems had always rhymed before. What right did the author have to throw up his or her hands this way? During one of my mother's visits I called this to her attention and for several years we would recall that quatrain and laugh about it. Though it became funny, the first few re-readings of the book I still felt betrayed by the author and his or her failure to rhyme. After all he or she could have *tried:*

> I've a notion to cave in your skull with a thump.
> I've a notion to beat out your brains on a stump.
> I've a notion to kick your rabbity rump.

Whoever wrote that book is probably dead. But to his or her spirit I say, Come on, one more try. At the time it seemed extremely important that the poet had failed his or her obligation to that poem.

A huge fleshy woman, Miss Effie Aiken, my eighth grade teacher, ran a tight ship, taking no crap from the impulsive 12- and 13-year-olds who filled her class. I was already writing, if that's what I was doing. Well, I was putting words on paper. That's writing, isn't it?

One day, Miss Aiken read a poem aloud to the class. A poem by Tennyson, called "The Brook" and it was an experience that would last as long as that trout who swam out from under the Holden Street bridge in Longfellow Creek. I was truly moved, but how could I tell my fellow students how beautiful I thought that poem was? I was smart enough not to try. Poetry in those days was for girls, and I kept my feelings to myself. Hadn't Tennyson caught the running water rhythm of a creek with his refrain:

> For men may come and men may go
> But I go on forever.

And wasn't that true? To a 12-year-old boy it seemed so. Didn't the creeks run forever, while we lived and died? Oh, that wisdom.

That experience, hearing "The Brook" read aloud, stuck a long time. In 1968, when staying in London, I took a trip to Lincolnshire and saw Tennyson's house, and also the creek (brook) that had "inspired" the poem, as we used to say.

The creek was lovely and the land it flowed through seemed not to have changed since Tennyson's time. I saw no recent houses, no roads that seemed new. It struck me how easy it must have been for Tennyson to imagine he owned the creek, possessed it utterly and forever. And though I knew it couldn't possibly be true, in some fanciful, probably egotistical way, I imagined for just a moment that I was the first person since Tennyson to see that creek. It was an easy delusion to come by because, except for my companion, I remember seeing no other people, only two cemeteries in the yards of two churches not very far apart. What a lovely world for a poet to have lived in as a child. And it remains just as it was, remote, private, to my eye ignored by the rest of the world.

Recently I found a copy of "The Brook" in a collected Tennyson. It isn't very good. It is much longer than I remember and I'm sure Miss Aiken, bless her, read only the verse refrains.

In the late forties I found a book of poems by the English poet Bernard Spencer, called *Aegean Islands and Other Poems*. First published in Great Britain in 1946, it was published by Doubleday in the United States in 1948. It is far from the best, I know, but that isn't important. It has meant more to me than many books that were far better.

Spencer did it exactly the way I wanted to. He left home (though he went farther than I wanted to), and he lived near water and there he found his poems. In his case he lived in self-exile in both the Greek Islands and in Egypt, with a group of writers and scholars, George Seferis the one destined to become most famous. Spencer had a charm that can only come from a winning naiveté. What poem fell as innocently on the page as the first poem in his book?

Aegean Islands 1940–41

Where white stares, smokes or breaks,
Thread white, white of plaster and of foam,
Where sea like a wall falls;
Ribbed, lionish coast,
The stony islands which blow into my mind
More often than I imagine my grassy home;

To sun one's bones beside the
Explosive, crushed-blue, nostril-opening sea
(The weaving sea, splintered with sails and foam,
Familiar of famous and deserted harbours,
Of coins with dolphins on and fallen pillars.)

To know the gear and skill of sailing,
The drenching race for home and the sail-white houses,
Stories of Turks and smoky ikons,
Cry of the bagpipe, treading
Of the peasant dancers;

The dark bread
The island wine and the sweet dishes;
All these were elements in a happiness
More distant now than any date like '40,
A.D. or B.C., ever can express.

Aegean Islands and Other Poems, p. 3.

He took firm, tender and private emotional possession of a region where he was a foreigner, an intruder perhaps, certainly a stranger, and he felt it. And he lived his invented relation with the landscape out to some kind of poetic realization. I would have liked to have said "to poetic perfection" but that would be wrong. He didn't come close to executing most poems perfectly. But some kind of perfection lay in his acceptance of what he was, a bewildered innocent in the face of thousands of years of civilization and history and wisdom, what many of us have been at least once in our time if not forever. Spencer was not afraid to blurt out the simplest, most disarming truth:

> I was looking for things which have a date,
> And less of the earth's weight,
> When I broke this crust.
>
> From "Greek Excavations," *p. 14.*

> In the boulevards of these dead you will think of violence,
> Holiness and violence, violence of sea that is bluer
> Than blue eyes are; violence of sun and its worship;
> Of money and its worship. And it was here by the breakers
> That strangers asked for the truth.
>
> From "Delos," *p. 16.*

> and it may be, too, we are born with some nostalgia
> to make the migration of sails
> and wings a crying matter.
>
> From "Yachts On the Nile," *pp. 29–30.*

He was not afraid of his innocence, his poetic roughness. Literature, the important stuff, Eliot, Pound, Williams, was being offered in the classrooms at the University of Washington. They belonged to everyone, but Spencer seemed to belong to me. He had no real literary ambition, I felt, though I may be wrong. His poems seem to settle for a simple, direct validation of his relations with the world, often made crudely but honestly:

> *Egyptian Dancer at Shubra*
>
> At first we heard the jingling of her ornaments
> as she delayed beyond the trap of light,
> and glimpsed her lingering pretence

her bare feet and the music were at difference:
and then the strings grew wild and drew her in.

And she came soft as paws and danced desire at play
or triumphing desire, and locked her hands
stretched high, and in the dance's sway
hung like a body to be flogged; then wrenched away,
or was a wave from breasts down to the knees.

And as the music built to climax and she leaned
naked in her dancing skirt, and was supreme,
her dance's stormy argument
had timid workday things for all environment;
men's awkward clothes and chairs her skin exclaimed against.

Aegean Islands and Other poems, p. 34.

I felt my chances at ever writing anything so grand as literature were slim and I decided I would be happy to settle for a poetic world as limited and innocent as that of Bernard Spencer. Once in a while I might get lucky there and come off graceful.

Olive Trees

The dour thing in olive trees
is that their trunks are stooped like never dying crones,
and they camp where roads climb, and drink with dust and stones.

The pleasant thing is how in the heat
their plumage brushes the sight with a bird's-wing feeling:
and perhaps the gold of their oil is mild with dreams of healing.

The cold thing is how they were
there at the start of us; and one grey look surveyed
the builder imagining the city, the historian with his spade.

The warm thing is that they are
first promise of the South to waking travellers:
of the peacock sea, and the islands and their boulder-lumbered spurs.

Aegean Islands and Other Poems, p. 31.

Spencer was at the edge of things himself. To this day his reputation as a poet remains relatively obscure. He is seldom mentioned with the other better known poets of his time. He lived at the edge of islands, even one could say at the edge of civilization, a stranger whose only license to be there seemed to be his childlike love of place.

And he based many of his poems on places. It was Spencer's poems based on places, and a poem called "Copalis Beach" written by my friend Kenneth Hanson, that first gave me the idea of writing place poems, something I still do. Places were special to me, very special it turned out. In psychoanalysis where I tried and more or less succeeded in overcoming the problems I'd acquired in early life, I learned that I identified as strongly with places as I did with people. Could that be why one night long ago I wept just as violently for the loss of a house as I had for the loss of the two old people who had lived there, and with whom I'd lived for about twenty-five years? And did it follow that in my visual imagination I could not separate event from setting? That I thought where something happened was just as important as what had happened? Sometimes it seemed the place was more important than the event since the event happened and was done while the place remained. It often seemed that way when I wrote. If I could find the place I could find the poem.

Sometimes I'd see the place and invent the happening.

Montana Ranch Abandoned

Cracks in eight log buildings, counting sheds
and outhouse, widen and a ghost peeks out.
Nothing, tree or mountain, weakens wind
coming for the throat, even wind must work
when land gets old. The rotting wagon tongue
makes fun of girls who begged to go to town.
Broken brakerods dangle in the dirt.

Alternatives were madness or a calloused moon.
Wood they carved the plowblade from
turned stone as nameless gray. Indifferent flies
left dung intact. One boy had to leave

when horses pounded night, and miles away
a neighbor's daughter puked. Mother's cry
to dinner changed to caw in later years.

Maybe raiding bears or eelworms made them quit,
or daddy died, or when they planted wheat
dead Flatheads killed the plant. That stove
without a grate can't warm the ghost.
Tools would still be good if cleaned, but mortar
flakes and log walls sag. Even if you shored,
cars would still boom by beyond the fence, no glance
from drivers as you till the lunar dust.

Making Certain It Goes On, p. 205.

Sometimes I'd invent the place, then "see" it clearly enough
to invent the happening.

Cape Nothing

The sea designed these cliffs. Stone is cut
away odd places like a joke.
A suicide took aim, then flew out
in the arc he thought would find the sea.
He came down hearing "sucker" in the wind,
heard it break at "suck-" and all the time
tide was planning to ignore his bones.

Far out, the first white roll begins.
What an easy journey to this shore,
gliding miles of water over stars
and mudshark bones that laugh through tons
of green. You can time that wave and wind
by tripling your memory of oars.
The sea will con the gold from our remains.

Foam is White. When not, no dirtier
than bones gone brown with waiting for the sea.
When wind deposits spray on bone
bone begins to trickle down the sand.
Now the bones are gone, another shark

abandoned to the sea's refractive lie.
The moon takes credit for the boneless rock.

Bones don't really laugh beneath the sea.
They yawn and frown through green at time
and lie in squares to kid the moon
and drive stars from the water with the gleam
of phosphorus gone mad. Now a diver
poses on the cliff for passing cars
before he flies out singing "water, I am yours"

Making Certain It Goes Ou, p. 70

Sometimes I'd see the place and reinvent what had actually happened there.

Bear Paw

The wind is 95. It still pours from the east
like armies and it drains each day of hope.
From any point on the surrounding rim,
below, the teepees burn. The wind
is infantile and cruel. It cries "give in" "give in"
and Looking Glass is dying on the hill.
Pale grass shudders. Cattails beg and bow.
Down the draw, the dust of anxious horses
hides the horses. When it clears, a car
with Indiana plates is speeding to Chinook.

That bewildering autumn, the air howled
garbled information and the howl of coyotes
blurred the border. Then a lull in wind.
V after V of Canada geese. Silence
on the highline. Only the eternal nothing
of space. This is Canada and we are safe.
You can study the plaques, the unique names
of Indians and bland ones of the whites,
or study books, or recreate from any point
on the rim the action. Marked stakes tell you
where they fell. Learn what you can. The wind
takes all you learn away to reservation graves.

If close enough to struggle, to take blood
on your hands, you turn your weeping face
into the senile wind. Looking Glass is dead
and will not die. The hawk that circles overhead
is starved for carrion. One more historian
is on the way, his cloud on the horizon.
Five years from now the wind will be 100,
full of Joseph's words and dusting plaques.
Pray hard to weather, that lone surviving god,
that in some sudden wisdom we surrender.

Making Certain It Goes On, p. 215.

However it worked, the process was based on the visual and involved a faith in the mystique of place, a notion treated disdainfully by some poets, notably Charles Olson. I would not defend it. That would be defending my poems, a tasteless and futile thing to do. I can only remark that in my case it seemed to work. At least I got a lot of poems, some of them as good poems as I'm capable of writing.

But do I mean reinvent, or do I sometimes simply rediscover? In the case of "Bear Paw," the result of a visit to the Montana battlefield where the Nez Perce finally surrendered, when I first saw that site I felt nothing. It seemed a dull place with no distinguishing features when I stepped from my car and looked at it. No one else was there. Then I walked through the campsite and up the embankment on the other side. When I turned and looked back from "the rim," the edge of the scene, the last camp of the Indians, the approach of the soldiers, the teepees burning, the fear and confusion, the cries, the soldiers dying, the Indians dying, the wails, the tears, Chief Looking Glass dying practically, if the marker could be believed, at my feet, Chief Joseph's surrender speech, the final line of that speech, "I will fight no more forever," came clear, all provided one more sad time by the empty land.

Small Waters and Tiny Words

SINCE I'M willing to speak to anyone who wants to speak with me, and rarely try to avoid anyone, I think of myself as accessible. If anything, I've suffered from getting too emotionally involved in the lives and problems of others, of lacking what we call, mistakenly I think, objectivity. So I'm taken aback from time to time when I hear myself described as standoffish.

Then, on reflection I have to admit that I grew up standing off, sort of at the edge of things. From the time I can remember I was living with my grandparents, silent people who communicated little, and who left me to my own devices for hours. For long periods I seemed barely a part of their lives. They gave me no work to do though they worked very hard themselves. I think it was harder for them to explain what they wanted done and how to do it than to do it themselves.

So, I was at the edge of their existence. And our house was at the edge, too, for my entire boyhood the only house on our side of the block, thick rich woods all around it, willows, cedars, dogwoods, alders, hazel nut trees (filberts), red hawthorne, ferns, moss, grass, salal. Our side of the block was special, our house standing alone and the woods mine alone to play in.

The woods to the north held three rain ponds. To a small boy two seemed sizable, though I suspect now that they were ten feet across, if that. The third was very small but I liked it best. The pond of water collected at the bottom of a stump of what had been an enormous tree, perhaps three feet in diameter at the base. The stump had been hollowed out and the inside burned. The inner walls were charred black, and coating that black, growing from it, flared a bright green moss.

The rain pooled at the bottom of the stump reflected that rich green and black. The surface glowed like obsidian and emeralds.

When I leaned over the edge of the stump and looked straight down I saw my face and behind it the sky, the white clouds moving north. Once I went there to play and found a garter snake swimming in the pond. I waited for it to leave before I sailed my bark submarines, my fern cruisers. I recall a honeysuckle growing wild is somewhat rare in the Pacific Northwest, and I assumed that something unique about my rain pond warranted honeysuckle growing there.

My late Aunt Sara told me that when I was three or four, my grandparents couldn't find me one day and they called and called. They finally found me at the rain pond "fishing." I had cracked a long twig in the middle, the half of it hanging down, my "line," was in the water, the other half, my "pole," gripped hard in my fist. Since the pond was close to the house I could have heard them calling and can only assume that "fishing" had my attention's priority. I don't remember that, but I remember I used to drink the rain water because I believed it was "poisoned" or "diseased" and that by drinking it and not getting sick, not dying, I could successfully defy whatever in the world might threaten to destroy me. I drank water from ponds, swamps and ditches to prove my immortality, but I told no one. My immortality was my secret, shared only with water. At least, that's how I like to remember it.

Grandmother was a bit cracked, quite primitive at times such as mornings when she held prolonged conversations with herself. I'd wake up and hear her in the kitchen: who on earth can she be talking to? I'd go out and find only her, babbling away.

On the other hand, Grandfather often whistled barely audible tunes to himself but seldom spoke. He seemed to carry inside himself his own portable radio which he turned on when he pleased to avoid boredom.

Given our lean cultural holdings we grabbed at almost anything that offered escape or amusement. Each day we read the comics thoroughly. Once someone in Moon Mullens announced a stranger was coming to visit. Grandmother became excited and said that she was sure the stranger would turn out to be Daddy Warbucks. "That can't be," I whined in frustration. "Daddy Warbucks is in Little Orphan Annie. He can't be in Moon Mullens too." But Grandmother held firm. She was convinced Daddy Warbucks was on his way. She always liked Daddy Warbucks because he showed up just when Little Orphan Annie needed him. She may well have spent much of her life wishing for a Daddy Warbucks. Her own father had hanged himself in a Michigan barn when she had been eight. Then her oldest brother, Fred, had taken over as head of the family. I gather he had been mean to her.

I never could determine if I wrote poems to make sure things remained where they belonged, or to free things to wander in where they were not expected but would be welcome all the same.

Our house was on the edge of Seattle, less than two blocks inside the city limits, in a district that was then a town, isolated from the parent city by miles of woods and undeveloped land, and whose reputation for violence and wild behaviour seemed to put it at the edge of civilization. Seattle itself is practically on the edge of the nation.

Seattle was a strange city, more Scandinavian than anything else in character. Downtown, it often seemed inhabited by silent people, everywhere but in the Pike Place Market where the Italians, Greeks and Orientals hawked their produce with loud voices and colorful spiels and gestures. President Calvin Coolidge paraded down 4th Avenue and thousands of people lining the streets to watch him made no sound. In the '30s Seattle was reputed to have a suicide rate second only to Berlin. One explanation went that suicides were people running away from themselves and their lives, and that after one reached Seattle there was no place left to run to. They had reached the edge. The Aurora Bridge was barely completed before people started throwing themselves from it. Certainly the repressive liquor laws and Blue Laws were characteristic of the cheerlessness of that city, though that has all changed now. Once fun seemed as out of style as a week of cloudless days. Seattle was gray, cool, windy, cloudy, moody, and oppressively quiet.

Bad things were happening in that house at the edge of

the city. My grandmother's selfish possessive love for me, and her resentment of men in general and of what she perceived as their sexual freedom and irresponsibility, as well as her sudden bursts of gratuitous cruelty, were producing a spoiled, confused, extremely neurotic young man. My grandfather's silences seemed like a lack of support, and that didn't help matters. "There's no worse pain in the world than childbirth," Grandmother told me when I was too small to understand. "Does it hurt the man too?" I asked in serious innocence. "No," she said bitterly, "all a man gets out of it is the pleasure." And I thought of sex as something bad a man did to a woman. If I was ever to love a woman I must never do anything that awful to her.

One day Grandmother announced that we, she and I, were going on a picnic. I was still quite small and, though unable to articulate what I felt, I knew that she was doing this for me. It was one of her few attempts to relieve the boredom of a child living with relatively old people. Grandfather had the car at work so we set out on foot with our picnic basket. Time of year? It must have been July or August because the bracken was brown and crisp, and I seem to remember dust.

We walked perhaps half a mile or a bit more to the inter-section of McKinnon Road and Trenton Street. Suddenly Grandmother said, "Down here. We'll have our picnic here." "Down here" turned out to be a vacant lot that plunged below road level on the southwest corner of Trenton and McKinnon, two fairly busy streets. The lot was ugly with dry fallen small trees, summer dried ferns and no grass, a terrible place to picnic with traffic going by just above us. I realized that Grandmother just didn't want to walk farther. We ate in silence, and I couldn't help but be impressed with the pathetic attempt it was to show me a good time.

That picnic, the failure it was, never left me, and every so often in my poems there's an allusion to a failed picnic or a picnic held in the wrong place.

Four years ago, maybe five, my wife and I were staying at a friend's summer house on Marrowstone Island in Puget Sound. One afternoon, watching TV news from Seattle, we saw a segment about some young people called on to help weed out the thick brush that had overgrown Longfellow

Creek. In an interview one young man of high school age stated that he had lived a block and a half away all his life and had never known a creek ran there. He and the reporter were at Holden Street where it crosses the creek.

It seemed impossible that a creek that had been so important to me, where I had gone again and again to fish during my boyhood years, now flowed unnoticed and unknown. And where Holden Street crossed the creek and the boy and reporter talked, more than forty-five years before I had stood on a relatively crude wooden bridge, six years old, and seen Longfellow Creek for the first time. Cousin Warren, ten, had brought me, I'm sure, since the distance from my house, well over a mile, was too far for me to have come on my own at that age. Several boys were there, Warren's chums, all four years or so older than I. Seven or eight feet down ran the creek, a steady, smooth flow of clear water, less than a foot deep, about four feet across. It flowed out of thick watercress and on the other side of the bridge vanished into more cress, tunneling its way north to the sea though many stretches I was to find later, ran open and were easy to fish, as was the stretch right below us on the bridge.

_____ a fish line into the water, an earthworm on the hook. The boy controlled the line by hand, having no pole. For a short time the worm hung quietly in the water. I remember it hung there steady so the boy must have had a sinker on the line, too. Suddenly a trout appeared, seemingly out of nowhere, black along the back, perhaps six inches long, sleek, hovering, barely swinging its tail to hold firm in the pour. It stared at the worm. The moment it appeared, the boys yelled. I'd seen my first trout. The surprise of its sudden appearance, the excited cries of the boys, the beauty and gracefulness of the fish, the suspense as we waited to see if it would take the bait, I would never forget.

Many years later, arranging my first book of poems, I put the poem based on that experience at the beginning because, though it is not the earliest poem in the book, it seems to me to have grown out of the earliest experience that could rightfully be called an impulse to write.

Trout

Quick and yet he moves like silt.
I envy dreams that see his curving
silver in the weeds. When stiff as snags
he blends with certain stones.
When evening pulls the ceiling tight
across his back he leaps for bugs.

I wedged hard water to validate his skin—
call it chrome, say red is on
his side like apples in a fog, gold
gills. Swirls always looked one way
until he carved the water into many
kinds of current with his nerve-edged nose.

And I have stared at steelhead teeth
to know him, savage in his sea-run growth,
to drug his facts, catalog his fins
with wings and arms, to bleach to black
back of the first I saw and frame the cries
that sent him snaking to oblivions of cress.

Making Certain It Goes On, p. 3.

By the time I was old enough to go to dances I was too
timid to dance. I would slip to the edge of the dance floor,
near the band where I could listen to the music and watch the
others dance. Sometimes I would see a boy whisper something into a girl's ear and the girl smile, her teeth dazzling in
the spotlighting of the hall, and I wondered if I would ever
learn those secret words and make a girl smile. I felt most at
home at the edge of things and alone.

Say on the edge, on the bank of the Duwamish River. The
last stanza of an early poem, "Duwamish," goes:

But cold is a word. There is no word along
this river I can understand or say.
Not Greek threats to a fishless moon
nor Slavic chants. All words are Indian.

Love is Indian for water, and madness
means, to Redmen, I am going home.

from "Duwamish," *Making Certain It Goes
On,* p. 46.

On the edge of the ocean; the edge of the nation.

La Push

Fish swim onto sand in error.
Birds need only the usual wind
to be fanatic, no bright orange
or strange names. Waves fall
from what had been flat water,
and a child sells herring
crudely at your door.

The store has a candy turnover
amazing to the proprietor.
He expected when he came
a Nordic rawness, serrated shore,
a broken moon, artifacts
and silence, large sales of corn.

Smelt are trapped in the river
by a summer habit, limit
of old netting rights ignored.
Who but an officed lawyer
far away has read the treaty,
his sense of rightness rounded
in a bar? The broker's pier
is measuring the day in kings and jacks.

Your land ends at this border,
water and stone, mobile in tide,
diffuse in storm, but here.
The final fist of island rock
does not strike space away. Swim
and you are not in your country.

Making Certain It Goes On, p. 7.

The fear is always there. If you return home you risk madness. If you leave your country, your home, you face the unknown. Poems could start on the edge of things, on the border between home and the void. But who would write them?

Well, whoever wrote them would have to be tougher and wiser than I am. Someone who could return home and stay there long enough to find the poem and not go mad, and who wasn't afraid of his feelings when they came.

The Way A Ghost Dissolves

Where she lived the close remained the best.
The nearest music and the static cloud,
sun and dirt were all she understood.
She planted corn and left the rest
to elements, convinced that God
with giant faucets regulates the rain
and saves the crops from frost or foreign wind.

Fate assisted her with special cures.
Rub a half potato on your wart
and wrap it in a damp cloth. Close
your eyes and whirl three times and throw.
Then bury rag and spud exactly where
they fall. The only warts that I have now
are memories or comic on my nose.

Up at dawn. The earth provided food
if worked and watered, planted green
with rye grass every fall. Or driven wild
by snakes that kept the carrots clean,
she butchered snakes and carrots with a hoe.
Her screams were sea birds in the wind,
her chopping—nothing like it now.

I will garden on the double run,
by rhythm obvious in ringing rakes,
and trust in fate to keep me poor and kind
and work until my heart is short,
then go out slowly with a feeble grin,

my fingers flexing but my eyes gone gray
from cramps and the lack of oxygen.

Forget the tone. Call the neighbor's trumpet
golden as it grates. Exalt the weeds.
Say the local animals have class
or help me say that ghost has gone to seed.
And why attempt to see the cloud again—
the screaming face it was before it cracked
in wind from Asia and a wanton rain.

Making Certain It Goes On, p. 54.

And someone who wasn't afraid to go the other way and risk
the void.

Northwest Retrospective: Mark Tobey

What life is better—stone and stone?
Freaks are honored in the east with shrines,
even marked and worshiped, even painted
if some color amplifies the strange.
In the market men are selling color
cheap as fruit. On canvas what faint
line extending, splits and lives,
returns and multiplies, and never ending
stiffens like a fighter's wrist, becomes
a net and traps our eyes with salmon,
or is silk and floating, or is quiet
like a map? What drums are driving
migratory ants through charming lakes,
and if beholders weep, what painter
needs their tears to mix tomorrow's oils?

That's where harmony was contraband,
and later where the loot was owned,
and later where the cirrus circled
Mars and left white trails of pain
that hung for centuries. (A line
of poetry is not a painter's line,
and in museums flight is not allowed.)

Beyond Van Allen rings, the stars
don't glitter, arrogant as moons.
When did we start? Light-years ago.
Why did we come? No matter. We
are not returning to that world
of ditch and strain, the research terms:
cryogenic fuels, free radicals,
plasma jets, coordinated fusion.
Only the last, in all this void, applies.
A universe is fusing in our eyes.

Why return to air and land, when
free from weight and the weight
of hope, we float toward that blue
that kisses man forever out of form.
Forget the earth, those images and lies.
They said there'd be no wind out here,
but something blows from star to star
to clean our eyes and touch our hair.

Making Certain It Goes On, p. 47.

A space traveler would write the poem. An Indian. But above all, a tough man, one who opted for reality over sentimentality. Years later my first wife and a friend and I would go house haunting, one of our favorite pastimes. There's nothing to it: just find an empty house and haunt it. This day, a Sunday, the house we haunted was right in the city, near the downtown area, on Boren Avenue, a major arterial until the freeway was built years later.

It had been a big house, probably an expensive one for its time. Then it had fallen to bad fortunes, and had become a boarding house, with small rooms partitioned off, one of those places where poor people end up alone in the bowels of our cities. Much debris had been left for us to rummage through, old letters, sentimental small items like dolls and pennants from some happier time, I presume. Also left was a heavy framed etching that hung on the wall of what had been the living room when the building had been a home, what was probably called the sitting room after it became a boarding house. The etching, done by a man named J. O. Anderson in

New York in 1891, was a lovely landscape with a canal, a sea beyond the canal, a sturdy stone country home surrounded by trees and a charming road leading from the viewer to the house. Two sailboats floated on the canal. I wanted very much to live there. But was it real or an idealized dream of a place Anderson wanted to find? Certainly where it hung was real enough, the drab old frame building where the lonely and dispossessed ended their lives. How many had been carried out to be buried by the county, no mourners at the graveside, or a mourner who was not a relative but only another near-derelict waiting his or her turn for the same anonymous end?

1614 Boren

For Guy Tucker

Room on room, we poke debris for fun,
chips of dolls, the union picnic flag,
a valentine with a plump girl in a swing
who never could grow body hair or old
in all that lace (her flesh the color
of a salmon egg), a black-edged scroll
regretting death: "whereas—Great Architect—
has seen it fit—the lesser aerie here—
great aerie in the sky—deep sympathy."
Someone could have hated this so much . . .
he owns a million acres in Peru.

What does the picture mean, hung where it is
in the best room? Peace, perhaps. The calm road
leading to the house half hid by poplars,
willows and the corny vines bad sketchers used
around that time, the white canal in front
with two innocuous boats en route,
the sea suggested just beyond the bar,
the world of harm behind the dormant hill.

Why could room 5 cook and 7 not?
These dirty rooms were dirty even then,
the toilets ancient when installed,
and light was always weak and flat

you say, make sure it's alone in a cold garage,
the mechanic's hammer banging you mute.
Make sure only you hear the address.
Make sure your car when fixed
will not break down between the home in the sketch
and the home you deny, the boy with your mouth
who shouts goodbye from the roof.

Sail easy on the freeway. Your next home
has never been photoed. Your next home town's where
so little goes on, the hum of your refrigerator
joins the slow river leaving for home.
Isn't it familiar? Rain hitting the south window first?
Dark corner where the warm light can cringe?
If you go with rivers, not roads, the trip
takes longer and you weave and see a lot more.
When you say, 'I live here,' animals
you hadn't thought of for years live on your lawn.
They insist you remember their names.

Making Certain It Goes On, p. 372.

With all due credit to the intelligence of Miss Retivov, earlier I had tried to catch my final time in my grandparents'
house. They were long dead. Grandmother first and three
years and two months later, Grandfather. The house went to
my mother and her two sisters and they sold it. I'd moved out
long before. Still, I had lived there about twenty-five years,
and I always felt it was there, and that if I could not find the
social stability necessary to make it through life—for I was so
maladjusted at times it seemed I might not be able to hold a
job—I could always return to that house. But now it would
not be there for me. Almost all the furniture had been removed,
though the two wooden chairs remained in the kitchen and I
sat in one under the bare light bulb shining overhead. Why
didn't we ever have lamps like other people? The drab empty
rooms, the shadows, the memories, the sudden realization that
this night when I walked out I could never return again, became
overwhelming. I broke out of control into violent sobbing. I
couldn't stop for a long time. Years later, pre-Retivov but after

"1614 Boren," I would find a poem in that final evening there, but the emotion had long gone and I would create another.

Last Day There

All furniture's gone. It hits me in this light
I've always hated thinned the way it is
by tiny panes, when I leave now the door will slam
no matter how I close it and my groin will throb
hungry as these rooms. Someone left the snapshot
on the wall, two horses and a man, a barn
dark gray against gray light I think was sky
but could be eighty years of fading. Once I called
that unknown farmer friend. He stared back
ignorant and cold until I blushed.
What denies me love today helps me hold a job.

This narrow space I slept in twenty years,
a porch walled in, a room just barely added on.
I own this and I know it is not mine.
That day I found locked doors in Naples, streets
rocked in the sea. The sea rocked in the hands
of brutal sky and fish came raining from volcanoes.
I see the horses swirl into the barn. I hear
two shots, no groans. When I say I'm derelict
the horses will return to flank the farmer.
Again, the three die gray as April 7, 1892.

I'll leave believing we keep all we lose and love.
Dirt roads are hard to find. I need to walk one
shabby some glamorous way the movies like.
I'll rest at creeks. I can't help looking deep
for trout in opaque pools. I pass a farm:
it's home, eviction papers posted to the door,
inside a fat ghost packing wine to celebrate
his fear of quarantine, once outside, pleased the road
he has to take goes north without an exit ramp,
not one sign giving mileage to the end.

Making Certain It Goes On, p. 233.

I might note that in both "Houses" and this poem I'm much more receptive to that sentimental side of self that I rejected so disdainfully in "1614 Boren." But I'm older and have come to accept much of what I am, and I don't worry what others think about it.

But that wasn't my last day there, it turned out. I would return some twenty-five years later, this time with some film makers doing a movie about my work and my life. We went to the house to shoot some outside footage. My late Aunt Sara and I did a scene on the front steps. Also, I walk around the house and into the backyard in another bit of the movie.

But a surprise waited. A man lived there. He apologized for not having cut the lawn. He obviously drank quite a bit, and was self-deprecating, constantly apologizing for something or other he hadn't done though it was clear he might never do it—such as cut the lawn or sweep the house. I'd always entertained the idea that had I bought the house from my mother and aunts and remained there alone my writing would have been different. I fancied that I would have written less but better. My poems would have been wilder, perhaps longer. I'd carried this inside me for twenty-five years, playing the scene of what I would have been over and over. And now I saw in the last tenant with terrible clarity the man I would have become. It gave me the creeps.

I asked if we could come in and, eager to please us, the sad man said of course. I found the interior much changed. New walls up, old walls down. A few things remained. I went through the basement, too. A lot of memories came back, of course, but not much definite feeling. Instead I was moved by the diffident man who lived there alone and who supported himself with a menial job at a shop where they made doors for houses.

Doing the House

This will be the last time. Clearly
they will tear it down, one slate shingle
at a time and the man here now, last
occupant, face the color of old snow

will leave for the cold he is certain of,
sweating more than last night's bad wine.
He is the man I would have become.
When he leaves he wires the door
and padlocks the wire. When he comes home
he knows his is the one unkept yard
on the block. The weeds, he believes,
are the weeds that will cover his grave.
The style's so old the house does not belong,
not even alone, the way it stood '14
to '44, brush on three sides
not much better, scrub hawthorne
and salal and the dogwood threatening
to die, huge now in some neighbor's
backyard and blooming a white
I don't remember like the walls
yellow as sick eyes inside where I move
room to room, one wall gone, another
for no good reason put up blocking
the kitchen from the room where we ate.
We called it the eating room
and my claim on this has run out.

It's nice of the last man here
to let me come in. I want to tell him
he's me, menial job at the door plant,
table set just barely for one. I want
to tell him I've been writing poems
the long time I've been away and need
to compare them with poems
I left here, never to be written, never
to be found in the attic where hornets
starve and there's no flooring.
Are they wild? Do they ring sad and real
as the years here would have become,
as real and unseen as women
would have been dreamed, curled
in the corner where light still
has a hard time? And later, Lord,

later I would have prayed
and begged to be forgiven for the blood.

This will be the last time. The road
outside's been paved twenty years,
the road no one ever came down
long as I waited, except for a bum
who whistled, "I'll Paint the Clouds
with Your Sunshine." Now the bus
downtown's routed by, every ten minutes
fresh diesel fumes. Across the street
only three of the old homes remain,
one where a sad man lived,
a man who drank himself to the grave
and drank his way into my poems
at least twice. He was the first sad man
I remember. I preferred sadness
to anger and I preferred him
for too long a time. My last gesture
will be at the door, facing east.
It will be a look at the hill
two blocks away, that delayed dawn
every morning and stood between me
and a nation. I live east of that hill.
Thanks to the man with a face the color
of wet salt, the second true sad man
on this block, it is not madness
for the first time I have gone home.

Making Certain It Goes On, p. 325.

I remember that I told Annick Smith, the movie director, of my fantasy about living all that time in the house and what I felt my poems would have become given those circumstances. "Don't be foolish," she said. "If you'd stayed there, you would have stopped writing years ago."

Self-Interview

Q: You were married fourteen years yet I understand you seldom mention your ex-wife in the autobiographical work you're doing.

A: True. I don't mean to slight her or imply that she was not important in my life. She was very important. But our relationship was a close one, very personal, and she is alive and hopefully will be for a long time. Writing about her in any depth would be a violation of our relationship.

Q: Was the breakup difficult?

A: Agonizing for me and I'm sure for her too.

Q: Were your friends upset by the breakup?

A: Yes, many of them were but most didn't choose sides and I'm grateful for that. Jim Wright told me recently that he had been terribly sad about it because he had never known a couple that had been so close. I guess that's true. We were much closer than most married couples I know. We suffered through some terrible times together. I don't believe a marriage is a failure because it ends badly. I think ours was necessary for both of us. We helped each other to survive and each made it possible for the other to go on. We'd both had a bad shake from life and we respected each other's pain. I blame myself for the breakup of the marriage though she was the one who had the courage to separate.

Q: Doesn't she appear in some of your early poems?

A: She certainly does. Frequently. Many of my early poems took their impulses from experiences we shared. We went everywhere together. We loved the same places and things. We used to drink late into the night together, talking intimately about our lives and affections.

Q: Where did you go?

A: Often to the ocean. We loved the ocean. We used to rent a cabin between Copalis and Pacific Beach on the Washington coast. We loved it in the winter when the ocean was wild and stormy and few people were around. Later, others got the same idea and the coast became crowded, at least by our standards, even in winter. We would go down to the beach and build a fire with the driftwood, and stare at the ocean, drinking and talking away. The driftwood supply was limitless and later in the evening we would build the fire to Wagnerian heights. We made our way back to the cabin in the dark where we cooked dinner. We would sit and talk for hours. We took a radio along and at night we would pick up stations from all over. Reception is wonderful at night on the Washington coast. We sat fascinated listening to stations from the Dakotas, California, the southwest and midwest. When we picked up a remote station we were delighted. Our needs were that simple. Jim was right. We were unusually close.

Q: You dedicated a book to her, *Good Luck in Cracked Italian.*

A: Yes, I'd told her I would several years before the book came out, and I keep promises.

Q: And you did an early poem for her?

A: Yes, one of several beach poems I did years ago. The poem grew out of a camping trip we took one year to a beach near Kalalock. In that area the trails leading to the beaches are numbered for identification. This particular trip we went down Beach Trail 6. We carried sleeping bags, hot dogs, buns, mustard, beer and a kitten. Barbara kept the kitten inside her sweater that was tucked in her jeans, so her arms were free to carry other things. We stayed there four days on the beach. I went back to the car a couple of times and drove to Kalalock for more hot dogs or beer, but otherwise we stayed right there. We hadn't brought the radio and so we left the world and its news behind for four days. It was a slow and beautiful four days. We put the sleeping bags on a bed of dry round pebbles rounded from years of sea wash, and now beyond the reach of the waves. It was surprisingly soft sleeping. The small rocks shifted to accomodate the contours of our bodies. From that trip, I took this poem.

Near Kalalock

Throw sand dollars and they sail alive.
One dead salmon slides to immediate maggots
and the long starch of his side begins,
the chunk of belly gone in teeth
beyond the sonar stab, in green too thick
for signals from our eyes. Tan foam tumbles
and we call the bourbon in us wind.

We put this day in détente with a pastoral
anxiety for stars. Remember when our eyes
were ocean floors and the sun was dissonant
and cold, unlike today. Scream at waves
go back you fools or die, and say once
light was locked in a horizoned hunger.

A crack wind breaks the driftwood's white
from stark to cream. East is lost
but serious with lines: defeated slant
of grass, the cirrus pointed and the sudden
point of sun, the lean of ocean
on our throats, bacon-baited knocks
of sea perch in our palms.

Now the shore is speared by ancient orange,
let a trickle say a beach is bleeding.
Tonight the sea will come like the eyes
of all cats in the world stampeding.

Making Certain It Goes On, p. 3.

Q: Didn't that phrase "remember when our eyes were ocean floors" become part of the dedication of *Good Luck in Cracked Italian*?

A: Yes. It refers to a time we camped on the bank of the Quinsam River on Vancouver Island. That's way north of Victoria, in the Campbell River area. We slept under some tall alder trees. They had bare, thin, long trunks and all the branches and leaves were at the top. That's unusual for alders. I think it's because the soil was sandy. Anyway, when I woke up in the morning, high over us the leaves and branches at the top of the trees were shifting in the wind. It was lovely, like sleeping on an ocean floor and waking to see the surface shifting fathoms above. We both loved that sight and we lay there a long time watching the sea surface of leaves swaying against the blue sky.

Q: And after the camping near Kalalock?

A: We went to Forks, the only town of any size between Port Angeles and Hoquium on the coast, and took the fanciest motel we could find. That was out of character for us. Usually, we took the oldest place we could find, ate in the oldest cafés, drank in the oldest, most run down bars. But we were dirty, and we showered four days of sand and grime from our bodies, put on some clean clothes and found the best restaurant in town where we drank martinis and ate sea food. I remember how happy Barbara was. She said of the motel, "Doesn't that room look beautiful?" It did too. The clean rug, the bed with fresh sheets.

Q: What about other poems addressed to her?

A: Oh. Lots of those. In many of my early poems where I seem to be addressing someone, I imagined myself speaking to her. Take "At the Stilli's Mouth," for example. It was Sea Fair time in Seattle. I hated Sea Fair and so did Barbara. Sea Fair posed as a festive week, sort of our answer to the Mardi Gras in New Orleans. But it didn't ring true. There was something phony and promotional about it. The men behind it had about as much festive sense as Howard Hughes. Seattle is not by nature a festive place anyway. For a long time it ran second only to Berlin in suicide rates, though that was long ago. If anything, Seattle was a town of introspection, the last corner of the nation. From there, there was no place else to go but inward. Now, of course, it is like most other cities. Cities are about the same everywhere, though I still love Seattle because it's mine and my affectionate connections with the past are there. Anyway, with civic and business hotshots behind it, Sea Fair gained momentum. And Sea Fair week was capped by a hydroplane race on Lake Washington. Some boat from Seattle had gone back to Detroit and won the Gold Cup, hydroplane racing's prize trophy. Now, I doubt that until the

Gold Cup came to Seattle most people in Seattle had ever heard of it. Suddenly, blown up by the papers, it became something we had to win to keep it from returning to Detroit. Like most western places that suffer from years of feeling ignored, Seattle suddenly assumed itself to be in the national eye. From the publicity that raged in the papers, you'd have thought that the Sea Fair hydroplane race was comparable to the World Series or the Super Bowl. Hydroplane racing is a rich man's pastime, of course, and Seattle people who two years before had never heard of the Gold Cup or even of a hydroplane ringed the shores of Lake Washington. All TV channels carried the race. It must have been Seattle's silliest period. One year, because the scoring rules were so involved, no one knew who had won the race until hours after it was over. Hundreds of thousands of people went home bewildered and wondering why in hell they had just spent the whole day, some of them the night before, on the bank of the lake. After a few years the public began to realize that the race was boring and interest fell off. But when the race was at the height of its popularity, Barbara and I decided to spend Sea Fair Sunday out of town and we went to a place we'd not been before, the lower reaches of the Stilliguamish River north of Seattle. It seemed unique, the river slowed down, seemingly without current, the flat land it runs through at the end. It's untypical of the Pacific Northwest. It seemed like an unpopulated Holland. I think knowing that thousands of people had flocked to Seattle that day and that we were alone and had the place to ourselves affected the way we saw it. It was fun driving and walking about that place. It seemed to be topographically special. How deserted and lonely it was. We walked along the diked bank of the river and we explored an abandoned house. Barbara shared my love of places that seemed ignored by the world. At the end of the poem, where I say "Listen," I was saying it to Barbara.

At the Stilli's Mouth

This river ground to quiet in Sylvana.
Here, the quick birds limp and age

or in flight run out of breath and quit.
Poplars start and then repeat the wind
and wind repeats the dust that cakes the girl
who plays a game of wedding in the road
where cars have never been. The first car
will be red and loaded with wild grooms.

August rain says go to blackmouth,
violate the tin piled derelict against
the barn and glowing like the luck
a fugitive believed until he found
this land too flat for secrets
and the last hill diving on him
like a starved bird. The crude dike,
slag and mud and bending out of sight,
left gray the only color for the sky,
wind the only weather, neo-Holland
printed with no laughter on the map.

That hermit in the trailer at the field's
forgotten corner, he has moments, too—
a perfect solo on a horn he cannot play,
applauding sea, special gifts of violets
and cream. In bed at 5 P.M.
he hears the rocks of children on his roof
threatening his right to waste his life.

With the Stilli this defeated and the sea
turned slough by close Camano, how can water die
with drama, in a final rich cascade,
a suicide, a victim of terrain, a martyr?
Or need it die? Can't the stale sea tunnel,
climb and start the stream again
somewhere in the mountains where the clinks
of trickle on the stones remind the fry
ending is where rain and blackmouth runs begin?

Now the blackmouth run. The Stilli quivers
where it never moved before. Willows

change to windmills in the spiteless eye.
Listen. Fins are cracking like the wings
of quick birds trailing rivers through the sky.

Making Certain It Goes On, p. 53.

Q: You mentioned an abandoned house. Several of your poems are about abandoned houses. Did you often seek out empty homes and go through them?

A: Yes. We called it "house haunting" and just now it struck me the disdain we secretly felt for normalcy, for married couples who go house hunting. We preferred old rundown out of the way places and weren't interested in putting up a normal front to the world. It's more complicated than that I suppose. Maybe our decrepit houses indicated some way we felt about ourselves. I believe no matter how much money we had we always thought of ourselves as poor. I remember we used to spend money foolishly so we would be broke by payday. When we decided to go to Italy, we saved enough in fifteen months to make the trip.

Q: Could you get back on the subject?

A: What was it?

Q: Empty houses.

A: Sorry. Yes, we went house haunting often. Our attitudes reflected our past lives. Barbara had moved around a great deal as a child and went into empty houses eager to see what was there. Going into an abandoned house held no fear for her. I lived in that same house for almost twenty-five years, and I went into abandoned houses apprehensive and afraid, feeling that I was trespassing and might be caught. I don't mean just illegal trespassing, I mean a kind of psychic trespassing too, violating someone's life and memory, someone I didn't know. The one in this next poem we found on Orcas Island. We took several vacations on Orcas Island, and we went right after Labor Day when all the tourists had gone home and we had that big beautiful island all to ourselves. Anyway, the house, the poem.

Houses Lie, Believe the Lying Sea

Forget the keep-off sign. That cow
is no detective paid to guard this house
and the barricade is rot. Inside
the stove is moldy. Sunlight rays
through slits to spot the dust we breathe.
Rooms are sick for light. That male doll
fractured in the corner means
the rage of children went remote
in sea light and the humming flies.

The well still works. Pump, and water
coughs out brown. Did a father weep
and shout at weeping children: we are poor?
And when they moved without a buyer,
did the mother turn Chinese with shame?
An empty house can teach a rat despair.

Decay is often moss, green when grass
is dirty, tan or dying. Someone's due
to tend the cow. The meadows slant
a way they didn't when we entered.
Those rooms will be remembered vaguely
years from now in Greece. Who's for loving
on those rags, that broken glass?
Let's go loving where the ocean
scatters on the rocks to die like homes.

Making Certain It Goes On, p. 89.

Q: You seem to assume a history of despair, almost pathos.

A: Yes, I see that now.

Q: Aren't you being coy? Where did you get the children raging, the father weeping, the mother humble with shame?

A: Out of my fertile imagination, I suppose. Of course, I grew up in the depression and was well aware of deprivation and what it does to people. Then, I suppose the state of disrepair the house was in may have triggered some of the melodramatic images. I'm not ashamed of having corn in my poems. All good art has a measure of schmaltz. I like that poem because the ending is healthy and seems to come naturally. A lot of reviewers talk about the anguish and despair in my poems, yet I'm really somewhat optimistic, though considering what we face it's a short term optimism. Anyway, the wind help us if poets lose sight of certain basics about the human condition.

Q: Do you think of the wind as God?

A: I suppose I do, except I don't believe in God. I believe the wind is like God because we can see and feel its effect but not see it.

Q: But isn't that true about other things, for example electricity?

A: Yes, and I hate you for bringing that up. I suppose the fault lies with me. I want to but can never accept theoretical explanations of electricity, and I've never been able to accept electricity as a concept because I don't understand it. On the other hand I accept wind BECAUSE I don't understand it, and would refuse to listen to a theoretical explanation of it.

Q: Aren't you rather narrow?

A: Hopelessly.

Q: How about another poem involving your ex-wife?

A: This is one I like very much still. Although I speak to my ex-wife in the poem, she didn't share the experience that triggered it. One afternoon my boss at Boeing, Jack Davis, who died a few years back, John Popich, a buddy from my softball days, and I drove to the Washington coast to fish the north fork of the Hoh River the following day. We arrived in the dark at Kalalock where we camped. The ocean was glowing with phosphorus. When fish die in the ocean, as I understand it, their bones release a small amount of phosphorus. These small amounts collect in pockets and every so often a pocket, which is a fairly large deposit, is washed ashore. Literally, the foam gleams when this happens. That night was very dark and though the ocean was close we couldn't see it except for the stark white phosphorescent glow of the waves as they crashed on the sand. How lovely. What a haunting and eerie sight. I also borrowed from the experience that triggered "Near Kalalock," the time Barbara and I camped at Beach Trail 6. I imagined us back there again, but this time with the waves throwing the phosphorescent foam on the sand. The first four lines of the third stanza are taken from the early flashback sequence in Ingmar Bergman's "The Naked Night." The wolf fish I saw in an aquarium somewhere, Hoodsport I think. God what an ugly fish. It makes a bullhead look like Caesar Romero.

Road Ends at Tahola

My nostrils tell me: somewhere *mare nostro.*
Here the wolf-fish hides his lumpy face in shame.
Pines lean east and groan. Odors of a booze
that's contraband, are smuggled in by storms.
Our booze is legal Irish and our eyes
develop felons in the endless spray.
Mare nostro somewhere, and eternity's
a law, not a felony like here.
That derelict was left for storms to break.

One ship passes denting the horizon,
creeping down the world. Whatever gave us pride
(food en route to Rio) dies. The wake could be
that wave we outrun laughing up the sand.
Night comes on with stars and years of dead fish
lighting foam with phosphorus they left.
All day the boom was protest, sea against
the moon. *Mare nostro* somewhere and no shame.

Remember once, a scene, a woman naked
clowning in the sea while armies laughed.
Her man, a clown, had courage and he came
and hauled her (both were sobbing) up the stones.
If I were strong, if wolf-fish didn't dive
beyond the range of scorn, you'd be alive.

I can't say *mare nostro*. Groaning pines
won't harm you, leaning east on galaxies.
I know I'm stone. My voice is ugly.
A kelp bed is a rotten place to hide.
Listen. Hear the booming. See the gleam,
the stars that once were fish and died.
We kiss between the fire and the ocean.
In the morning we will start another stare
across the gray. Nowhere *mare nostro*.
Don't claim it and the sea belongs to you.

Making Certain It Goes On, p. 78.

I took the title from a highway sign just north of Moclips, about ten miles from Tahola, an Indian reservation town. Quinault tribe. Barbara and I visited that forlorn rundown village many times. I love it there.

Q: Wait a minute. Tahola isn't near Kalalock. Just where does the poem take place.

A: In my imagination I suppose I move our camp at Beach Trail 6, north of Kalalock, south about fifty miles or whatever to Tahola. Maybe all beaches are one. Some of the details are about Tahola. For example, the pines leaning east and the derelict ship battered by storms. Also, the contraband booze. That's from a story the tribal chairman, Horton Capoeman, told us. He runs a café in Tahola. He told Barbara and me about a French ship that ran aground off Tahola many years back. The ship was loaded with booze, brandy, wine, and the Fed's put a guard around the ship to keep the Indians from getting the liquor. But the Indians slipped through the cordon in their dugouts and got the booze ashore. "God," Capoeman said, "if you think those Indians didn't have a time." Bless them. Bless them all. I think that happened in the early part of the century.

Q: So we've got salvage, which was really theft, over sixty years ago, a movie, a passing ship, a wolf fish you saw in an aquarium, phosphorus deposits left by dead fish, a derelict ship being battered off the coast of Tahola, etc. etc.—do you often write that way, borrowing from various sources and experiences?

A: When I'm lucky. I seem to enter a state of suspended cynicism. Where relative values and locations are forgotten. I say cynicism because a cynic believes nothing has value, which is to say all things have equal values. It's easier to write if you can free your mind of moral and mundane distinctions. Love is no more or less important than a wolf-fish or a grounded ship. In real life we have to act as if one is more important than another, but when they become words it is easier to use them imaginatively if they are all equal.

Q: Aren't you talking about aesthetic distance?

A: That term doesn't mean a damn thing to a writer. That term was probably invented by a critic. If a writer invented it he ought to be ashamed. One does not get distant, one gets close.

Q: Are you saying poets are amoral?

A: Just the opposite. Most poets I know have an unusually strong sense of right and wrong. That's why they can enter the state of suspended cynicism without feeling overly threatened. Most people who worry about morality, ought to.

Q: If relative values are ignored, don't you run the risk of being trivial?

A: Yes, and often I am. That's the risk. Taking the grains of sand seriously in the wrong way. But this state of suspended cynicism can also unlock hidden ways you feel about things that would remain obscure if you worried about truth, justice, morality and, most of all, sincerity. If you have to risk being overly sincere or being affected, be affected. False things become real if we live with them long enough—in some poem I say, "The real is born in rant and the actor's gesture."

Q: Does formal verse help?

A: Sometimes. Writing in forms makes it much easier to enter the state of suspended cynicism. When you concentrate on the "rules of the game" being played on the page, the real problem, blockage of the imagination, often goes away simply by virtue of being ignored. That's why I write more formal poems when I go dry. But when I write a poem I like in some regular stanza form, I have the nagging feeling I've cheated.

Q: So finally what comes is real and honest?

A: Hopefully, though it's a bit rarer than I'd like. In that state of suspended cynicism, real feelings begin to show and if the poet is lucky he's not afraid, or if afraid, he's courageous enough to finish the poem. In most of my poems, and I think most poems of any poet, we settle for something secondary but no less authentic. We fail to discover our real feelings, so we create them and believe in them for the duration of the poem. In good writing, the reader would have a tough time telling the difference. I know the difference in my own mind. I don't know how I know, but I do.

Q: You're the Director of a Creative Writing program. Do you feel these programs are valuable?

A: Absolutely. It's generous of universities to support them, though, and in some schools there's bad feeling between creative writers and academics. Happily, there's very little of that at Montana. George Garrett said somewhere: "All serious students of literature should take creative writing. At least they might acquire a measure of common humility." In many English departments, I think academics find creative writers lazy, ignorant, self-indulgent, standardless, egocentric and slovenly. And creative writers find academics petty, pompous, inhuman, dull and arrogant. Unfortunately, we both have plenty of supportive evidence.

Q: Which side of the English department do you think is more important?

A: The academic.

Q: Why?

A: Because teaching literature is a durable purpose. I can imagine writing programs being dropped but never the lit courses. Writers will write no matter what else they have to do or where they are.

Q: But don't you think the wrong job can destroy a poet?

A: If what you are doing for a living stops you from writing a poem, you are no poet. I get tired of people who worry about how poets make a living, about whether a Ph.D. isn't killing the creative urge. Wright and Stafford have Ph.D.'s and have taught lit. for years. What demonstrable effect did it have on their poems? Personally, I admire great academics. Hillis Miller is one of the best and most worthwhile people I've ever met.

Q: Can you teach creative writing?

A: You damn right I can.

Q: So the classes have value?

A: The best justification for writing classes is not the writing itself, though that's important, but that people can come together to share fundamental human concerns. What the humanities, literature, art are all about it discussed in other classes. In creative writing classes it operates. We need writing classes the way we once needed churches, because, simplistic as it sounds, that's where we can reveal our feelings and admit they are important to us. Most people are called on to practice gross forms of inhumanity just to make a living. A close friend of mine, a writer, Rick DeMarinis, told me a terrible story about being at Boeing when President Kennedy was assassinated. Rick said that as the reports came over the public address system the only reaction of the engineers he worked with was to grow silent and bend closer to their drawing boards and intensify their attention to the immediate job in front of them. Whatever that nameless thing is that makes us human, that is the thing that is kept alive in writing courses, some recognition that our lives, no matter how drab, wretched and frustrating they have been, are all we have and in nearly all cases are preferable to death. Simple as this is, it ought never be forgotten, least of all by people who call themselves educated.

Q: Do you see a great difference between yourself, poets in your generation and the young poets today?

A: Our concerns are often different. Poets in my generation, a lot of us, grew up in poor, often degrading circumstances. For example, both James Wright and David Wagoner saw their fathers enslaved to lousy factory jobs. When we were kids, making a living, even finding a job, was tough. We have had to struggle with memories of a working class past and acceptance of a middle class present. Dave has found this easier than Jim. Jim feels enormous loyalty to his past and it still pulls at him in terrible ways. Dave finds it easier to use his past in his work, I think, and also to accept his present status. But for both, and for many of us, the past has been something to deal with. The Depression, threats of poverty and dispossession, loyalty to defeated people we still love and desire not to be like, and then a feeling of having violated our lives by wanting to be different—oh, very complicated matters. Most young poets rebel against the middle class, but that's what they are, middle class. The idea of destitution is foreign to them though they may not have much money. They are far more secure in areas we were not. Certain problems, very basic ones, don't concern them as much. However, the problems of writing a good poem probably are the same for everyone. Nor is there any less suffering in the young poets than in the older poets. It's only a matter of different concerns.

Q: You must have had a lot of students from remote rural areas as well as from cities. Do you have any ideas regarding the differences in the two groups?

A: I'm glad you asked that. I find I have more success with people from relatively isolated areas and small towns. This is in part due to my limitations, limitations imposed by my sensibility. But then, any poetry writing teacher, no matter how he guards against it, is telling the student: write like I do. That's the best way. It's unavoidable, I think. In fact, if you didn't do that, you'd be too eclectic to be a good teacher. However, I have noticed some problems with young poets from large cities.

They often have a tendency to be up on things, to know what is going on now, and they try to avoid duplication. Consequently, they concentrate on being original rather than being themselves. Sometimes they try to lose themselves by becoming one more member of a poetic movement they find fashionable.

They write as if they know they have an audience. This leads them to ignore the possibilities that sounds of words offer and to worry about what they are saying, often even before they've said it. A poet is like a drummer alone in the ballroom of a deserted hotel. If he plays well enough, a passer-by might pick up his ears and step inside to see what is going on. But he can only play the way he likes because when he starts, at least, he is the only one listening. Solipsism will never be a crippling problem because, by its very existence, language implies more than one person lives. Talking to yourself is not insane, it is only primitive. During the composition of a poem it's best to know you don't have a friend in the world.

They, young would-be poets from the cities, often lack emotional possession of their materials. Private personal relations with the world are either missing or distrusted. If everything is already experienced by others as well as yourself, you have nothing unique to share. In Fellini's film, 8½, a director finds himself creatively impotent. In this state, he rejects both friends and distasteful acquaintances, as well as himself. In an effort to find his lost creative impulse, he willfully explores his childhood and his sexual fantasies but without success. When his creative impulse returns, he accepts all people he has been rejecting, and everyone who had touched a responsive chord in him, negative or positive, is urged to take a part in his new movie. Art then becomes the generous act of accepting the totality of one's own life, not just those moments, places and people one happens to like or thinks are important.

Young poets from cities find the writing of serious lyrical poems difficult because the poem seems too restricted a form for this generous act of total acceptance—and one reason may be that their lives contain more than the form can accommodate. This may be why a "big" poet, like Whitman, is an attractive model for urban poets.

You don't have to be a renegade WASP from a small town to write a good short lyric poem but you may have to be that lonely.

No problem a poet has, regardless of where he comes from, is prohibitive. City poets are no better or worse than rural ones. Poets turn liabilities into assets and there are countless ways of doing that.

Q: Do you ever feel like rewriting early poems?

A: Yes, but it seems dishonest and I don't do it.

Q: Auden did it all the time.

A: I know. It may mean he was interested in being right and that results from a strong sense of humility. He is in effect saying: The history of my mind is not as important as what my poems now say. I can't feel that way. I say, my poems say: my life is important and by implication so is yours—I'm cheating here—Jim Wright told me I was saying that in his review in APR—before that I wasn't sure what I was saying though I had a vague notion that I'd been dramatizing my life for a long time to make it seem interesting. If I changed an early poem, I'd feel like I was saying that I prefer to have been a better person than I was, say, at thirty-four. For me, my poems have always fought for self-acceptance, and that means accepting myself as I am now and as I was then. I'm at the age where I'm losing the sense of regret. To me, things just happened and there's nothing I can do about it. Stafford says I'm forgiving people in my past but I'm really forgiving myself, or perhaps reaching that point where forgiveness is unnecessary.

Q: Have you ever been jealous of the popularity of other poets?

A: Not deeply, nor for very long. I know I never thought Ginsberg was a very good poet and I was surprised by his fame. When I finally met him, I realized that he is so important as a social force that whether his poems are good or not is unimportant. He is a great human being and that's what counts. Besides, I came to know that success and fame were frightening to me. They can have it. My God, do you realize the demands put on Ginsberg and to a lesser extent, Snyder? If they weren't each good people, it would shatter them.

Q: Is Ginsberg the greatest human being you've met?

A: No. But he's one of them. I think the jazz clarinetist, Jimmy Noone, is the greatest person I've met. I talked to him in 1944 in Hollywood, a few months before he died. I met Earl Father Hines and he is up there. Zutty Singleton, the jazz drummer, is also right up there.

Q: Old jazz musicians? Is there something special about them?

A: I think so. They, the ones I've mentioned, were so open and warm and honest. Ginsberg is like that. One thing that strikes me is how Ginsberg and Snyder are so unlike their followers. Both are very down-to-earth and practical about basic things. Their devoted followers often seem vague and ethereal.

Q: Why do you think jazz musicians are so great?

A: Because they do something out of sheer love? Playing jazz for a living is a terrible life. The people you play to are often drunk and unappreciative, and you make so little money at it. At least the old timers made little. Yet, you tell them how much you love their music and they beam like little children. The old jazz musicians, many of them, were warm as their music.

Q: What about poets?

A: I like most poets I've met, but only Ginsberg approaches being the great human being some of the old jazz musicians are, and for the same reasons: openness, attentiveness, giving at all times.

Q: Who are your favorite contemporary poets?

A: Levine and Stafford. It's easy to find good things to say about many others though. I don't keep up on my contemporaries. After a while you just go your own way and wish the others well. One poet I could never get with is Creeley, but recently Stafford and I read with him and I got with Creeley's work for the first time. I picked up strength from his humanity while we were on the stage, and I began to understand the warm searching quality of his poems. Of course I will always feel close to my northwest buddies, Wagoner, Hanson, Kizer, Vi Gale, John Haislip, Stafford.

Q: What about younger poets?

A: Oh, so many good ones. Albert Goldbarth, Gary Gildner, Jim Welch, lots of them.

Q: Welch was a student of yours?

A: Yes. I am proud of that too, unreasonably so because I know a teacher does only a small bit for a writer, but that small bit can be a great help. I expect Jim may turn more and more to fiction in the years to come. Whatever he writes, it will be very good.

Q: Where are we now? We've come a long way from your ex-wife.

A: Haven't we. Well, we've been apart ten years now. She's remarried and to a very sweet man. He even has some money, I understand. So she did well the second time around.

Q: Do you have hard feelings about the marriage or about her?

A: No. I wish her well. She's a brave, resilient woman. She's seen and overcome terrible hardships in her life.

Q: How about the last ten years for you?

A: On the whole, it's been lousy. My drinking kept increasing until my health went bad. I had love affairs that were disasters. I've felt bitterness and resentment toward women. My job seemed the only source of stability for a long time. Whenever I left my job at Montana, either to go to Europe in '67–'68 on a Rockefeller grant or to go to Iowa in '70–'71, I went to pieces. But when my health made me stop drinking, I began to see that a lot of my grief was old and shopworn and only the booze had kept it alive. Maybe that's one reason I kept drinking. I couldn't bear to let go of old selves because they had been sources of poems. When I quit drinking, I found a lot of new poems, some new selves and my old degrading past had died. And recently I lucked out on life. I found a great woman and I love her. I've never been this certain about a relationship and I'm happy.

[Hugo married Ripley Schemm in 1974.]

Q: How about one more poem?

A: This is the title poem from my second book. For years my former wife and I spent many weekends at Lake Kapowsin. We loved going to the small unpretentious tavern in Kapowsin after we'd fished the lake. We ate hamburgers there and drank beer late into the night, playing old tunes on the juke box and chatting with the locals. It was easy to find people to talk to. We were both warm and friendly people, and my ex-wife was very beautiful so men were eager to make her acquaintance. One year we came to Kapowsin in May, the first trip there for that year and the tavern was gone. We both felt a terrible sense of loss. Places we shared like that meant much to us. To find only a few charred remains where we'd spent so many happy evenings made us terribly sad. I notice now that only in the word "our," last line, second stanza, do I indicate the speaker is not alone. Maybe that means something.

Death of the Kapowsin Tavern

I can't ridge it back again from char.
Not one board left. Only ash a cat explores
and shattered glass smoked black and strung
about from the explosion I believe
in the reports. The white school up for sale
for years, most homes abandoned to the rocks
of passing boys—the fire, helped by wind
that blew the neon out six years before,
simply ended lots of ending.

A damn shame. Now, when the night chill
of the lake gets in a troller's bones
where can the troller go for bad wine
washed down frantically with beer?
And when wise men are in style again
will one recount the two-mile glide of cranes
from dead pines or the nameless yellow
flowers thriving in the useless logs,
or dots of light all night about the far end
of the lake, the dawn arrival of the idiot
with catfish—most of all, above the lake
the temple and our sanctuary there?

Nothing dies as slowly as a scene.
The dusty jukebox cracking through
the cackle of a beered-up crone—
wagered wine—sudden need to dance—
these remain in the black debris.

Although I know in time the lake will send
wind black enough to blow it all away.

Making Certain It Goes On, p. 102.

Q: A good place to stop.

A: I suppose. I hope I haven't sounded too pompous.

Q: Only here and there a little.

A: I depend on you to tell me when I go wrong.

At Boeing, early
1960s.

The Boeing Bombers; Hugo is at far left, first row.

At Hugo's first house in Missoula, Montana, June, 1966 (PHOTO COURTESY CAROLE DE MARINIS).

Harold's Club, formerly the Milltown Union Bar, Laundromat & Cafe. The laundromat was in the side-building on the right (PHOTO COURTESY BOB CUSHMAN).

Opening Day of Fishing Season, Montana, May 18, 1967.

With William Stafford, 1969 (PHOTO COURTESY WILLIAM STAFFORD).

Mid-1970s, James Welch in background.

Summer, 1974.

I Have the Money and Can Pay for the Past

(—"Letter to Wright from

Gooseprairie")

The Problem of Success

ONE MORNING a few years back in Iowa City, I got an early morning call from a friend. I was living in a trailer house at the time. My drinking had reached dangerous dimensions and my stomach crawled with pain most of the time.

My friend told me that a woman I'd been with the night before had been to see him. She had cried about the evening she and I had spent together. I couldn't recall much of that evening. I had been too drunk. I remember having dinner at her house in Solon, and going with her to my favorite bar there, Heitman's, after.

I called her immediately and she was very upset about our talk in the bar. I can remember none of it. But as I was trying to piece bits together it came to me suddenly that I was suffering a breakdown and had been for several days. This was the fourth time in the last ten days or so that I'd had a conversation with a woman I'd liked, drunkenly calculated to insure her alienation. The realization was staggering.

I'd better point out that I like most people and want people to like me. That's not unusual, I know. But with me it is an outrageously important matter and always has been. I don't apologize for it nor do I understand it completely. It, and I, are childish, I suppose. To be alienating people was not like me. It meant I was out of control when I drank.

I'd expected trouble months before, but I didn't recognize it right away when it came. Living alone in cramped quarters like that with a generous five days out of every seven off, I often drank late into the night listening to the radio or watching TV. And of course really dwelling on matters of personal concern. Months before, around Christmas, I had sensed trouble was coming and I had phoned my analyst, whom I hadn't seen in years, in Seattle, and told him I expected something was wrong. Would he save me some time that summer when I was due to teach the Roethke courses at the University of Washington. He said he would.

I'd had a couple of signs shortly before the truth hit me, leaving me terribly depressed, nervous, ashamed. Jack Marshall had come one day to the undergrad workshop I was teaching and a couple of hours later had phoned me at my trailer. He said if I wanted to talk, please feel free to call him, and he gave me his number. When I'd hung up, I thought, what a funny call that was. If I wanted to talk, why wouldn't I just go down to his office? But of course he was telling me I needed help and I didn't catch it. It was an act of great sympathy on Marshall's part because his own life was unhappy and complicated right then. Later he told me he had seen deep despair in me that day in class. I knew, after talking to the woman I'd dined with the night before, that I was worthless as a teacher and, I thought at the time, as a human being. I blamed it on the booze, though I was vaguely aware that my success and popularity there as a teacher had something to do with the trouble. I wasn't writing at all despite all the free time.

I know most people in mental hospitals are there for toxic psychosis, meaning they scrambled their brains with booze often beyond functional repair. I was terrified. I called Jack Leggett, the Director, and told him I was in no condition to teach. He agreed and with the most unforgettable and affecting kindness urged me to take off. School had but two weeks to run.

My hands were shaking and my impulses were wild and without purpose. For the first time in my life, my sense of humor deserted me. The next few days are a blur. I was virtually helpless. I remember calls from Missoula. I don't know how many supportive calls I got from Carolyn Kizer in North Carolina during that period, but they seemed priceless and still do. I remember Bill Fox calling, urging me to stay a few days with him before I drove west. He was afraid for me. I should not be driving in that condition. But I had to get out of there. Iowa City had suddenly become a scene of unbearable degradation for me. I remember saying goodbye to the two secretaries Roberta and Gail. I loved them both and I think I was in tears. I remember Jack Myers helping me in my trailer. I remember students helping me pack in my office. I remember saying goodbye to Marvin Bell, whom I had come to be quite fond of, in the parking lot and bursting into uncontrollable sobbing. I remember saying to him a terribly dishonest thing. I said, "If only they hadn't turned on me," meaning the women that I had deliberately though unconsciously alienated. And I knew it was dishonest, but I had to say something to account for this and I was too weak to blame myself aloud though already I was blaming myself inside. I remember Bell saying something like, "No one puts out as much for others as you and takes so little in return." Maybe I cried at that too. I seem to have had plenty to cry at then. Today, if I were an actor and had to cry in a scene, I would think of the kindness of Bell, Leggett, Fox, Myers, Kizer, Roberta, Gail, and many others, including the women I'd misused to grease the road down, who were assuring and understanding in the weeks to come. I had also tried to alienate women with long distance and I'd spent over 500 dollars in calls, but I simply didn't have the talent to be objectionable over the phone.

The drive west was a nightmare, what I remember of it. I remember once leaving the freeway early, about three or so, somewhere in South Dakota, a terribly drab little place, not even a town really. It was warm and I bought some beer and an ice chest with ice because the dreary little motel had no refrigerator in the room. I remember sitting there alone in the room watching TV and drinking beer and hating myself. I remember a pheasant wandering out onto the freeway somewhere and starting up too late as I exploded him and my right headlight doing 80. Later in Missoula when I told the story about the pheasant and how a truck driver told me what stupid birds they are, one of my colleagues said, "I don't know if the pheasants are stupid for not getting out of the way or we are stupid for going 80 down a freeway." And I thought, I may have to leave the academic scene. A pheasant takes out my right headlight and some young academic makes a major sociological point. Can't we let anything alone? I remember a gas station somewhere and drinking a cup of coffee and suddenly being aware that the attendant was staring at me. I knew I looked terrible. I was shaking, dirty, and depressed. I doubt that I signed one credit slip legibly during the entire trip. As I neared home I put up early one afternoon in a motel in a small Montana town about 250 miles out of Missoula. The psychic pressures were fatiguing and I couldn't drive as far per day as I normally could. Getting back meant everything at that point and I made several calls to Missoula. The calls had to go through a switchboard in the motel office and I remember once I could hear the woman who, with her husband, ran the place, yelling in a nasty voice, in the background, "Why don't you write a letter." She was quite hostile to me, maybe a little crazy, and I remember thinking if I can bear her and not make a scene I'll be home tommorrow. Everything seemed to take on terrible proportions and my inner voice kept telling me I could make it, when it wasn't telling me how damned awful I was. In Missoula, the worst possible happened. After a month of temporary quarters, a month where old friends dropped by to have a beer now and then, visits that were important to me but bewildering to them, I moved back to the house where I'd lived before and where I assumed I'd be living again after I returned from summer teaching in Seattle. Shortly after I got to Missoula, the landlord called to tell me I had to move. They were tearing the house out to make room for a fancy motel. It was the wrong news at the wrong time. I've suffered from a fear of dispossession all my life. And of course at that time, my fears were surfacing. I was helpless. Friends packed for me and moved my things to a colleague's basement for storage while I sat at the table drinking beer and sobbing, a useless slob. If I ever needed the trappings of security it was then. That house seemed of monumental importance that day I walked out of it.

In Seattle I received several letters from people in Iowa, apologetic, supportive. One phrase ran, "If only we could have been more understanding————." I wrote back assuring them that no one there had caused the trouble. Hardly. I had been treated wonderfully there by my colleagues, by the students, by the administration. I was well liked. A popular teacher. I gave a reading to a packed auditorium, SRO, and it went well. If anything, I'd been a smashing success there and I was vaguely aware that that had been at the root of the problem.

Psychoanalysis is under attack these days, perhaps justifiably. Many analyses are unsuccessful and that makes the process suspect. Then I think people expect too much from it, and even suspect that some doctors understandably make the error of trying to be too much to the patient. I'm not knowledgeable enough to defend or attack analysis. I can speak with certainty about mine however. It saved me, if not from death, certainly from a life of dereliction. My doctor is good at what he does and he's also quite down-to-earth, a good quality for a doctor if the patient is an artist. It took him a month to put it together, but of course there wasn't time for anything but an intellectual understanding. Why, he asked, are you afraid of success? I didn't know.

He pressed on. What were the most painful memories I could remember from the analysis years before? Well, the most painful memories were not the most painful times. The doctor once told me my emotions came out pure like chamber music without memories to support them. But as for memories, these two were the most painful. When I was eight, a beautiful girl, Rosalie Burns, six, who lived across the street, died of scarlet fever. I hadn't remembered that until the analysis. I'd repressed it. When I remembered it, I found myself sobbing terribly and the doctor asked why I was crying. Because I'd broken the Burns' window with a rock I'd hit with a tennis racket. Mr. Burns was a young virile man and I idolized him. He made my grandfather replace the pane. Since I felt my grandfather was too old to be doing such work, my shame was compounded. By some peculiar childhood logic, I stood responsible for Rosalie's death.

The other involves my cousin, Eileen, who came to live with us when I was three. She was eight and her mother had died a couple of years before. Though I had remembered Eileen lived with us for five years, leaving when I was eight, in fact she really only lived there sporadically. My memory turned out to be wrong on that point. One early evening she was playing with a boy named Johnny Daly. He was her age, about 12. So, I was seven or so. Johnny Daly was recovering from severe body burns, hidden under his shirt but I had been told about them. He was teasing Eileen, and to show Eileen my affection for her, I jumped on his back. Of course I was much smaller and by this courageous act I would demonstrate my love. But I'd forgotten about the burns and he fell screaming in pain. I can remember standing alone far back in the backyard, in the potato patch, the grownups despising me, Eileen despising me. Shortly after that Eileen moved away and to my mind there was a connection. As a matter of sad interest but without importance to the dynamics of the experience, a few years later Johnny Daly died aboard a Japanese prison ship in the early days of WWII.

Although I don't remember Eileen's departure, I wrote a poem about it. In those days, I often would imagine extreme situations in order to write. In this case I imagined we had grown up together in a cruel religious orphanage. The poem was included in my second volume. I wrote the poem because I discovered in the analysis that I had loved her very much. Before the analysis, I'd convinced myself I hadn't cared for her.

Eileen

Why this day you're going so much wind?
When you've gone I'll go back in alone
and take the stillest corner in the house—
the dark one where your dark-eyed ghost
will find me whipped and choking back my rage.
I won't show my hatred to their food.
I have to live here with these shaking hands.

Find a home with heat, some stranger
who's indifferent to your dirty dress
and loves you for that quiet frown
you'll own until you die or kiss.
The wind is drowning out the car
and raising dust so you can disappear
the way you used to playing in the fern.

Some say I'll be too big for them to hit,
too fast to catch, too quick to face the cross
and go away by fantasy or mule
and take revenge on matrons for your loss
and mail you word of faces I have cut.
Be patient when the teasers call you fat.
I'll join you later for a wordless meal.

Then I'll stroke the maggots from your hair.
They come for me now you're not here.
I wax their statues, croak out hymns
they want and wait for dust to settle
on the road you left on centuries ago,
believing you were waving, knowing
it was just a bird who crossed the road
behind you and the sunlight off the car.

Making Certain It Goes On, p. 85.

In Iowa in my cramped trailer house, drinking late into the night, I had gotten into the habit of dwelling on painful episodes of my past, though more immediate ones than the two just described. In both instances, I made a mistake and the result was that a girl was lost. In one case, dead, in the other, gone away. The success and popularity constituted an interruption of this dwelling which had become a psychic necessity and I deliberately set out to reestablish the pain. The pattern had to be the same: make a mistake and lose the girl. If the woman died or went away or rejected me, I'd be free again to wallow in those dirty images of self, other experiences where I was humiliated, rejected, degraded. The louder the acclaim, the stronger my urge to overcome the interruption. Of course, I only used women I liked for my dark purpose, since the rejection had to be painful. Sober I didn't want those nice women or anyone else rejecting me. When it came to me that morning in Iowa City what I was doing, I could have exploded with fear.

Since then I've had little trouble, but I have had time to think about success and the problems it can cause. And I've thought much about American poets, including several I know personally. I've come to a few conclusions, none well developed, and for the most part intuitive and far from final.

What triggered all this is a passage I reread recently in *The Dyer's Hand*. I love that book and I reread it every so often even though generally I don't like to read. Auden says:

> The sudden paralysis or drying up of the creative power occurs to artists everywhere but nowhere, perhaps, more frequently than in America; nowhere else are there so many writers who produced one or two books in their youth and then nothing. I think one reason for this may be the dominance of the competitive spirit in the American ethos. A material good like a washing machine is not a unique good but one example of a kind of good; accordingly one washing machine can be compared with another and judged better or worse. The best, indeed the only, way to stimulate the production of better washing machines is by competition. But a work of art is not a good of a certain kind but a unique good so that, strictly speaking, no work of art is comparable to another. An inferior washing machine is preferable to no washing machine at all, but a work of art is either acceptable, whatever its faults, to the individual who encounters it or unacceptable, whatever its merits. The writer who allows himself to become infected by the competitive spirit proper to the production of material goods so that, instead of trying to write *his* book, he tries to write one which is better than somebody else's book is in danger of trying to write the absolute masterpiece which will eliminate all competition once and for all and, since this task is totally unreal, his creative powers cannot relate to it, and the result is sterility.
>
> In other and more static societies than in the United States an individual derives much of his sense of identity and value from his life-membership in a class—the particular class is not important—from which neither success nor failure, unless very spectacular, can oust him, but, in a society where any status is temporary and any variation in the individual's achievement alters it, his sense of his personal value must depend—unless he is a religious man—largely upon what he achieves: the more successful he is, the nearer he comes to the ideal good of absolute certainty as to his value;

the less successful he is, the nearer he comes to the abyss of nonentity.

From The Dyer's Hand (Vintage Books Edition, 1942),
pp. 331–332.

This may be valid insight. I don't know. But for poets, exactly the opposite may be true, at least in some cases. If one writes because basically he feels worthless unless he does, then the feelings of worthlessness become indistinguishable from the impulse to write. When people tell a young poet he is good, they may be doing him some disservice because they are telling him he is not worthless and unwittingly they are undercutting what to him is his need to write. I'm not suggesting that we run around telling young poets how awful they are to insure they keep on writing. I'm fatalistic about writing. I think writers just go ahead and do it, whatever happens. But I know of cases other than mine where the poet's behavior has been adversely affected by "success." Yes, I really am great and everything I put down is great so I don't have to work hard anymore. Yes, I am great and can treat fellow human beings anyway I like. No, I am not great. I am unworthy of all this praise and once they see how outrageous I really am they'll leave me alone and I can get back to writing. I am great and will be a part of literature, therefore I must change my style to insure growth worthy of an artist of stature. In the last case, of course, the writing itself is being affected and that's bad. If the poet has a choice between writing the same poem over and over, being monotonous and boring, and willing style changes so that every poem of every book is new and different, being novel and eclectic (styleless), he is far better off being boring and monotonous. If the style is honest, it won't change any faster than the personality—not very fast at all. Most good poets are quite boring read very long at one sitting.

It would be ideal if some system could be developed that could determine a writer's capacity for success and then just enough acclaim, money, whatever, could be doled out to keep the writer going.

Two American short stories: Hemingway's "Soldier's Home" and Faulkner's "Barn Burning." In Hemingway's story, the protagonist, Krebs, is by birth and background an insider who, as a result of experience and his own sensitivity, feels alienated and outside. In Faulkner's story, the protagonist, Snopes, a little boy, is by birth and background an outsider who wants desperately to be in, to be a part of what, from his disadvantageous position, seems a desirable life. His father is criminally insane and in his own mind can justify anything he does. Snopes is torn between loyalty to his father and a desire to protect "decent people" from his father's viciousness. At the end, he informs on his father and as a result the father is killed while committing a crime.

Not so much from birth and circumstance, but by virtue of how they feel about both themselves and their relationships with the world as revealed in their poems, nearly all modern American poets see themselves (or really are) either Krebs or Snopes.

Krebs	*Snopes*
William Carlos Williams	Hart Crane
John Crowe Ransom	T. S. Eliot
Wallace Stevens	Theodore Roethke
e. e. cummings	Robert Lowell
Ezra Pound	William Stafford
Richard Wilbur	James Wright
W. S. Merwin	Galway Kinnell
Stanley Kunitz	E. A. Robinson
James Dickey	Louise Bogan
Allen Ginsberg	A. R. Ammons

I could list others, but I'd be cheating even worse than I am now. I'd be relying not on their poems for evidence but solely on my personal knowledge of their lives. For example, I know David Wagoner quite well and have a reasonably accurate idea of how he feels about himself, but how he feels about himself is not clearly defined in his rewarding and intelligent poetry.

Of the two, the Snopes poets would probably have a harder

time handling success because the Krebs poets could be successful without feeling that in some terrible way they had violated their heritage. The Krebs poets would not feel that their heritage had some deep emotional claims on their loyalties. They could write their best poems without fingering their fathers. The Krebs poets would also tend to feel that if something is wrong in their relationships with the world, the fault might not be entirely their own.

For all the possible differences, both groups would find success hard to adjust to. For a Krebs poet, success could mean accepting values he knows are phony. In a Snopes poet, success could mean he has cast aside all those people, including himself, whom he believes are doomed to failure and whom he continues to love. In both cases, the obvious extreme result would be self-hatred, and possibly creative impotency.

I'm not sure any of this is defensible and I suppose I don't care. Like things occur to me and I throw them out.

I know this is true: "success" is less important than how the poet feels about his work. People who don't write can probably never understand this. We are all babies and we love good reviews, applause after our readings, compliments—expecially from people we respect—money, fame, even if those things are sometimes frightening. But the way one feels when he has finished a poem he likes is what finally endures. And to look back over your work and be able to say, whatever else, it is mine and it is as honest as I could be then—that is worth all the pain you went through to do it. If it is good, that is for others to say, and if they say it, it is delicious topping.

James Wright

❧

I THINK I met him in a café. He was seated and I was standing. Someone was seated across from him. We said how much we admired each other's work and went on too long until he made some wisecrack about how silly we were being. That broke the ice.

I'm surprised to find that *The Green Wall* was published as late as 1957, surprised because I was jealous of Jim's success and fame and by 1957 I should have known better. Once I got to know him, my jealousy seemed ridiculous. Ultimately I would realize that all jealousy is ridiculous. But for a brief time I resented James Wright—four years younger than me and already an established poet. What was worse, he deserved his reputation. I realized that when I read *The Green Wall*. I knew nothing then of the pressures of "success," especially on someone like Jim. The luckiest thing that ever happened to me was the obscurity I wrote in for many years.

Theodore Roethke, my wife and I were invited for dinner at the Wrights'. Libby served ham, boiled potatoes, vegetables, bread and salad. Roethke prided himself on being a gourmet, and I worried about what he would say to such a plain meal. (He had once remarked about "the swill served by Seattle hostesses" and that utterance had found its way back to a very fine cook who only a few days before had had him to dinner. She never forgave him and years later when she was into voodoo she took credit for Roethke's death.) I was relieved when Roethke simply said, "Very good, Libby." Later we got into a discussion on writing poems. I remember Jim saying, "It's rhythm finally that makes it work, isn't it?" Roethke nodded.

Gooseprairie, Washington, on the bank of the Bumping River. Jim, Libby, my first wife and I rented a large cabin there. Jim had no interest in fishing, but Libby went with me to the river and we caught several small trout. Libby remarked on how strongly they pulled on the line. That night we cooked the fish. Soon after dinner, three elk appeared in the meadow outside the cabin. We stood on the porch and marveled at their dignity, their long necks erect as they ran off slowly and proudly with their sure gait.

That night we drank all our beer, which was plenty. Jim and I talked about humor writers. Eventually we discussed Benchley. We agreed Thurber and Perelman were more polished artists, but Benchley seemed funnier, one who revealed the absurdity of everyday existence. He was also insidious. We started quoting him from memory, and couldn't stop. Though we soon ran out of quotes, we went on, repeating passages over and over. Our laughter seemed like it would never stop. We were howling. Tears ran down our faces. We never tired of Benchley stories, no matter how often we told them.

The next morning, we went to a local store run by Ed and Zetta Bedford. Like others who live in remote places, they had abandoned gentility years ago. They were neither friendly nor polite. And they charged plenty for beer, knowing we were miles from the next store. On another trip with other friends, I once stopped Ed Bedford, who was driving in the mountains, and asked directions to the Upper Bumping River. He immediately started to yell at me angrily: What in hell was I doing up there. I had no business fishing the Upper Bumping when the Lower Bumping had plenty of fish. The roads were bad and we'd all better get the hell out of there. He had just towed some people out of the mud and damn it he was tired of us city people coming there and causing him trouble.

Bedford only increased my resolve to go on. The fishing that day in the Upper Bumping was splendid.

Jim and I took instant dislike of the Bedfords. For years afterwards we called each other Ed, and our wives Zetta. We grabbed at ploys like the Bedfords, and we hung on with an obsessive grip.

Jim and I liked the humor inherent in hostility. We both loved Alfonso Bedoya (in *Treasure of Sierra Madra*), his voice rising in progressive anger saying, "Badges? What badges? I don't have to show you no stinking badges." We used to say that to each other on occasion, often substituting "Poems" for "badges" or "beers" or "kindness." Jim also was fond of Bogart's line, "They're not putting anything over on Fred C. Dobbs." He loved the absurdity of the name Fred C. Dobbs, the way it implied a lack of distinction.

Somewhere along the way of our early days together in Seattle, we either invented or stole the line, "Get out of the car, and get out of the car fast." We used to say it to each other often, trying to affect the accent of a New York gangster. For some unknown shared personal reason, we found that funny. We seldom tired of anything no matter how often we repeated it.

Jim gave a reading one night at Hartman's Bookstore in the University district. He read a couple of poems by Jean Clower and one of mine. He also read bits from earlier writers he loved, H. L. Mencken, Ring Lardner and I think Robert Benchley. That was typical of him. He was always generous to other writers, known or unknown. I think he was a unique writer in that he loved to read as much as he loved to write, and he had the most genuine appreciation of writing I've ever seen in anyone. He was anything but snobbish, and one of his loves included Max Shulman's *The Feather Merchants,* a popular humorous book about World War II and a soldier who stayed in the States for the duration. It didn't bother Jim that the "literary merits" of what he read and loved were not up to the standards presumed by his profession. Reading was too important to bother with "good taste."

My wife and I took Jim, Libby and their son Franz to our favorite spot, Lake Kapowsin. It was natural for us to want to share places we loved with others. But in our innocence, we failed to recognize that not everyone's sensibility was the same. Some people we took there looked on that Lake with disdain or disinterest. The Wrights didn't let us down. They loved it too.

We picnicked at a table above the lake. When Jim sat on one end of a bench, it started to tilt and he caught himself awkwardly on one hand and giggled. I still couldn't interest him in fishing but he did go out in the row boat with me, and together we admired the dark water, so rich it fed new young trees that grew out of dead logs. The mossed stumps, the cat-tails and the redwinged blackbirds that perched in those cat-tails and swayed with them, the monster heron who climbed from some obscure place in the acres of rushes and reeds and authoritatively swept over the water. That bird had a right to feel superior, and we knew it.

On the way home, as we neared the U.S. Naval facility at Pier 91 in Seattle, Franz, perhaps five at the time, suddenly shouted, "Look. Look. It's our country's flag." Jim and I said that to each other whenever we saw an American flag. Like other obsessively repeated private jokes, it never failed to amuse us.

I suppose because we were both from working class back-grounds and because we felt the consequences of those back-grounds in ourselves, we favored stylish, graceful, near-elegant Sugar Ray Robinson over that rough Utah miner, Gene Full-mer. A mutual friend, from a far different background, favored Fullmer. Jim and I watched the fight at my place. Fullmer was tough. He had never been knocked down. He looked like you couldn't knock him down with a top maul.

I can't recall the round. Robinson was keeping his right hand busy with a series of short chops and short hooks to Fullmer's face. Fullmer was blocking the blows well. Suddenly Robinson, who must have shifted his weight to his left foot, caught Fullmer on the chin with what looked like a short left upper-cut. The blow didn't seem all that powerful (Robin-son's knockout punches always seemed too smooth to be any-thing but light taps) but Fullmer stopped for a moment, then tumbled over. Jim and I were screaming as the count neared ten. We exploded with joy when the ten came. We danced. We sang. We laughed. Mostly we laughed and traded our own descriptions of what had just happened.

A mutual friend, who supported Fullmer, was a dreadful needler and Jim couldn't wait to phone him. The barrage went on for some time. I remember Jim saying, "Don't give me that shit. Next you'll be telling me it was a tank job."

We also saw the second Robinson-Bobo Olson fight, I think. Perhaps we just talked about it afterward. Robinson put Olson away with a similar move, shifting his weight to his left foot and throwing a quick left that seemed like nothing more than a crisp, light blow. Jim said more than once that Olson fell asleep on his feet. It was a good description. Olson didn't fall so much as he crumbled, didn't crumble so much as he slowly melted down into the canvas. That was the second time Robinson knocked Olson out, and both fights came after Olson had been knocked out by Archie Moore, when he had added some pounds and tried to fight light heavyweight. Jim was sure Olson had never recovered from the Moore knockout. "Moore changed Olson's jaw to glass," Jim told me. Jim once told me that he'd rather write the poems of—I can't remember what poet he was in love with at the time—than do anything else except win the heavyweight championship of the world.

If you saw the old graveyard in Mukilteo, Washington, and didn't feel the urge to write a poem, you probably had no soul. The graveyard was only one vacant lot, next to a big white house with red trim. Most of the people buried there were children or Chinese who had died in the early part of the century. A few tall pines grew at the back edge, and beyond that the land fell off to railroad tracks below and the sea beyond the railroad tracks. I wondered once what Valéry would have made of that graveyard and that sea.

I took Ken Hanson there, but I think someone else took Jim. I don't remember being there with him. Anyway, the three of us ended up with Mukilteo poems. We decided to try to publish them together. How we decided on that I don't know, for Jim had left Seattle by then. I think it was in the late fifties and Jim had taken his first teaching position at the University of Minnesota.

Ken and I asked Jim if he would handle the submission. We agreed to a common title, settling on Ken's "Graves at Mukilteo." Ken felt, as I did, that since Jim's reputation was soaring and we were unknown, that his submitting the poems increased our chances of getting the three in print together. In one letter, I suggested in my shameful ambitious way that Jim try *The New Yorker* first. Jim had been in *The New Yorker* and so had Ken. I hadn't but I was sure I wanted to be.

Jim turned the idea down. He sent me a letter and said

that he was sure my lines about a boy getting his first in the tall grass back of Laroway and Wong (invented names on gravestones) would insure rejection by *The New Yorker.* "*The New Yorker*," he wrote, "just automatically assumes that their readers neither fuck nor die." Later he got them taken by the now long defunct *New Orleans Poetry Journal.*

Twenty years later, J. D. Reed, James Welch and I would try the same thing again. This time the subject was a bar in Dixon, Montana, and the title agreed on would be mine, "The Only Bar In Dixon." And where else would they appear but in *The New Yorker.*

One of Jim's favorite stories, one he told me several times, was about a radio program he'd heard one night late while riding in a car in Pennsylvania. It seems that a radio station in Clint, Texas, had a powerful transmitter located across the border in Mexico. Since the transmitter was outside the U.S., the FCC had no control over what the station broadcast. The commercials were the pits, according to Jim. That particular night the powerful station was coming in clear in Pennsylvania and an oily voiced announcer was giving a pitch for a porous plastic figurine of Jesus. The figurine was hollow and had a cork in the top of Christ's head. The accouncer's big line was, "Pour beet juice in Christ and he bleeds for you." Jim would repeat that line several times, imitating the announcer's voice and drawing out the word, "bleeds." Then he'd start to giggle at the tastelessness of it and say, "Bottom of the barrel. Bottom of the damned barrel."

It was while we were living in a rented brick house in early 1960 that Jim returned from Minneapolis to defend his Ph.D. thesis, a brilliant one on Dickens. He stayed with us for a month. He was drinking more than I'd even seen him drink and he talked ceaselessly. He found a record he liked in our collection, something by Delius, and he played it over and over every moment he was in the house. At times he was great fun, but of course he was also trying, telling the same stories over and over, playing the same record for eight or ten hours at a stretch.

He came home one day from his thesis defense, and soon after, when he was drunk, kept saying, "I made it. I really made it." He got hung up that night on a review he'd published, a most favorable review, of a poet who, he'd learned after the review came out, suffered from cerebral palsy. He was afraid people would think he knew about the poet's condition before he wrote the review and so had written the review out of kindness or perhaps sentimentality. I argued that he had, after all, commented only on the poems and had used quotes from those poems to support his approval of the book. I couldn't see how the poet's health had anything to do with it. Somewhere during that long evening, I must have gotten through because, as he was about to go to bed, having just washed down a fried egg sandwich with a big glass of "dago red" in a most sloppy hedonistic way, egg and wine coursing down his chin, he suddenly screamed, "You're right. You're right. What the hell has cerebral palsy to do with poetry. Dear (poet's name), fuck you." My wife and I went to bed giggling.

He stayed on, playing the Delius constantly. He seldom stopped either talking or reading aloud from some book. To survive, it was necessary to ignore him and the music at times, to blot it all out—the same music, the same talk, the same reading, again and again. A few times we made excuses, left the house with Jim in it, and made our way to a tavern where we could talk with each other and where the juke box had more than one tune to play.

He was there when we were evicted, two sad young people who couldn't fit in a world of well-kept lawns and revered gardens and nice clean houses. We found a house, not far away, but old, wooden, rundown, in a neighborhood that didn't take itself seriously. Students, laborers and old poor retired people lived there, people who didn't care how we lived. When Jim saw it, he said, "It's more like us." I felt good he'd included himself.

A few friends came to help us move. Jim drank wine and read aloud from some book while the rest of us carried out boxes and boxes of books and records, and our few other possessions. Our friends shot Jim dirty looks as they struggled by with loads or came back for more. He was oblivious to the situation, that he was the only one not doing any work. Jim and I shared that too, a distaste, even a fear of physical work. I remember when they had moved, Libby had done all the packing. She also had to do the driving as Jim never learned to drive a car. At least he hadn't yet in the early sixties. I believe Jim, like me, felt acute anxiety when faced with physical work. I'm still that way. When I mow the lawn, I do it so fast I wear myself out and end up panting and sweating. I could never paint a house. I can't pace myself, couldn't find the patience. It isn't laziness. It's an inability to work calmly and easily, a desire to have the job done and out of the way.

Jim stayed on a few days in our new find. We were far more relaxed. Not only was the junky old house "more like us," but our landlord and landlady, whom I had known slightly before, had gone to California. The landlord had to run from a serious traffic violation committed while drunk, one of many on his record, rather than stand trial before a new traffic judge out to make a name for himself by handing out harsh sentences. Our landlord faced six months in jail if he didn't leave the state. All we had to do was mail the rent every month. Besides, the rent was considerably less than that for the brick home and we had more money for the essentials, beer and what Jim called "That great American philosopher, James Beam."

The day he left, we took him to the train, relieved he was going. He had found the Delius almost the moment we'd moved into the new rental and his behaviour hadn't changed in the new surroundings. Yes, we were glad he was finally going. Or were we? An unexpected thing happened in the railroad station. We stood there yelling old jokes, jokes really only between us, things like "Look. Look. It's our country's flag." or "Get out of Seattle, Bedford, and get out fast." And we were still yelling them when the train pulled out. Then he was gone and we suddenly turned to each other, my wife and I, and shrugged with a sadness we both felt. We didn't have to say it: some winning energy, tiresome yet important, had just left our life. We felt empty now that he was gone.

I saw him a few months later, on purpose. It was in the fall of 1960. My first book had been accepted by Minnesota Press, thanks to Jim. When he found out I'd submitted it there, Jim walked into the Minnesota Press offices and told them he strongly supported my work. I suspect that's why they took it.

I had decided to use my vacation (I was working at Boeing Company) to see Jim and Libby. I took the train to Minneapolis and a cab to their house. He and Libby were buying the house and he told me that 'owning' a home was a great relief— the idea that no one could throw you out. It was a real source of stability, he told me, and we, my wife and I, should try it. Stability was important to him, I knew, for by then he'd been hospitalized with a nervous breakdown. Libby too had been having problems and, as I recall, had been taking electric shock treatments though she wasn't taking them when I was there. Their house was old, plain and homey. Jim took me to the English department and introduced me to some of his colleagues. I sensed some strain in some of them, uneasy feelings in Jim's presence.

One night we went to a faculty party, and it was there I began to feel Jim's alienation from the others. One young man was particularly disdainful of Jim, and of me as well. He made no effort to hide his sneers when Jim or I spoke. He was in every sense a bourgeois. In him I saw the one quality I've seen in many minor academics and cannot find sympathy for. He had acquired knowledge not out of love of the works he'd read, but to appear superior to others. That he felt superior to Jim and to me was only too evident. I remember his name and learned only recently he has died. I have to add that I've been lucky enough in the last few years to know some of the great academics, such as J. Hillis Miller and Louis Martz, and I've never seen in them any trace of that presumed superiority. Maybe that's why they are superior. Whatever, I saw in that young man the difficulty Jim must have had as a member of a university faculty.

Jim stayed up drinking back at his house and once I woke up to go to the bathroom. It must have been four in the morning and though I was groggy, I remember hearing Jim on the phone. He was talking to a colleague and was quite hostile. In my fog I worried about him and his future.

I went to a class of Jim's and heard him lecture. He was good, I thought, and the students seemed to like him. I left Minneapolis shortly after that and would not see Jim again for seven years.

A year or two later, out west, Jim Dickey told us that Jim Wright had been fired at Minnesota. It was an odd dismissal, sudden and complete. No extra year to look for another job, normal in such cases.

I'm hazy on this next bit. I remember I was in Bloomington, Indiana, and had received a letter from Robert Bly, with a copy of the letter from Allan Tate to Jim, specifying the reasons for Jim's dismissal. Bly urged me to write on Jim's behalf and felt it had been Tate's duty to back Jim and protect Jim, the way Heilman had protected Roethke at Washington. I tried to write a letter but felt futile. It bothered me that I didn't know what had happened. For although Tate's letter was specific enough, I didn't believe the reasons he gave were the real reasons Jim had been let go. I'd been in the work-a-day world long enough to know that people are seldom dismissed for incompetence. They are usually dismissed because other people don't like them, though incompetence is given as the official reason. Besides, I'd heard Jim lecture and didn't think he was incompetent, despite Tate's letter and the "evidence."

The next time I saw Jim was in 1967 in New York, where he had taken a job at Hunter College. He had remarried and I met Annie for the first time. Jim and I were both quite drunk and I recall very little of that brief meeting except that he told me they had been right at Minnesota to fire him. He didn't elaborate. He simply said he'd deserved it.

1972 was a great year at the University of Montana. Allen Ginsberg, Gary Snyder and Mark Strand read there that year, and then Jim came, not to read, just to visit. He seemed much as he had been in Seattle in 1960. He drank constantly and he played one record, a Stan Getz recording, all day and all night until he went to bed. He was on his way to give the Roethke reading in Seattle but generously offered to read for nothing at Montana. I think we got him some money at the last minute.

When he awoke in the morning, he would drink a water tumbler full of straight bourbon. Then he would return to bed for two more hours. His energy was at the usual high level and he talked ceaselessly. I had been living alone for eight years. I'd had to stop drinking the year before Jim's arrival, and at times had to block him out to keep my sanity, it seemed. One Sunday, to escape his constant chatter I turned on the TV and watched a movie. He kept talking but I put the volume high enough to crowd him out and directed all my attention to the film. At one point in the evening he suddenly cried, "Oh, my God, Dick. I can't stop talking. No wonder I have no friends."

During that visit I told him of a minor crackup I'd had at Iowa the year before and how ashamed I'd felt afterward. "I've had six," he said. I was astounded. I'd never known Jim had had six breakdowns. And all had resulted in hospitalization. I'd seen so little of him over the years I had no idea of the crippling depths of his anguish.

He would walk around the house naked for hours. "In the army," he said, "They called me Adam in the Barracks."

Jim said a lot of things that visit. I remember some of them well. He was genuinely happy in his new marriage and he hoped I'd marry again too. "It's hard to find someone who knows what being a poet means," he said. "Annie knows. She's rare."

Once he started talking about the older generation of poets, Tate, Ransom, mostly. "We really did something, Dick, our generation. We really made a break from all those guys and that stuff they peddled." He also told me, while we were mentioning our divorces, that he felt, looking back on it, that he and Libby had to get married to escape Martin's Ferry. Neither of them could have done it alone.

The morning of the day he was to read, I found an article in the newspaper about a man who had gone into St. Peter's in Rome and started beating on Michaelangelo's *Pietà* with a hammer. He'd managed to damage it before they could stop him. I mentioned it to Jim who was shaving. Later, when I was shaving, I knew he was reading the same article because he yelled, "Oh, Jesus Christ, does he have to be named Lazlo Toth?"

Jim gave a good reading that afternoon. Students and faculty alike loved it. He was in good form though somewhat drunk. In his remarks between poems he indicated once that he did not believe in God. That was a typical attitude in many poets of my generation, especially those who had come from working class backgrounds and who had suffered the boredom and repression of churches that today seem long out of date.

After the reading, a young woman approached Jim and started arguing with him. She was, she declared, a Christian. Her accent was Scandinavian, perhaps Swedish. Her religious fanaticism reminded me of some dotty old women in my hometown during the depression, especially a Mrs. Morley who couldn't talk about anything except Christ, Our Saviour. Jim surprised me by inviting the young woman to come with us.

She didn't let up in the car. How could we survive without accepting Christ? Only Jesus would lead to true happiness. Then I did something very unusual for me. I suddenly pulled the car over and ordered her out. (I didn't think to say, "Get out of the car, and get out of the car fast.") Jim reproached me a bit. "You shouldn't have done that, Dick."

I replied, "I had to listen to that shit when I was a kid. I sure as hell don't have to listen to it now."

"It's important to them," he said quietly.

Jim had read in the afternoon because that night a well-known scholar and social critic was scheduled to speak. By the time I got Jim fed at some local restaurant we were late to the lecture. We didn't get to hear most of the talk. When we arrived, the speaker was advising people to change their lives. If you have a job in the Post Office, quit and become a fireman for a while. I sensed Jim's hostility and realized I should not have brought him. He was drunk and the speaker was upsetting him.

When time came for questions from the floor Jim was on his feet instantly, shouting, "Have you ever been to———" he gave some address in New York that sounded as if it could be Harlem.

The speaker cooly answered that the address sounded specious to him.

"It may be specious to you, but if you go there and start advising people on their lives you'll get answered with a knife,"

Jim screamed. I knew what was bugging him. The speaker had presumed that workingclass people enjoyed the same cavalier mobility as upper-middle-class people. That they could just change jobs with no emotional complications. Jim had seen his father enslaved to a lousy factory job during the depression and knew what terrible fears bind people to jobs. I knew too. For years I assumed that if I lost a job I might very well never find another.

But I felt a little embarrassed that the speaker suddenly found himself in an inhospitable situation in Montana. My colleagues told me afterward that Jim's outburst was understandable and that his reaction was justified. Jim told me later that he resented the condescension with which the speaker had treated the Montana audience. "These are sophisticated people here," Jim said, "and he had no right to take a superior attitude." I wasn't sure Jim was right. The speaker had struck me as smooth and a bit cold, but I'm not truly sensitive to condescension and so had missed that, if in fact it had been there at all.

Jim turned out to be a big hit and several people said to me at the party later, "I like your friend." I spoke to the lecturer briefly and tried to be as gracious as I could without seeming to patronize him for I was still embarrassed and, while I couldn't agree with the substance of his talk, I did want the man to feel good about Montana hospitality. Jim, at some point, sidled up to him and said, "Have you ever had a job?"

Until he left, Jim went on with the same pattern, playing the Stan Getz record over and over. Getting out of bed in the morning, drinking a water glass full of straight bourbon, then going back to bed for a couple of more hours. He attended my workshop, which I held at my house, and in answer to a question from a student, loudly announced that Roethke had been a "prick." Roethke did have an unfortunate way of putting students down or dismissing them, and I wondered if the speaker had, with what Jim termed condescension, reminded him of some painful memories involving Ted.

Alone with him for hours at a time in my house, I couldn't help noticing a peculiar change in him that had happened over the years. When he talked about his past he seemed to be trying to replay old pain, but there was something phony about it, as if the pain were no longer there to be relieved, though the anguish in his remark about having no friends was real. I wondered if a doctor hadn't made some break-through. I felt the very real hope that he was in much better shape than he realized. Now if he could reduce his drinking. It was killing him.

A bad thing happened during Jim's final night there. He tried direct dialing a Seattle number and in his drunkenness kept getting it wrong. I asked him to call the operator to get "credit" for the wrong numbers he'd dialed. He couldn't seem to do that right, either. I said, "Here, I'll do it." I must have let some irritation show in my voice because he suddenly flew into a rage. He glared at me and stood with clenched fists and threatened me. "No one talks to me like that," he yelled. Only an hour before he had bragged about slugging a colleague at a party in Minneapolis, and I had no doubt he wanted to slug me then. In a disdainful voice he offered me a hundred dollars to help pay my telephone bill.

I was frightened, but somehow managed to placate him. I assured him everything was all right. It was the only time the strain of being sober and alone in the house long days with a drunk had shown in my voice. I felt terrible about it and, after I got him to bed, I sat there shaking.

The next day I took him to the plane. He was drunk again by the time we left the house. At the airport I watched him board the plane, his legs slightly spread to insure his balance as he climbed the aerostairs. I believed I would never see him alive again.

Not so many months later Jim published a long glowing essay on my work in the *American Poetry Review*. I was touched and grateful. He was too honest to say anything he didn't mean. But I couldn't help wondering if he was trying to make up for that bad scene his last night in Missoula. I hoped he didn't feel he had to.

I next saw him in December 1975 (I think). I gave a reading at the YMHA Poetry Center, with Thom Gunn. I didn't know Jim was in the audience. I wanted to give a good reading because several people I admired were there—Richard

Howard who introduced us, Stanley and Laura Kauffmann, Stanley and Jane Moss, and Jeff Marks who had come from Philadelphia. I knew where those good people were sitting, and though I was reading for them maybe more than for those I didn't know, I avoided looking at them while I read—I suppose I glanced once or twice at Richard Howard who sat in the first row and so could be easily seen despite the lights that made much of the audience obscure from the stage.

After the reading, people collected in the lobby and Gunn and I went out to greet our fans. To my surprise Jim and Annie were there. Jim told me he didn't drink now. I kept hugging them. I hugged them over and over. We said almost nothing.

The next time I saw Jim was the last time. January 1980, at The White House. Mrs. Carter had invited American poets to a national celebration honoring American poets. I'm not sure how the poets invited had been selected.

After hearing Philip Levine, Maxine Kumin and Sterling Brown read, I went upstairs with the others to meet the President, the First Lady and Mrs. Mondale. I was dazzled by it all, not just the White House, or meeting the President—though I had never met an American President before—but by the numbers of poets I admire. It was manic. I would start saying hello to one poet and another would be on my back: Hey, Dick. Reporters asked me questions—I was amazed they knew who I was. A glamorous blonde society lady talked to me at length about something or other. But mostly, poets. Seeing all those remarkable people reminded me more strongly than ever that poets are people I like. With a few exceptions, poets seem to me among the best people I've met. I was dizzy with it all, happy and talking too fast in my excitement, not making much sense I suppose. Just sort of babbling. Not really in control.

Then someone tapped my shoulder. It was Jim, Annie was behind him. He looked fine but his voice sounded terribly strange, like it was coming from another throat, almost as if he were acting as a dummy to a ventriloquist somewhere nearby.

"Dick," he said, "I don't want you to hear any rumors and

wonder what is going on. I have throat cancer." The news would have been unbelievable anywhere. There, it was bewildering as well. "They'll operate in about three weeks and they expect to get it all. It will be all right."

In that swirl of poets and reporters and politicians, I can't recall how long we talked or how we got separated. A couple of months later I came into my house in Missoula and Matt, my stepson, told me Jim's death had just been announced on National Public Radio.

I should let this go at that. But I don't want to. I have to say that Jim Wright did a lot of things for me and I know that I'll go out inconsolable because I did far less for him. Now there's no way I can make up for it. I wrote three poems for him, one after he was gone. None were worthy of him and that's why I haven't included any of them here. So, I want to say, I wish I had done something for him. But then I remember a thing Jim's Grandmother used to say, and he was fond of quoting, "You wish in one hand and you shit in the other and see which one fills up the fastest."

No one carried his life more vividly inside him, or simultaneously in plain and in eloquent ways used the pain of his life to better advantage. What maims others often beyond repair maimed him too, but in some miraculous way it also nourished his great talent. It was miraculous too that his obsessive repetitive mind never limited his artistry.

In 1963, my first wife and I found ourselves in the Greyhound Bus Station in Wheeling, West Virginia. When I think of Jim I sometimes also think of that depressing place, the pathetic looking people, poor and discouraged. I knew that Martin's Ferry was across the river, but I couldn't see it. I asked someone where it was, and the man pointed upstream and said it was just around the bend. I looked a long time across the river as if my gaze might penetrate the bank that stood between me and the place where Jim had started, and just once I would see it.

But the bank held solid and firm, and now I let that bus station say a lot about where Jim came from and why it was necessary for him to leave, to get away. And why he did get away. And why he didn't.

Last Words to James Wright

I'll call you Bedford, Ed. That's what you called me.
The plane lifts off the runway, circles left across
the mountains, straightens and heads east.
I'm reading in New York and Zetta's coming.
Ed was you, was me, our private ploy.
He lasted 30 years. Now one of Ed is gone.
And what's one Ed alone? You told me January 3
they'd operate in time and damn it, Jim,
I took that as a promise. I really did.
Ed Bedford, you bastard, you lied.

This time, the branch is broke. In early work
you urged the criminal, the derelict,
the dispossessed to run between the stars.
You wanted words to sing the suffering on
and every time you asked the words came willing.
I'm toasting you in heaven, four miles over Billings.
When I see Zetta, your wife
I'll kiss her. I'll call her Annie for luck.
I'm scared as hell nothing's going to work.
Ed Bedford, you bastard, you lied.

You're the only man I knew outside of me
quoted Robert Benchley, same passages in fact.
You need every laugh you get
when your home town's stocked with broken souls.
You left and couldn't leave that dirty river town
where every day the dirty river rolls.
I'll toast you on the Minneapolis layover.
As Rodney Dangerfield puts it, Ed:
"It's not easy, life. Not easy at all."
Make it scotch and dirty river water.

Now the New York leg, non stop. The midwest
moves back in the dark, now and then

the dull electric burn of town, the dark again.
Off left, some shining major city. Remember, Jim,
when they seemed glamorous, filled with magnificent women
you'd never find at home. That and the need to run,
the gift that sent a raw boy non stop
over a green wall, over a green world,
star to star, buddy to dubious saints.
What poet ever found a synonym for shame.

Those saints in solitary where the dirty river rolls,
they know each life clicks off and on,
the off darker than a shabby habit,
the on more blinding than a stray star in the kitchen.
Jesus, Jim, the starker the fact I'm facing
the less I want to sing. Sorry, Ed,
to be so godddam serious. We've got your poems.
We've all got at least two names.
But which one gives and keeps his word?
Ed Bedford, you bastard, you lied.

Ed Bedford, you bastard, you died.
What a chill. We circle the Statue of Liberty.
I feel no liberty at all on the final approach.
I feel a little drunk and a lot more empty,
like passing through some unknown factory town
knowing it must be home.
Be glad of the green wall you climbed across one day.
Be glad as me.
I forgive you, Ed, even if I did swear never.
What's a lie between Eds? What's one more dirty river?

Making Certain It Goes On, p. 423.

New York tour, 1974

1979

With Richard Blessing (left) and David Wagoner (right), May, 1980.

James Wright creating a curse for Ed Bedford (PHOTO COURTESY ANNE WRIGHT AND JOHN UNTERECKER).

Montana, Fall, 1981 (PHOTO COURTESY PAUL ZARZYSKI).

With stepdaughter
Melissa Hansen, July,
1974 (PHOTO COURTESY
IRVING BROUGHTON).

With stepson Matthew Hansen, 1979, at the cabin on the Teton River, Montana.

With Ripley at La Push, Washington, August, 1980.

With stepson Matthew Hansen, University of Montana, June 1982; Matthew has just graduated with High Honors; Hugo has just received the Distinguished Scholar Award.

Honorary doctorate, Montana State University, June, 1982.

He Is the
One Who Waves

(—"Salt Water Story")

Dialogue with Richard Hugo

WILLIAM KITTREDGE: Driving up here I was telling Ripley I felt very unsure about doing this, and she said that you felt your mind had changed after the operation. Is that true?

RICHARD HUGO: In the poems.

KITTREDGE: In the poems?

HUGO: I don't know why I find myself writing poems based on fiction, more and more. I fictionalize things and then write as if they actually happened. They sound almost like narrative poems. I suppose it was a way to get going again. I had post-operative depression and I also hadn't written for quite a while before I went into the surgery. After surgery, for months I felt: What's the use of doing anything. I'm told this is the usual reaction to major surgery. Now I find I am doing different kinds of things than I had done before. They seem like slow moving narrative poems.

KITTREDGE: Do you think you're searching for a kind of story?

HUGO: I hope not. I think perhaps I'm writing a little bit like a man named John Bensko, whom I chose as a winner in the Yale Series of Younger Poets. I make things up, and then write as if they actually happened.

KITTREDGE: Ray Carver was drinking pretty heavily and he quit. He said he thought nobody just quit drinking to start writing again. He had the same kind of depression when he quit drinking. Did that happen to you years ago?

HUGO: When I quit drinking? I can't remember; it was so long ago, but probably, I think, there were several days where there are chemical reactions setting in and that causes depression. But once that was over, I found it was almost like materials had piled up inside of me for years and years awaiting release. At the time I was drinking, I was down to five or six poems a year and then all of a sudden I burst loose and I had that "hot" streak—eight or nine years—you remember? That probably will be the most prolific time I will ever have as far as poems are concerned.

KITTREDGE: You were coming up with a new poem every couple of days—terrific stuff.

HUGO: Well, thank you, I was satisfied with a lot of those things I was doing. I think a lot of them were pretty good poems, at least for me, and it was almost like I could have written them earlier but I just delayed them. I had stored them all up and then suddenly they were escaping. That's how it seemed.

KITTREDGE: Annick Smith suggested that you had gone through two changes like this, one when you quit drinking and the other one with this operation. Do you feel like there is any resemblance between the two experiences?

HUGO: You mean that she thinks that the operation parallels the experience ten years ago when I stopped drinking. I hadn't thought of it. I think maybe I had better hold that in abeyance while I think about it. That's interesting. There isn't any doubt that they are kind of turning points and they are just about one decade apart, you see. In fact today, oddly enough, is the anniversary of my operation. Right now. This is the 13th, isn't it? I was operated on January 13, 1981.

KITTREDGE: In the morning?

HUGO: No, as a matter of fact it was in the afternoon. It lasted a long time. I was under for six and a half hours.

KITTREDGE: What were your feelings—I suppose terror . . . ?

HUGO: No, I didn't feel any of that. I'll tell you how I got through. I acted as if nothing was happening. I just ignored it. And the doctor, my surgeon, told me that I was a good patient and a bad patient for the same reason. He said I was a good patient because I refused to admit I was sick, and, therefore, I just let them go ahead with their work and didn't give them any problem. On the other hand, I was a very bad patient because since I wouldn't admit I was sick I got extremely impatient because I wasn't getting well faster. And, so that's how I got through it—I just acted like I wasn't sick. There wasn't anything to do anyway. I was in their hands. They have a thing called intensive care after the surgery and they induce amnesia through drugs. I have almost no memory of it at all, but apparently it lasted for two days and two nights, and during that time I spoke with a lot of profanity to one of the nurses who asked my wife if Mr. Hugo wasn't given to extremes. And my wife said, you mean in language, and the nurse said yes, blushing a little bit. I have no memory of that at all, but apparently I spoke just vile language. I mean I wasn't swearing at her, I was just swearing, and apparently at the fates for this and so forth. But I don't remember it. That whole time passed fast because of the drugs, you see. And I was able to give up smoking. It's very easy to give up smoking in a hospital. They just keep bringing you drugs. They bring you much better things than cigarettes. My goodness, they bring you all kinds of goodies. And all of a sudden a week has gone by and you haven't had a cigarette. You realize you don't care anymore. So it's not hard to give up smoking in a hospital while they keep the drugs coming. It might be a little hard after a while to give up the drugs. But whenever you're going to climb the walls—they're very generous—they'll bring you something right away.

KITTREDGE: Tell us what you feel has happened to your writing since the operation.

HUGO: Well, so, far, I have only been able to write poems and one essay which I wrote on request. I haven't heard about that essay, by the way. It seems to have disappeared back east somewhere.

KITTREDGE: What was it?

HUGO: Oh, it was an essay on influences for a book on influences that they asked me to contribute to, and I was awfully pleased they had asked. I think probably most of my influences were the ones everyone had who came up in my generation. I mean, there was Pound and Eliot and Yeats and all those giants in the background. But, I think, also that it may be necessary for a young poet to find a poet he likes who is a little outside the main stream. A poet he can sort of call his own. And for me there was a poet named Bernard Spencer, an English poet who died in the early sixties. His first book, *Aegean Islands and Other Poems,* I liked a great deal, and it remained an influence for a long time. It wasn't only an influence but something I held up as a kind of ideal. It was a book of poems written by someone about a foreign country, about things that happened in a foreign land, and that seemed fresh and different—a very naive and innocent poetry. I mean, he's a bewildered expatriot, that's generally the role he is playing in the poem, and he is constantly surprised by what he finds. It's a beautiful book of poems. Incidentally, his collected poems have just come out from the Oxford University Press, edited by a man named Roger Bowen who wrote the introduction. He's a professor at the University of Arizona.

Spencer wrote a lot of poems of place. I mean not so much of events, but of place. So he was very appealing to me, Spencer. But I could never approximate the way he lets words fall on the page with complete utter innocence. He's a wonderful poet but not very highly thought of in England. He didn't write a great deal. I understand that he was somewhat depressed. I was just looking at the forward here in the book, by Bowen, and it seems he didn't go at it as hard as some other poets.

KITTREDGE: Can you suggest some of your favorites of Spencer's poems?

HUGO: Oh, yes. Oh, yes. "Olive Trees" is a favorite of mine. "Aegean Islands, 1940–41" is one of my favorite poems. "Egyptian Dancer, Shubra," and "Delos." There are some beautiful poems in here. I reprint them in the essay. "Greek Excavations," "Base Town." What lovely, lovely poems some of them were.

Other than that I have just been writing poems. I want to start on a mystery novel. A lot of people want me to. They seem to like that first mystery novel I did, and I would like to do a better job this time because that was—you know—I was a novice, I mean that was my first one. And I didn't know how to do it; I had to cheat a little on the form to get it done. But I think I'd like to play it fair and square this time, and I have been in contact with a forensic pathologist who has come to Missoula and who is in charge of the crime lab. The state crime lab has been established here. It's the first time we have ever had one in Montana. The doctor has taken me around the crime lab and I've talked to people there, and to him. He's a very generous man named Ron Rivers, and I have been particularly interested in skeletal identifications, and he's been very generous about that—how one identifies skeletons. It's amazing what they can tell from bones and how they can tell it and so forth. So, I'm just about set.

KITTREDGE: To get started? That's terrific news.

HUGO: I hope I'm just about set. Well, of course, I can't give the story away. Let's just say I'm going to use the same detective and his same boss, and he'll have the same girlfriend. And so I'll have a set of knowns to work off of. It'll start out in Plains, Montana. It'll go back east to some city, I'm not sure which one yet, and then will come back finally to Plains. I kind of think this one may end up in Seattle, but that's all I can tell you.

KITTREDGE: When you say poems, how many poems? I've seen four in *Rocky Mountain Magazine*.

HUGO: Yeah, and I just got one taken by *The New Yorker* and one taken by the *Atlantic*. I have two out now to the *New Republic*, and have three that I haven't submitted sitting around. I'm waiting to decide where to submit those. And I get some requests for poems, but I've become a little greedy about where I send my poems because I have the family and I need the money, and now that higher paying publications will publish me sometimes I tend to submit to them first.

KITTREDGE: You can't be blamed for that, my God.

HUGO: I want the money. It's that simple a matter.

KITTREDGE: I had a friend years ago who used to demand— this was ten years ago—that he get $5.95 at least for a poem because a poem was always worth a bottle of Jim Beam.

HUGO: Jim Dickey had that attitude, you know. I remember when I was an editor of *Poetry Northwest*, he refused to let anyone publish his poems without paying him. And I remember one time I sent him a check, five dollars of my own money, so we could publish one of his poems. There is much to be said for that attitude. I mean there is a price on everything else, and especially, I think, if one lives in a city, especially an eastern city, like New York where you pay for everything. Then it doesn't seem wrong to charge for a poem too. Of course, out here, in the smaller towns in the West, I think we tend to think more in terms of just doing things for nothing. And that's a nice healthy attitude, but not a very profitable one.

KITTREDGE: How do you feel about the notion of poets being more politically involved in society?

HUGO: Well, I mean, you can do that whether you're a poet or not, I suppose. But I don't think that poets are a particular political power. I think they do become so in certain countries. I believe in Russia people are in awe of poets and the poets enjoy a different kind of reputation there. I understand that when a book of poems is published in Russia, it is published in an edition of 100,000 copies and it sells out within a week. I don't know of any poet in America who could sell 100,000 copies in a week. Not in a lifetime.

KITTREDGE: You have any personal feelings of yearnings for that kind of audience?

HUGO: No, not at all. I think maybe unconsciously I do because I notice that I sort of take pride in knowing our Senator and our Governor. And it used to be that I would shy away from people like that. Now I kind of enjoy chatting with them, or feeling that I am worthy of chatting with them.

KITTREDGE: Of course in Montana it's possible.

HUGO: They're lonely too if they're from Montana.

KITTREDGE: I can't imagine chatting with the Governor of Massachusetts. You talk about a novel and you say your new poems have a lot of narrative in them. I was just wondering what the implications of that are, and I was wondering what kind of story it is you are looking for?

HUGO: I seem to want to create a story about a community and measures being taken to insure that this community keeps going and survives. And I want to create a story about an individual who finds his way out of circumstances that point toward a tragic ending, but then to reverse the flow of the story and have the person doing okay at the end. That kind of thing. In other words, the reversal of the old Elizabethan wheel of fortune.

Here's what I try to do. I take a narrative poem but leave out the transitions. You remember that poem in the *Rocky Mountain* called "O-Mok-See at Nine Mile," about the old man looking at his shoes? What happens is that I think I am using a narrative line but allowing the detail to stand firm in a kind of symbolic stance. In other words, the symbolism of the events and the detail become all the starker because the poem itself is written in a narrative framework. I think that's what's happening. At least, I hope that's what's happening. I don't know how well it works. I have a new poem called "Bannerman's Island" about an island that is just up river from the West Point Military Academy. In fact you can see it from the Military Academy. Interesting place. Bannerman was a man who made a fortune from gunrunning and he built a Scottish-style castle on this island. He had bought the island and built a castle on it and then had wild game imported. They would bring over a tiger and let it loose on the island. It was a small island, just a little place on the Hudson River. Then he would go out and hunt this tiger down and kill it. It wasn't exactly what you would call the sport of kings. And I guess they brought elephants in there and lions, and let them loose on this island and this guy would go out and gun them down. But, of course, they had no place to go, you see, no way for them to get away. That island isn't even a quarter of a mile long. There's nothing to it. Just a little island in the Hudson River. It's an attractive subject, of course. It's one of those subjects that I think Stafford would call a bonus of the world. It almost writes its poem for you, given details. And then, of course, to have it sitting there almost in the shadow of this modern military school, which also has a tradition behind it. And the fortress, the armory there high up on the bank of the Hudson, overlooking the Hudson. Lots of material.

KITTREDGE: It sounds very cinematic.

HUGO: In a way I suppose it is. What happens as near as I can tell is that a contrast sets up. In the slow, apparently narrative, style of the language, the symbolic meaning of things becomes even starker because of the contrast of symbolism to this slow narrative rhythm of the line. In other words, a person seems to be speaking almost casually about things. In contrast to the casual language—the casual rhythm of the language—the symbolic meaning seems to become even starker and more vivid. But it doesn't always work and I still have the same problem that I have in other ways of writing—and that is that I tend to fall into too monotonous a form. That is to say, the rhythms tend to set up too monotonous a pattern and so I have to break that.

KITTREDGE: One of the things that strikes me again is how much you have been talking about the juxtaposition of disparate elements. I keep finding in fiction that the real energy comes from a collision, a conflict, you know.

HUGO: Yeah. I understand. In certain kinds of poems—I wrote an elegy for my father and I wrote an elegy for Jim Wright—and in those poems I tend to go back to more standard rhythms—a harder driving kind of rhythm to set up a very strong beat and so forth, which will free me to say certain things and lead me to say certain things. But I find elegies very hard to write. I have written one that I liked fairly well for my father who died a couple of years ago.

KITTREDGE: Getting back to the subject of careers. It's my impression that Roethke became more metaphysical in the last book. Do you think that's true?

HUGO: That might be. I'd have to go back. I haven't looked at Ted's stuff in years and years.

KITTREDGE: I just wondered if there was any impulse to move in that direction yourself.

HUGO: I don't know. I'm only interested in getting the poems. So I don't concentrate on that other matter so much, about whether I'm being more metaphysical or less metaphysical. I don't think about those things, so I couldn't give you a very good answer on that. But I'm sure you're right about Roethke, that there was a change. I'd have to go back. What was his last book?

KITTREDGE: *The Far Field.*

HUGO: *The Far Field* was the last book he did. I tried to teach him many years ago. I didn't do very well. In fact, I find him very hard to teach. Louis Martz teaches him at Yale. Of course Louis Martz is terribly bright about poems, a great scholar and critic, and teacher, and I'm neither. But Martz said that he finds Roethke hard to teach except for the North American Sequence.

KITTREDGE: Why do you think that is?

HUGO: I don't know.

KITTREDGE: It doesn't seem on the surface—to me—what you would call difficult poetry.

HUGO: No. But there is something about them. It's hard to talk about. I think that there are a lot of good poets like that. I think Yeats is hard to teach for that reason. And one reason I think that Stevens enjoys such popularity isn't just that he was a good poet; of course, he was. But that he was kind of a kitchen sink. He gives you a lot to talk about. And, you know, when you're sitting up in a classroom and you've got fifty minutes to fill up, it's better to have a rich flamboyant, esthetic kind of poet like Stevens than it is to have, say, someone like William Carlos Williams who's spare. And I think that one reason Stevens is so well regarded on campus is simply that he's a good poet to teach. For one thing, he's difficult and you can get in there and worry things to death. Whereas with some poets everything seems so spare. Things are left out and what is included seems all on the surface, direct and readily available. I almost feel like saying "here." With Roethke, however, it's a different matter. He is difficult, but I find—I don't know what to say about him exactly. I think it's because you can't exactly say what's happening in his poems.

KITTREDGE: With a poet like Stevens, there are a lot of things to name. With Roethke it's pretty darn difficult to name what in the hell he is talking about exactly?

HUGO: That's right. He's playing games sometimes that he played as a child. That is to say, he's demonstrating ways his mind used to behave when he was a child making up nursery rhymes, trying to recall fears and so forth, and sometimes the jumps get very difficult to follow. Sometimes the language is meant, I think, to approximate manic states. Sometimes he is sane in the poem, and sometimes he isn't, and I think that makes it hard to follow too. I don't think I would ever try to teach Roethke again, except for simpler poems. But there are people who do very well. One problem, as Dick Blessing pointed out in his book on Roethke, is that you can't crawl the lines the way you can in Stevens. That is to say, the new criticism was sort of fashioned to talk about a certain kind of poem and it was the kind of poem you could talk about as if it were a refrigerator. That is to say, if you took it all apart and studied all its parts, then somehow you would understand the whole. It was no good, of course, for a great poem, that is to say for epic poetry. You obviously can't do that with Homer. That would be silly. Roethke was also the kind of poet that you can not crawl the lines and find this meaning or that meaning, as Blessing points out. You can't say, well, let's see if we can understand this poem more fully, because in a way you're never going to understand it more fully. It's a curious sort of poetry, and I think for that reason Roethke may not do as well as Stevens in your university systems because I think he is more difficult to teach.

KITTREDGE: I know that holds true of lots of works of fiction. For instance, one of the things that everybody teaches is *Heart of Darkness*. It's very easy to teach. Take it apart like a Model-T and put it back together again. But nobody teaches *Benito Mereno*, which is a greater work of art, I think, and much more difficult to talk about. It deals with the same thing, really.

What do you think about writing from the perspective of a foreign country?

HUGO: I know that I was disappointed in my Italian book [*Good Luck in Cracked Italian*, 1969]. I wanted to go to a foreign country and write a book that I liked. And the first time I did it, I went back to Italy where I had been in World War II. Now that book didn't have many good poems in it. I think the thing that worked best in its favor was that it had a certain kind of unity to it. In fact, it was probably the most unified book of poems I've ever published. But Gary Thompson, you remember him.

KITTREDGE: Certainly. He was a student here.

HUGO: He told me one time that my trouble as a poet was that when I got in a foreign land I talked only for myself. That when I was in America I talked for a lot of other people as well as for myself. I wasn't aware of that. I couldn't see that much of a difference but I suppose it's there. When I got the invitation from the Guggenheim Foundation to apply and felt, since everything was coming my way, that I was going to get it, I talked to Ripley about it. She showed me pictures of Skye, in Scotland. I thought, well, I've always been disappointed in my book of Italian poems. I like the unity of the book but I didn't think it had very many good poems in it, and I always wanted to do a good book of poems in a foreign setting, outside of America; and Ripley, in the early fifties, had gone to the University of Edinburgh for graduate school. She was studying the Ninth Century Celtic lyric manuscripts, and to facilitate her studies she studied the Gaelic. She then came back. Her father took ill when she was halfway through the program, and she came back and finished up her degree at Montana. But when she was studying Gaelic she went over to Skye to practice, because they speak the Gaelic in streets in towns there. She showed me some pictures of Skye. I liked the looks of the place. It was desolate and bleak and beautiful. Castles in ruin. Rivers and lakes (lochs, if you will). Beautiful sea coasts. I thought, this is for me. So I proposed to go to Skye to do a book of poems if they would give me the money, and they gave me the money so we went to Skye. So I took Melissa and Ripley and we got the Guggenheim and a sabbatical at the same time. That gave us enough money. So we went over and lived on Skye. That's how I came to do the book of Skye poems [*The Right Madness on Skye*, 1980].

There was one thing I believed at the time or at least thought might be true.

KITTREDGE: What is that?

HUGO: If I went to a country where the language around me was not always foreign, where my own language, more or less, was available, it might be easier to write a book, so that this time I would go to a spot, and it would have to be somewhat remote. I always like the out-of-the-way places, as you know. This time I would go to—what about the Hebrides? Go and try a book of poems there. I think that worked this time. I liked that book. Somehow I was able to absorb the history of the place and some of the traditions very rapidly when I got there. Of course it's my kind of landscape. It's something of the weather of Seattle and some of the vegetation is very much like Seattle. On the other hand, the bareness, the starkness of it, the open quality is very much like Montana. So it's almost like having two homes in one. So I had two of my favorite landscapes around me in one way or another. One of my favorite weathers is windy, rainy weather. Skye's very far north. So far, in fact, that in the summer there is only one hour of darkness in June. And it is so far north that one would expect extreme cold. Yet it rarely gets cold there because of the Gulf Stream in the Atlantic Ocean. As long as the wind remains out of the west, you get usually warm but very strong, fierce winds, a lot of rain, about seventy inches a year, and winds that go from forty to sixty miles an hour and stay that way for as long as a week. So that was a little more extreme than Seattle. I was awfully pleased that I was able to go to a foreign land the second time, this time to get poems. Now my language wasn't always available to me; that is to say, they speak the Gaelic in bars and in the streets, but also they'll speak English with their Scottish lilt and brogue and so forth.

Things are changing there too. I think that at one time people spoke the Gaelic all the time. I remember in the main town, the biggest town, Portree, where Melissa went to school— I visited the school one time. I was invited there and in a class, I think fifth grade, students were asking questions so I decided to ask a question. I asked how many people in the class spoke the Gaelic and turned out that only about three or four of them spoke it. On the other hand, out where we lived on Trotternish, I went to a grammar school there and asked the same question in the eighth grade class and every student spoke it. So once you get out in the country in Skye, that's where traditions still are. But, you see, a lot of Lowlanders have come over and a lot of English have come over and settled in Portree. So they don't know the language and it's not being passed on there. Anyway, I heard a lot of English and I could converse with people in the pubs and so forth. The Gaels are not overly friendly people, at least on the surface. When you first meet them, there's not a lot of throw-away charm that you might get in cities, but when you get to know them they're very generous and helpful. The only place where we ran into much trouble was out on the island of Lewis. Some of the people there have a rather bad reputation for being unfriendly anyway. Not only to foreigners but to their own people.

In Italy, you see, I was never quite sure where I stood with the people because I couldn't understand what they were saying. I mean I can speak a little Italian and I would converse with them in Italian and so forth, but they all converse in dialects, you see, when they're not talking to you. So at one time I lived in a place in Southern Italy for three months and there was no one to speak English to. A very lonely situation. And so I didn't hear my language at all unless I talked to myself.

KITTREDGE: That probably, as you say, accounts for some of the differences. I have the sense that the Italian book is predominantly by a visitor, an outsider, someone looking at things in a place where he accidentally was years before.

HUGO: Yes. I think that's right. That probably sums it up very well.

KITTREDGE: And in the Skye book, some of the poems, particularly the stronger poems, seem to me almost as if an inhabitant had written them.

HUGO: I don't know how it happened. Part of it, I suppose, was that I am just more mature as a poet perhaps. I've had more experience. But I was able to get some real personal investment in the poems in the Skye book that I probably couldn't get into the poems in the Italian book. They just didn't quite have the depth, I think, that these poems have. Anyway, I finally did something I had always wanted to do. I got out of my home country and into another one and I got a book of poems out of it. Also got a mystery novel out of it because I wrote the first drafts of that mystery novel there.

KITTREDGE: Like getting out of your skin?

HUGO: Yeah. Well I think one thing was that Montana, of course, is vast, and there are a lot of poems lying around just to be picked up, and most of my Montana poems the last few years have come from east of the Divide since I've gotten to know that area better through Ripley; that is where she comes from. But I probably needed a new hunting ground. You know I probably did. That's a funny way, I suppose, for a poet to think about it, but I do think of the world as a kind of hunting ground for poems and that I can find them lying around here and there. Hopefully always inside of myself ultimately. But I am a landscape poet, I guess. I respond pretty much to the place where I live.

KITTREDGE: You need new landscapes once in a while.

HUGO: I think that's true, but, you see, this wasn't too new and that probably helped. Italy is so beautiful. My God, Italy is just breathtaking with beautiful places, and it's different, especially Southern Italy. Even the attitudes of the people are not what we are used to in America. Northern Italy is a little more like the United States. It's more bourgeois and one sees the same kind of thing one sees in America. But when you get down to Southern Italy that surely is a foreign country, and it's a different kind—oh, it's breathtakingly beautiful, the towns, the old towns, the sea—quite different, but the Hebrides are more what I am used to, coming from around Puget Sound in Seattle. That wind and that rain and a lot of dark skies.

KITTREDGE: Wonderful landscapes.

HUGO: Yeah, I am about to submit, I think, another book of essays. It would be a sequel to *The Triggering Town,* but it won't be about writing so much this time. The essay is a form I really wish I knew. In fact, I kind of think I would like to see classes in essay writing if there was anybody who could teach them very well. I don't know who that would be. But I think the art of the essay is a wonderful art and I'd give anything if

I could write a really good essay. I think I've only written one that was real good, and that was the one on softball, "The Anxious Fields of Play," and the reason that it turned out so well was that Theodore Solotaroff helped me with it so much. He's an astute critic and understands what makes essays work and so forth, and oh, he sat hard on me on that, but it was to my advantage that I got in there and did it right. You know, I try to do the others as well as I can, but I'm always aware that there is some kind of trick to making essays work.

KITTREDGE: My feeling is that the essay is largely anecdotal, more anecdotal than a lot of other forms.

HUGO: That's right. That's true.

KITTREDGE: I remember when I first started trying to write for magazines, Terry McDonell, a wonderful editor, was editing *Rocky Mountain*. He's editing *Rolling Stone* now. He sent me a copy of Larry McMurtry's essays, *In a Narrow Grave*, and he said here, this is how to do it. Remember, he said, one anecdote can take the place of endless pages of "bullshit philosophizing."

HUGO: Yeah. That's right. I think when a poet goes to work in prose, especially essays, he feels some sense of luxury now that the form is no longer tight. Now I can really fool around, I have all the time in the world, and that isn't true. I mean what Solotaroff taught me, and other people, is that it isn't that much different. It really isn't. I mean, you've got to keep moving; you can't sit there and repeat yourself. You can't say something and then philosophize; you can't discuss your own meanings right in the middle of things and slow things down that way. It isn't so much different.

KITTREDGE: No, I don't think it is either.

HUGO: In a poem perhaps rhythms and tonalities tend to be more of a cohesive force than they do in prose. That is to say, in prose there is more of a logic to the progression and I think there is more of a clarity to why one thing follows another. In poems somehow it seems that things follow each other for musical reasons. And that is not true in fiction so much, somewhat perhaps in fiction, but almost never in an essay.

KITTREDGE: One of the things about *The Triggering Town* that I really like is that it's a useful book for writers.

HUGO: Oh, thank you.

KITTREDGE: And there are so few useful essays, you know. With these, when you sit down to write you can think, oh yeah, I remember what Hugo said.

HUGO: Thanks. You know Norton is going to come out with a paperback.

KITTREDGE: Oh really, good. The great thing about that is that finally it's feasible to use it in the classroom, where it was a pretty expensive item before. I think a lot of people will use it.

HUGO: I hope so. I read a lot of books on writing and they're quite helpful in one way or another, but most of them, finally, prove to be books about reading. That is to say, they talk about what is wrong about a piece of writing from the standpoint of the reader and, while this can be very helpful in some ways, it doesn't tell the writer what to do. That is to say, a piece of writing goes wrong for a reader for a different reason than it goes wrong for a writer. And so what I try to do when I teach writing is to get in behind the poem, act as if I had written it myself, and say where did I go wrong. Now sometimes I don't always bring this off. Of course I can't always bring it off because I run into poems that are so strange that it's impossible to feel that I could have written the poem.

KITTREDGE: That happens to me in teaching fiction writing. I know that there is a certain kind of story and a certain kind of sensibility that you run into a lot in the West. Sometimes you can be successful in helping those people. But there are others, as you say, other kinds of sensibilities, particularly East Coast urban sensibilities. I have a lot of trouble there.

HUGO: Oh yes. I don't think I could teach very well in the East, and, you know, they have wonderful writers there, but I wouldn't know where to begin to talk about some of the kinds of poems I see coming out of Eastern cities. And I admire them. They're fine poems, very well done, but if I had a class of say W. S. Merwin's or John Ashbery's, I don't think I would be much help to them. I'm better off in the West. That's limited, but I think any creative writing teacher is somewhat limited. I think there are certain kinds of things you can do.

I have always had good success teaching Indians and I don't know why. Not that every Indian I have had has turned out to be a good writer, but that would be true of any group. I had Jim Welch, and I had Bobby Hill in my classes. I don't know why I feel confident teaching Indians. I think it is maybe that their culture enables them to be individualistic in a natural setting—that is to say, their religion so often had in it the possibility of going out and identifying oneself with an individual spirit of some creature so that you had names like Mitchell Small Salmon or John Beaver or Joe Many Hides and so forth. I find that attractive. I think also the fact that the majority of Indians in the United States are not urban is very important. I am not very good with urban peoples as a teacher. I would say that of all the minority groups, the Indians prove to be the best students for me to teach. I think it's because, although I am not really rural myself in background, I tend to identify with rural sensibilities much faster than with urban sensibilities.

KITTREDGE: I find that true for myself, too. What are you working on now? You're preparing a lecture on Wallace Stevens?

HUGO: Right. Yes, alas, I have committed myself to that. Well, I think I am about to start revising one essay, and maybe I'll revise one other, and then I'll have the book done and then I'll mail it out.

KITTREDGE: What's this book going to be called?

HUGO: I think maybe *The Real West Marginal Way*.

KITTREDGE: That's a wonderful title.